The
Sanctification
of
Don Quixote

The Sanctification of Don Quixote

From Hidalgo to Priest

Eric J. Ziolkowski

The Pennsylvania State University Press
University Park, Pennsylvania

Library of Congress Cataloging-in-Publication Data

Ziolkowski, Eric Jozef, 1958–
      The sanctification of Don Quixote : from hidalgo to priest / Eric
J. Ziolkowski.
            p.   cm.
      Includes bibliographical references and index.
      ISBN 0-271-00741-9
      1. Don Quixote (Fictitious character) 2. Cervantes Saavedra,
Miguel de, 1547–1616—Characters—Don Quixote. 3. Fielding,
Henry, 1707–1754. Joseph Andrews. 4. Dostoyevsky, Fyodor,
1821–1881. Idiot. 5. Greene, Graham, 1904– Monsignor Quixote.
6. Holy fools in literature. 7. Christianity in literature. 8. Christian
life.
      I. Title.
PQ6353.Z56 1991
809.3'9351—dc20   90-14210
                                                                        CIP

It is the policy of The Pennsylvania State University Press to use acid-free paper for the first
printing of all clothbound books. Publications on uncoated stock satisfy the minimum
requirements of American National Standard for Information Sciences—Permanence of
Paper for Printed Library Materials, ANSI Z39.48-1984.

For my parents

Contents

Preface

The argument of this book is that to live a truly religious life in modernity is to appear (or to be?) quixotic, at least as such lives and the modern world are portrayed in the texts under consideration. While commentators have focused on the secularizing tendency of modern literature, my book delineates and examines within that literature a tradition that effectually sanctifies the hero of the first modern novel, *Don Quixote.*

The introduction elaborates my claim that the decline of religious consciousness in the West over the last several centuries has rendered questionable any earnest pursuit of religious values or ideals. Falling into opposition to the sociohistorical environment, any such pursuit consecrates quixotism as an important and typical sociocultural phenomenon. The book's three main parts attempt to substantiate this claim by examining the course of Don Quixote's sanctification (not to be confused with "sanchification"!) in post-Cervantine literature. The parts move chronologically, with each one covering a different century, beginning with the eighteenth and ending with our own. The first section of each part is extensive in focus, examining the developments within the religiously informed tradition in *Quixote* criticism from the given century: the sympathetic response to the knight in the eighteenth century; the Romantic interpretation in the nineteenth; and the religious view in the twentieth. Each part's second section has an intensive focus, analyzing the religious transformation of the Quixote figure in one particular novel that crystallizes its century's religious image of the Manchegan knight: Fielding's *Joseph Andrews,* Dostoevsky's *The Idiot,* and Graham Greene's *Monsignor Quixote.* My conclusion submits that religious existence, for the few who pursue it in the late modern world, entails quixotic suffering, which means that the religious person feels him- or herself to be temporally misplaced; like Don Quixote, the religious individual takes for real that which the contemporary world considers an illusion.

Except where indicated otherwise, all translations of foreign language texts in this study are mine. I use three different English translations of *Don Quixote:* that of Peter Motteux (1700–1703), as revised by John Ozell (1719), in its Modern Library edition (New York: Random House, 1950), in my discussion of Fielding in Part I; that of J. M. Cohen (Middlesex: Penguin, 1950), in my discussion of Greene in Part III; and that of John Ormsby (1885), as revised by Joseph R. Jones and Kenneth Douglas (New York: Norton, 1981), in all other places, including the headings to the study's three parts. As I reiterate in my text and notes, my reason for using the Motteux and Cohen translations where I did is that Fielding most likely read the former, and Greene acknowledges his use of the latter. My reason for using the Ormsby translation elsewhere is that his is by far the most accurate. All quotations of the original Castilian text are drawn from the Porrúa edition, with its prologue and biographical sketch of Cervantes by Américo Castro, and analytical index by José Bergúa (Mexico, 1966; 20th ed., 1981).

A useful tool for my research in the boundless body of Cervantine criticism was Dana Drake's *"Don Quijote" (1894–1970): A Selective, Annotated Bibliography,* vol. 1 (Chapel Hill: University of North Carolina Press, 1974); vol. 2 (Miami: Universal, 1978); vol. 3 (New York: Garland, 1980).

When Don Quixote pronounced ingratitude to be the worst of all possible sins, citing as evidence the common saying that hell is full of ingrates (pt. 2, chap. 58), he did not have scholars specifically in mind. Nonetheless, there is perhaps no other profession in which gratitude toward one's predecessors, colleagues, and supporters can be so much in order and yet so easily overlooked.

Having benefited from the assistance of a number of individuals and institutions while at work on this study, I will take this opportunity to thank them.

It was Anthony C. Yu, my former teacher and now my friend, who first encouraged my research on the religious significance of the *Quixote*'s theme in post-Cervantine novels; he, together with Langdon Gilkey and Lynn Poland, provided helpful responses to earlier versions of this work. Later, in a very different form as a book manuscript, my study was given valued readings by Ted Estess and Virgil Nemoianu, the latter of whom pointed me to Hans Urs von Balthasar's discussion of Don Quixote as a holy fool. The final honing of Part I benefited from an astute reading by James Woolley. I am indebted to my sister, Margaret C. Ziolkowski, for assisting me with the transliteration of Russian names and terms; and to my brother, Jan M. Ziolkowski, for identifying the *Physiologus* as the earliest source for the Christ-lion allegory. I also thank Frances Troup for her skillful clerical assistance; Stephen E. Lammers, for his interest in my work as a colleague, and for initiating me into some of the more obscure intricacies of the word-processing gnosis; the reference and interlibrary-loan staffs of the Joseph Regenstein Library and David Bishop Skillman Library for their promptness and efficiency; Betty Waterhouse for her scrupulous copyediting; and my editor, Philip Winsor, and the staff of the Pennsylvania State University Press, for their professionalism and panache.

In its earliest stages, my research on the subject of this book was supported by a pair of grants from two generous sources: a Junior Fellowship from the University of Chicago Divinity School's Institute for the Advanced Study of Religion, and a Charlotte Newcombe Grant from the Woodrow Wilson National Fellowship Foundation. The aforementioned institute stands as a fine tribute to its founder, Joseph M. Kitagawa, whose works, vision, and ideals have inspired me since my days as a student in his classroom.

My dedication of this book to Theodore and Yetta Ziolkowski can hardly do justice to their unflagging support as parents, critics, and avatars of scholarly rigor and integrity. They were there all along, draft after draft, reading, reacting, and opining. Needless to say, any errors or misjudgments that remain in the following pages are mine.

Finally, may I never be guilty of *desagradecimiento* to Lee Upton and Theodora Beatrice Rose for what is too much to convey in words.

Introduction:
Don Quixote:
Vehicle for Religious Expression

Miguel de Cervantes's *The Ingenious Gentleman Don Quixote of La Mancha* (*El ingenioso hidalgo don Quijote de la Mancha,* pt. 1, 1605; pt. 2, 1615) has been commonly viewed as "the first and unsurpassed model of the modern realist novel" at least since its tercentenary (1905), when M. Menéndez y Pelayo described it as such.[1] Over the centuries the *Quixote* has surely been the most widely read and most studied representative of the genre. It has gone through more than 2,300 editions in at least sixty-eight dialects and languages, becoming after the Bible the world's most widely translated book.[2] In giving

1. "Cultura literaria de Miguel de Cervantes y elaboración del 'Quijote,'" *Estudios cervantinos* (Buenos Aires: Plata, 1947), 97–144; here 135. (Throughout this study all translations of foreign language texts are mine wherever no published English versions are referred to.) The names of those who have adhered to Menéndez y Pelayo's view are innumerable: e.g., Anthony J. Cascardi in a review cites works of eight theorists from Ortega to Alexander Welsh as collectively showing that "the *Quijote* is the first modern novel because there is something quixotic about the novel itself" (*Cervantes* 2[1982]:185–87; here 185).

2. William Byron, *Cervantes: A Biography* (Garden City, N.Y.: Doubleday, 1978), 442.

rise to the novel as a genre and figuring directly in the development of almost every important novelist after Cervantes, the *Quixote* also engendered a theme that inspired repeated imitation: the conflict of fantasy, or the imagination, and reality. The inexhaustible adaptability of this theme, dubbed the "quixotic principle,"[3] was alluded to by Carlos Fuentes when he was asked once to name his favorite literary character. "I am Don Quixote," he replied. Declaring that he could therefore be Mr. Pickwick, Prince Myshkin, Madame Bovary, or Pierre Menard, he added: "I am myself plus all my intentions. I am myself plus all my readers. I imitate the past. The present imitates me. I am what I read. I read what I am. I am Don Quixote."[4]

The variety of literary guises assumed by Fuentes qua Don Quixote would not have surprised Américo Castro, who was keenly sensitive to the pervasive impact of Cervantes's theme on Western consciousness. In observing that the *Quixote* and Pirandello's drama *Six Characters in Search of an Author* (1921) share in "portraying the mutual interference of the real and the chimerical," Castro denies that the Italian playwright wittingly imitated Cervantes. Conscious imitation "is not essential, after all. As soon as a form of art is launched with genius by its creator, the atmosphere becomes impregnated with its properties, and the effective reflection of a theme or procedure appears where it is least expected."[5]

The number of novelists who have adapted the *Quixote*'s theme is inestimable. For Lionel Trilling, "all prose fiction is a variation on the theme of *Don Quixote*," posing "the problem of appearance and reality."[6] The permutations of Don Quixote and the quixotic principle might be accounted for by the array of factors discussed by W. B. Stanford as basic causes of variation in the successive portraits of any well-known mythical hero or theme: the different ways by which the authors adapting the hero acquired their information about the tradition around him; the amount of information to which those authors had access; the language(s) in which they presented their portraits of the hero; the authorial habit of assimilating old material to contemporary fashions and

3. Harry Levin, "The Quixotic Principle: Cervantes and Other Novelists," in *Grounds for Comparison* (Cambridge: Harvard University Press, 1972), 224–43.

4. Quoted in *New York Times Book Review,* 2 December 1984, 42.

5. "Cervantes and Pirandello," in *An Idea of History: Selected Essays of Américo Castro,* ed. and trans. Stephen Gilman and Edmund L. King (Columbus: Ohio State University Press, 1977), 15–22; here 17.

6. "Manners, Morals, and the Novel," in *The Liberal Imagination: Essays on Literature and Society* (New York: Viking, 1950), 205–22; here 209.

customs; problems of morality, such as the question of how to treat the hero's traditional morals; the authors' technical intentions (for example, regarding the question of whether to adapt the hero to a heroic, tragic, satiric, or other context); the authors' personal reactions to the hero's traditional personality; and above all, the presentation of the hero in his earliest definitive portrait.[7]

The last factor is especially crucial for understanding the adaptability of Cervantes's theme, as different transformations of the knight must reflect different views of his "definitive portrait" in the *Quixote*. As the predominant attitude among readers toward Don Quixote changed from ridicule to veneration with the rise of Romanticism during the late eighteenth century, he was, in Harry Levin's words, "discussed and revalued on the same plane of moral seriousness as Prometheus or Antigone." Anticipating the principles of reception theory, Levin states: "In the long run, the impact of any book is the sum of its various readings; and when these differ from the author's purposes, they reveal the readers' special concerns" ("Quixotic Principle," 233).

This study will concern itself not so much with *Don Quixote* as with Don Quixote, and more specifically with the religious dimension of his legacy in later literature. Together with the *extensive* examination of a specific development in *Quixote* criticism from the sympathetic response to the knight in the eighteenth century, through the Romantic approach in the nineteenth, to the religious view in the twentieth, the *intensive* focus will be on three novels that adapt the Don Quixote figure for religious ends: Henry Fielding's *Joseph Andrews* (1742), Fyodor Dostoevsky's *The Idiot* (1869), and Graham Greene's *Monsignor Quixote* (1982), with their respective depictions of Parson Adams, Prince Myshkin, and Father Quixote. Together with the *Quixote* these three novels establish a coherent literary lineage for at least four reasons.

First, all of them can be linked to the *Quixote* both textually and contextually. All three novels borrow from, and make explicit references to, the *Quixote*. For example, the famous subtitle of *Joseph Andrews* acknowledges Fielding's debt to the *Quixote,* and the narrator makes several allusions to the knight. Certain characters in *The Idiot* allude to Don Quixote and the quixotic hero of the nineteenth-century Russian poem "A Poor Knight." And the titular protagonist of Greene's adaptation believes himself to be the descendant of Don Quixote. At the same time, the *Quixote*'s influence on the three authors is confirmed by Fielding's scattered remarks on that novel in his

7. *The Ulysses Theme: A Study in the Adaptability of a Traditional Hero* (2d ed., Ann Arbor: University of Michigan Press, 1968), 2–7.

critical writings, and his early comedy *Don Quixote in England* (1734); by several of Dostoevsky's letters and journalistic writings, and his notebooks for *The Idiot,* where he formulates his idea of combining the personalities of Christ and Don Quixote in the character of Myshkin; and by Greene's autobiography *Ways of Escape* (1980), where he describes the great impact of Miguel de Unamuno's treatment of the *Quixote* on his own view of life.

Second, the three novels express different religious views through protagonists who, like Don Quixote, continually come into conflict with society as a result of their ideals, illusions, simplicity, compassion, and innocence: Fielding's latitudinarian Anglicanism through Adams, a parson; Dostoevsky's Russian Orthodoxy through Myshkin, who resembles a holy fool; and Greene's Roman Catholicism through Father Quixote, a priest.

Third, each of these quixotic figures must contend with a major problem or crisis facing his own religion. Adams confronts the pervasive contempt for Christianity and the clergy in Hanoverian England. Myshkin faces the threat of nihilism and atheism in nineteenth-century czarist Russia. And Father Quixote contends with the problem of faith and doubt in post-Franco Spain, which is presumably meant to represent the spiritual climate of the contemporary West in general.

Finally, the status of Fielding and Dostoevsky as classic Western authors, and of Greene as a major modern novelist, is indisputable. Though there have been other novels in which religious problems, concerns, or beliefs found expression through quixotic characters, usually for satiric purposes, these works by Fielding, Dostoevsky, and Greene in my judgment contain the three most significant cases of the knight's sanctification in fiction.

"Religion" in Texts: An Inductive Approach

To characterize Adams, Myshkin, and Father Quixote as religious transformations of Don Quixote is naturally to invite the question, What is meant by the term "religious" or "religion"? This problem has haunted the sea of religious studies like the Flying Dutchman, appearing periodically for engagements with some of the greatest minds on the shores of anthropology, psychology, sociology, *Religionswissenschaft* and the history of religions, but always sailing off again, ultimately unresolved, leaving behind an endless line of proposed definitions—descriptive, essential, functional, and normative—bobbing in its wake. Religion has been variously defined as "a propitiation or conciliation of powers superior to man" (J. G. Frazer[8]); "the feelings, acts, and experiences of individual men . . . as they apprehend themselves to stand in relation to . . . the divine" (William James[9]); "a unified system of beliefs and practices relative to sacred things" (Emile Durkheim[10]); a sense of the "numinous" with its train of experiential modalities, such as the *mysterium tremendum, majestas,* and *mysterium fascinans* (Rudolf Otto[11]); the expression of "Power" in its variegated forms, such as *mana* and *orenda* (G. van der Leeuw[12]); the "sacred" as it manifests itself in opposition to the "profane" through the "dialectic of hierophanies" (Mircea Eliade[13]); "a response to what is experienced as Ultimate Reality" (Joachim Wach[14]); or "a system of symbols" (Clifford Geertz[15]).

The plethora of definitions, of which those above are but a sampling, reflects the inability of scholars of religion to agree upon the nature and parameters of their subject. My inclination in considering the conjunction of religion and literature is to refrain, as did Max Weber, from defining the term categorically,[16] while acknowledging the usefulness of Paul Tillich's axiom that religion is the substance of culture, and culture, the form of religion. If any text has what Nathan A. Scott calls an "incorrigibly referential thrust"[17] toward concerns understandable as religious, then those concerns, to whose

8. *The Golden Bough: A Study in Magic and Religion* (abridged ed., New York: Macmillan, 1922; repr. 1963), 57-58.

9. *The Varieties of Religious Experience* (1902; New York: Mentor, 1958), 42.

10. *The Elementary Forms of the Religious Life,* trans. Joseph Ward Swain (1915; New York: Macmillan, 1965), 62.

11. *The Idea of the Holy,* trans. John W. Harvey (London: Oxford University Press, 1923; 2d ed., 1950), passim.

12. *Religion in Essence and Manifestation,* trans. J. E. Turner (Princeton: Princeton University Press, 1986), pt. 1 ("The Object of Religion"), 23-187.

13. *Patterns in Comparative Religion,* trans. Rosemary Sheed (New York: Meridian, 1974), chap. 1.

14. *The Comparative Study of Religions,* ed. Joseph M. Kitagawa (New York: Columbia University Press, 1958), 30.

15. "Religion as a Cultural System," in *The Interpretation of Cultures: Selected Essays* (New York: Basic Books, 1973), 87-125; here 90.

16. See his *The Sociology of Religion,* trans. Ephraim Fischoff (Boston: Beacon, 1963), 1.

17. "Criticism and Theology—The Terms of the Engagement," *Negative Capability: Studies in the New Literature and the Religious Situation* (New Haven: Yale University Press, 1969), 122-44; here 116.

expression the text gives form, must ipso facto be current in the substance of the culture that produced the text.

This does not mean that I seek, or think there must be, signs of a Tillichian Ultimate Concern—whatever that may be!—lurking beneath all literary works, let alone those that are the focus of this study. Nor, conversely, do I limit my probing to what Scott disparages as the "special iconic materials stemming from a tradition of orthodoxy which may or may not appear in a given work. Were [the religious dimension] to be so conceived, it might indeed then be something peripheral and inorganic to the nature of literature itself" ("Criticism and Theology," 132). Though I consider such "iconic" elements worthy of scrutiny insofar as they may reflect the differing religious or denominational orientations of the texts' authors and, hence, of the texts, this study's conclusion will reveal in the three novels another dimension that may be deemed religious in a broader, deeper sense: the experience of *quixotic suffering*.

In the three main parts leading up to the conclusion, I shall not attempt any comprehensive, essentialist estimation of what religion is. Instead I shall maintain a strictly historical, pluralist focus on what the three novelists and their contemporaries understood religion, and principally Christianity, to be, and how their particular views on it bore upon their adaptations of Don Quixote. My strategy thus squares with the theological method of David Tracy, who formulates his approach to the interpretations of the "contemporary situation" in "religious classics" as follows: "In place of Tillich's . . . 'ultimate concern,' let us search for *the particular forms* that those worthwhile, fundamental questions on the meaning of existence find in those classics" (emphasis mine).[18] In sum, I shall pursue an inductive method, allowing the understandings of religion to arise from the examined texts.

A tremendous paradox of this study is that it examines a particular tradition of literature and interpretation whose deepest religious purport is precisely its disquieted affirmation that religion is dying away in the Western world. The major literature of the modern West may indeed form what Scott calls "a canon that, in its predominant tone and emphasis, is secular."[19] However, stemming from the *Quixote,* the lineage of *Joseph Andrews, The Idiot,* and *Monsignor Quixote* expresses a profoundly religious anxiety in its critique of a

18. *The Analogical Imagination: Christian Theology and the Culture of Pluralism* (New York: Crossroad, 1986), 340–41.

19. Nathan A. Scott, "Religious Dimensions of Modern Literature," in *The Encyclopedia of Religion,* ed. Mircea Eliade, 15 vols. (New York: Macmillan, 1987), 8:569–75; here 569.

world characterized by—to invert the definitions already cited—the disappearance of (belief in) powers superior to man; the extinguishing of individual experiences of the divine; the breaking up of the unified system of sacred experiences and practices; the annihilation of the sense of the numinous and *mysterium tremendum;* the disarming of Power, whether in the form of *mana* or *orenda;* the denial and profanation of hierophanies; the deflation of Ultimate Reality; and the "deconstruction" of religious symbol-systems.

Most important, *Joseph Andrews, The Idiot,* and *Monsignor Quixote* sanctify their quixotic heroes in the only way appropriate to their secular contexts: by combining the highest virtues exemplified by Jesus and exalted by the Christian religion, with the figure of a religious paragon whose beliefs, actions, and words make him seem quixotic. In every time and place in history certain modes of human existence have been revered as sacred, such as the existential mode of the shaman among many archaic peoples, or that of the yogi in Brahmanic India. In the three novels to be studied, the modes of living, acting, and speaking as a good-natured man (Parson Adams), or a holy fool (Prince Myshkin), or in a spiritual struggle with faith and doubt (Father Quixote), reflect different aspects of the Christian ideal, but are made to seem quixotic by virtue of their discrepancy with the predominantly profane or secular currents of the modern West.

One hallmark of such literary "immortals" as Don Juan, Faust, and Don Quixote is that over time they transcended their original texts and evolved into "myths," each of which defines some specific existential mode or experiential type. Søren Kierkegaard's presentation of Don Juan and Faust as paradigms of different phases of aesthetic existence in *Either/Or* (1843), and Oswald Spengler's characterization of Western culture as the "Faustian soul" in *The Decline of the West* (1939), are matched by Paul Ricoeur's more recent description of "the pleasure in an obstacle" as that experience which "alone testifies to the heroic dimension, the Don Quixotic dimension of life contrasted to a Sancho Panza who is guided solely by the pleasures of possession, freedom from suffering, and ease."[20] As these figures were removed from their texts and mythologized, their names were appropriated as nouns and adjectives, so that someone can now be described as a Don Juan, as Faustian, as quixotic or a Quixote. The latter term, having departed from the melancholy Castilian

20. *Freedom and Nature: The Voluntary and the Involuntary,* trans. Erazim V. Koháč (Evanston: Northwestern University Press, 1966), 119.

connotations of *quijote* as "hombre exageradamente grave y serio o puntilloso,"[21] and of *quijotería* as "modo de proceder, ridiculamente grave y presuntuoso,"[22] now suggests in standard English a person who is idealistic beyond practicality, or inspired by ideals that are lofty, Romantic, and chivalrous, but also false, unrealizable, and rash.

Secularization and Faith

The colloquial connotations of "Quixote," complemented by the fact that seventeenth-century readers tended to view the Manchegan knight simply as a mad and ridiculous fool, lead to the central question: How and why did such a figure come to be viewed by Fielding, Dostoevsky, and Greene as a suitable model for the religious paragons that Adams, Myshkin, and Father Quixote are meant to embody? Put differently, How and why did the mode of existence exemplified by the most renowned and mocked madman in literature attain the positive religious significance reflected in *Joseph Andrews*, *The Idiot*, and *Monsignor Quixote?* Inspired by the preeminent classic of the modern Western-novel tradition, these three texts present themselves as what Tracy would call "provocations awaiting the risk of reading" (*Analogical Imagination*, 115) to the theologian or believer in their progressive portrayal of religion and faith as quixotic enterprises in the modern secular world.

I submit as a working hypothesis that Don Quixote's religious transformations reflect the struggle of religious faith and ideals in the increasingly secular modern West. The adaptability of the quixotic principle as a vehicle of expression for religious concern, and the knight's transformations into religiously significant personae, suggest an essential analogy between Don Quixote's relation to his surrounding reality and the relation of religious faith to the modern secular world. (Indeed, described by one of its own exponents as "a confused patchwork of potpourri, a jabberwocky of loose ends and bad fits, an unserious clown within the arena of academic disciplines,"[23] the area of religious studies appears as a kind of Don Quixote in the modern university

21. *Diccionario general ilustrado de la lengua Española,* 2d ed., s.v. "quijote."
22. *Diccionario enciclopédico de la lengua Castellana,* 4th ed., s.v. "quijotería."
23. Charles H. Long, *Significations: Signs, Symbols, and Images in the Interpretation of Religion* (Philadelphia: Fortress, 1986), 14.

curriculum—at least to some colleagues from other disciplines!) In this connection the idea of secularization and the analogy between Cervantes's hero and modern religious faith should be clarified.

Most scholars agree that the *Quixote*'s debut coincided with the dawn of the modern era marked by secularization, which connotes for Peter Berger "the process by which sectors of society and culture are removed from the domination of religious institutions and symbols."[24] The effects of this process are not limited to the sociocultural sphere: "As there is a secularization of society and culture, so there is a secularization of consciousness" (107-8). In the modern West this process led to the "demonopolization of religious traditions" (135), which entailed what Weber called "disenchantment" (*Entzauberung*), and what Rudolf Bultmann termed the "demythologization" of consciousness. By now, when skepticism has reduced God to a projection of certain economic conditions (Marx), society (Durkheim), or neurosis (Freud), it has become commonplace to question what the role of religious faith should be, or whether it should have any role at all.

Given the diminished authority of religious institutions and symbols from Cervantes's time to ours, certain striking analogies emerge between Don Quixote in his relation to his surrounding reality, and religious faith in its relation to the modern secular world. Each is governed by a particular representation of the world, chivalric or religious. Each seeks to act in accordance with that representation, through the practice of knight-errantry or piety. And each must struggle against forces that deny or undermine the legitimacy of that representation: reality and reason, or secularity and skepticism. If Don Quixote must fight to sustain his faith in the chivalric code at a time when that code no longer prevails, the modern religious individual must struggle to maintain his or her faith in a "system of symbols" (Geertz) at a time when the referents of those symbols are lost or denied. Just as the mad knight ignores the fact that chivalry is dead, so religious faith from Cervantes's time to the present had to sustain itself against notions that God has receded, as the deists suggested, or that God is dead, as Nietzsche proclaimed. In the words of J. Hillis Miller, "Post-medieval literature records, among other things, the gradual withdrawal of God from the world."[25]

24. *The Sacred Canopy: Elements of a Sociological Theory of Religion* (Garden City, N.Y.: Doubleday, 1969), 107.
25. *The Disappearance of God: Five Nineteenth-Century Writers* (Cambridge: Harvard University Press, 1963), 1.

The analogies between Don Quixote and religious faith help explain his adaptability as a vehicle for religious expression. The knight appears theologically significant insofar as his struggle to sustain his faith in his chivalric fantasy despite the antagonism of reality and reason is analogous to the struggle of the modern religious individual to sustain his or her faith in God despite the challenge of secularity and skepticism. Traditional religious symbol-systems seem discrepant with the secular spirit of the modern West in the same way that Don Quixote's chivalric code seems out of place in seventeenth-century Spain. Hence the Manchegan knight and modern religious faith seem anachronistic or literally "behind time" in their respective worlds.

According to Eliade's distinction, modern "historical man," in contrast to archaic "traditional man," forsakes eternal myths in favor of "freedom" and "novelty."[26] Unlike modern man, *homo religiosus* seeks to reexperience hierophanies, to recall sacred symbols, and to restore himself *in illo tempore* through the "eternal return." To this extent he finds a kindred spirit in Don Quixote, who seeks to reenact chivalric deeds, to revitalize chivalric symbols, and to restore the Golden Age. It was no mere coincidence that Don Quixote was exalted by the Romantics, who, in reacting against the rationalist excesses of the Enlightenment, sought to revitalize archaic myths and religious symbols. Nor was it merely coincidental that the Romantic idealization of Don Quixote led to comparisons of him with Christ, first in the writings of Kierkegaard, Turgenev, and Dostoevsky, and later as part of a religious trend in twentieth-century *Quixote* criticism extending from Unamuno to Greene. As one Unamuno scholar puts it, "As time passes and the West comes to gather awareness of itself, the inevitable necessity is clearly seen for making a comparison between Don Quixote and Christ."[27]

---

26. *The Myth of the Eternal Return, or, Cosmos and History,* trans. Willard R. Trask (Princeton: Princeton University Press, 1954; 2d printing with corrections, 1965), 154–55. Similarly, for Paul Ricoeur the definitive traits of "modernity" are "forgetfulness of hierophanies, forgetfulness of the signs of the sacred, loss of man himself insofar as he belongs to the sacred" (*The Symbolism of Evil,* trans. Emerson Buchanan [Boston: Beacon, 1969], 349).

27. Vicente Marrero, *El Cristo de Unamuno* (Madrid: Rialp, 1960), 178.

The Novel and Ambiguity

The analogy between Don Quixote and religious faith is further illuminated by the widely acknowledged kinship between the literary genre that the *Quixote* spawned, and the philosophical-cultural climate of the modern era. This kinship was first recognized by Jacob Burckhardt, who viewed the novel as "the epic of modern society."[28] But the task of defining the generic distinctions between epic and novel, and of analyzing the novel's natural affinities with modernity, was left to three of the most brilliant literary theorists of the early twentieth century: José Ortega y Gasset, Georg Lukács, and Mikhail Bakhtin, the first two of whom identify the *Quixote* as the first modern novel.

For all their obvious differences, Ortega, Lukács, and Bakhtin agree that the world mirrored by the modern novel came into being only through the destruction of the traditional epic's world and the cultural and philosophical conditions that supported it. According to Ortega the transition from epic to novel is a movement from the objective world of myth and romance into "the inner world in all its vast extension, the *me ipsum,* the consciousness, the subjective."[29] In the *Quixote* "the epic comes to an end forever, along with its aspiration to support a mythical world bordering on that of material phenomena but different from it" (138–39). Similarly, Lukács finds the internalization of the hero's adventures in the latter's "soul" to be the distinguishing feature of the novel, which in contrast to epic "tells of the adventure of interiority."[30] Where Lukács differs most strikingly from Ortega and Bakhtin is his pessimistic image of the novel as "the epic of a world that has been abandoned by God" (88). As "the first great novel of world literature," the *Quixote* "stands at the beginning of the time when the Christian God began to forsake the world; when man became lonely and could find meaning and substance only in his own soul, whose home was nowhere; when the world . . . was abandoned to its immanent meaninglessness" (103).

Like Ortega and Lukács, Bakhtin views the novel as the only genre "deeply

---

28. Paraphrased by Octavio Paz, *The Bow and the Lyre: The Poem, the Poetic Revelation, Poetry and History,* trans. Ruth L. C. Sims (Austin: University of Texas Press, 1973), 205.

29. *Meditations on Quixote,* trans. Evelyn Rugg and Diego Marín (New York: Norton, 1963), 138.

30. *The Theory of the Novel: A Historical-Philosophical Essay on the Forms of Great Epic Literature* (Cambridge: MIT Press, 1971), 89.

akin to" the new era of world history,[31] and regards its development as a movement away from the "idealization of the past" in such high genres as the epic, to an orientation toward "Contemporaneity, flowing and transitory, 'low,' present" (20). However, Bakhtin is alone in his effort to construe the shift from epic to novel against the popular cultural background of carnival and the marketplace. While finding its philosophical starting-point in the Renaissance's discovery of the human being's "inner world" (Ortega) or "interiority" (Lukács), the novel in Bakhtin's view discovers its authentic folkloric roots in the ancient and medieval tradition of popular laughter. The "absolute past" of the gods, demigods, and heroes is thereby "contemporized" and "brought low" in the novel, which represents its subject "on a plane equal with contemporary life, in an everyday environment, in the low language of contemporaneity" (21).

The novel as a genre thus partook of one of the most consequential cultural forces of the Middle Ages and the Renaissance: folk carnival humor. Fundamentally opposed to "the official and serious tone of medieval ecclesiastical and feudal culture,"[32] this force manifested itself in ritual spectacles of the marketplace, comic verbal compositions, and various genres of billingsgate. Because it "demolishes fear and piety before an object, before a world, making of it an object of familiar contact," laughter becomes "a vital factor in laying down that prerequisite for fearlessness without which it would be impossible to approach the world realistically" (Bakhtin, *Dialogic Imagination,* 23). What distinguishes Bakhtin's theory most notably from those of Ortega and Lukács is his perception of the role laughter played in annihilating the conceptual conditions of the epic:

> The novel took shape precisely at the point when epic distance was disintegrating, when both the world and man were assuming a degree of comic familiarity, when the object of artistic representation was being degraded to the level of a contemporary reality that was inconclusive and fluid. From the very beginning the novel was structured not in the image of the absolute past but in the zone of direct contact with inconclusive present-day reality. (*Dialogic Imagination,* 39)

While Bakhtin's concept of the novel's relation to epic may be "an affirming version of what the pessimistic Lukács means when he says the novel is the characteristic text of an age of 'Absolute sinfulness,' "[33] this difference need not imply a contradiction between the two theorists. On the contrary, they complement each other; they merely convey the experience of the novel's world from opposite perspectives. From Lukács's ideational, philosophical viewpoint the human being in the godforsaken world appears "lonely," while from Bakhtin's cultural, marketplace perspective the potentially alienating experience of the world's godforsakenness is assuaged by folkloric humor, which tends to subvert the ecclesiastical and feudal culture that legitimated God's authority. This is why Bakhtin describes the carnival experience as "the sense of the gay relativity of prevailing truths and authorities" (*Rabelais,* 11). Oblivious of any Eliadean terror of history, the marketplace revels in the "openendedness" of reality and contemporaneity, and finds folkloric humor precisely in the absence of any absolute meaning in present-day reality. Hence Bakhtin, in esteeming the *Quixote* as "one of the greatest and . . . most carnivalistic novels of world literature,"[34] singles out Cervantes, with Rabelais, Shakespeare, and Grimmelshausen as an initiator of "polyphony" (*Problems,* 33–34) in modern literature, and as marking "an important turning point in the history of laughter" (*Rabelais,* 66).

The acknowledgment by Ortega, Lukács, and Bakhtin of a special kinship between the novel and the modern era is complemented by the socioeconomic theory of Lucien Goldmann, a Marxist who discerns a "homology" between the novel and the market society. Also, the perception of the novel's world as a place marked by "meaninglessness" (Lukács) or "openendedness" (Bakhtin) anticipates views expressed by Goldmann and Milan Kundera. Goldmann draws on the theories of Lukács and René Girard to construe the *Quixote* and all novels following it as the story of "a search for authentic values in a world itself degraded."[35] According to Kundera, who shares the view of *Don Quixote* as the first novel and identifies Cervantes and Descartes as cofounders of the "Modern Age of Doubt," the *Quixote* inaugurated the "wisdom of uncertainty," furnishing the sine qua non of the novel as

33. Holquist, introduction to Bakhtin, *Dialogic Imagination,* xxxii.
34. *Problems of Dostoevsky's Poetics,* trans. Caryl Emerson (Minneapolis: University of Minnesota Press, 1984), 128.
35. *Towards a Sociology of the Novel,* trans. Alan Sheridan (London: Tavistock, 1975), 1. With Lukács's *Theory,* see also Girard's *Deceit, Desire, and the Novel; Self and Other in Literary Structure,* trans. Yvonne Freccero (Baltimore, Md.: Johns Hopkins University Press, 1966).

a genre, which mirrors the characteristic "relativity" and "ambiguity" of modernity.[36]

The *Quixote*'s ambiguity—the same term by which Tillich summed up the human condition during the midtwentieth century[37]—is perhaps the primary ingredient making Cervantes's novel and the genre to which it gave rise formally congruent with the philosophical and cultural climate of the modern secular world. Robert M. Adams points out that among the many elements of the *Quixote* that influenced later novelists were its "openness of form, ambivalence of judgement, and indefinite equivocation."[38] Octavio Paz has these qualities in mind when he asserts that, from Cervantes on, the novel's "essential impurity springs from its constant oscillation between prose and poetry, concept and myth. Ambiguity and impurity result from its being the epic genre of a society grounded on analysis and reason, that is, on prose" (*Bow and the Lyre,* 206). The "hero" and "reality" that the novel portrays are ambiguous as well. Unlike the epic hero, who never doubts his world's ideas, beliefs, and institutions, the novelistic hero doubts himself, and his self-doubt "is also projected on the reality that sustains him. Do Don Quixote and Sancho see windmills or giants? . . . The realism of the novel is a criticism of reality and even a suspicion that reality may be as unreal as Don Quixote's dreams and fantasies" (207).

In summary, the *Quixote* not only established a genre, but also engendered a character and theme that underwent repeated transformations. An essential formal element of the tradition of the novel, as established by Cervantes, is ambiguity, which reflects the human condition in the godforsaken modern era. Don Quixote's effort to sustain his faith in his chivalric fantasy against reality and reason is thematically analogous to the struggle of religious faith to sustain itself against secularity and skepticism. This analogy helps explain the adaptability of the quixotic principle as a vehicle of religious expression, as well as the religious transformations of Don Quixote in the three later novels to be examined.

Finally, the Quixote figure shares with the genre of the novel a subversive function that bears upon the knight's religious metamorphoses. For Frederick

36. "The Novel and Europe," *New York Review of Books,* 19 July 1984, 15–19; revised as "The Depreciated Legacy of Cervantes," *The Art of the Novel* (New York: Grove, 1986), 3–20. Cf. Manuel Durán, *La ambigüedad en el Quijote* (Xalapa, Mexico: Universidad Veracruzana, 1960).

37. "The Human Condition," *Criterion* 2 (Summer 1963): 22–24; see 22.

38. "Two Lines from Cervantes," in *Strains of Discord: Studies in Literary Openness* (Ithaca, N.Y.: Cornell University Press, 1958), 73–104; here 84.

R. Karl the novel is an "adversary" genre whose function is always subversion because it inherited the paradox introduced by the *Quixote,* "the archetypal novel": regardless of the novelist's intentions, "the novel form would itself force him into social attitudes, into a confrontation with routine activities, even to the extent of making him assume an adversary position without his consciously knowing it."[39] Like the novel as a genre, the figure of the mad knight is inherently subversive. If the genre is definable in some measure by its concern with "profane society" (11), and the *Quixote* represents "a farewell to the sacred in man" (26), then the knight appears as someone subversively seeking to embody a code from the sacred past (chivalry) in the world of the profane present (seventeenth-century Spain). Whether or not Cervantes intended this subversive aspect of Don Quixote to take on sacred significance, such significance is borne by his religious transformations.

Reminiscent of Jesus in ancient Jerusalem, or of Christ fifteen centuries later in the Grand Inquisitor's dungeon, Parson Adams, Prince Myshkin, and Father Quixote represent anachronistic, subversive, and above all, *quixotic* intrusions of the sacred upon the profane and godforsaken modern world. Let us consider more closely the prototypical theme of the novel from whose hero they are descended.

Reality Versus Our Representation of It

Almost four centuries of *Quixote* criticism have led to anything but a consensus regarding the question of what is that novel's central theme. As Leo Spitzer noted in 1948, "we are still far from understanding [the *Quixote*] in its general plan and in its details as well as we do, for instance, Dante's *Commedia* or Goethe's *Faust* — and we are relatively further from an understanding of the whole than of the details."[40] Such a problem would never have arisen had the *Quixote*'s readers simply accepted the author's claim in the prologue to part 1 that his sole aim is "to destroy the authority and influence which books of

39. *The Adversary Literature; The English Novel in the Eighteenth Century: A Study in Genre* (New York: Farrar, Straus and Giroux, 1974), chap. 1 ("Don Quixote as Archetypal Artist and *Don Quixote* as Archetypal Novel"), 55–67; here 61. See also Karl's introduction ("The Novel as Subversion"), 3–54.

40. "Linguistic Perspectivism in the *Don Quijote,*" in *Linguistics and Literary History: Essays in Stylistics* (Princeton: Princeton University Press, 1948), 41–85; here 42.

chivalry have in the world and with the public."[41] This line and the one echoing it in the novel's final paragraph were taken as literal statements of Cervantes's intention by his seventeenth-century readers, who apparently regarded his theme as simply the ridicule of chivalry books. In the eighteenth century, the novel's theme was generally interpreted as the satire of "enthusiasm," or of Spain, or some specific virtue hallowed by the Spanish people, such as honor.

However, the German Romantics of the late eighteenth and early nineteenth centuries turned their backs on the earlier view and transformed the knight into a profound symbol, finding that the *Quixote's* theme anticipated their own metaphysical, aesthetic, and artistic preoccupations. Ludwig Tieck, credited by some as having initiated the Romantic approach to this book, began in the years 1795-96 to extol Don Quixote's idealism against Sancho's vulgarity, and was followed in this view by other critics. Less than a decade later, the *Quixote* was sanctified as a Romantic masterpiece by F. W. J. Schelling's exegesis of it as a symbolic depiction of the universal conflict of the ideal (*das Ideale* = Don Quixote) and the real (*das Reale* = society). This interpretation persists today. As will be seen in Part II of this study, nineteenth-century variations of it include A. W. Schlegel's notion of Cervantes's theme as the dialogue of chivalric poetry (represented by Don Quixote) and prose (embodied in Sancho), and Heinrich Heine's view of the *Quixote* as an allegory of the soul and the body. Twentieth-century variants include Giuseppe Toffanin's suggestion that the thematic key to this novel is the Italian Renaissance debate over "the problem of the universal and that of the particular, the laws of poetry and those of history,"[42] and Joseph Wood Krutch's contention that its underlying theme is the opposition of the knight's "Platonism" and the squire's "Aristotelianism" or empiricism.[43]

Reacting against the reduction of Cervantes's theme to such abstract, objectified, or intellectual principles, other twentieth-century scholars have

41. Miguel de Cervantes, *Don Quixote,* trans. [John] Ormsby, rev. and ed. Joseph R. Jones and Kenneth Douglas (New York: Norton, 1981), 13. All quotations of the *Quixote* in the Introduction, Part II, and Conclusion of this book are from this edition of the Ormsby translation. In Parts I and III quotations of the *Quixote* will be drawn from the English versions of Motteux and Cohen that informed Fielding and Greene respectively. All citations of the original Castilian text are drawn from Miguel de Cervantes, *El ingenioso hidalgo don Quijote de la Mancha* (Mexico: Porrúa, 1966; 20th ed., 1981).

42. *La fine dell'umanesimo* (Turin: Bocca, 1920), chap. 15 ("Il Cervantes"), 211–21; here 214.

43. "Miguel de Cervantes," in *Five Masters: A Study in the Mutations of the Novel* (New York: Cape, 1930), 63–105; see esp. 81–82, 86–101.

construed the *Quixote* in radically different terms. According to Américo Castro its major theme is "the interdependence, the 'interrealization' of what lies beyond man's experience and the process of incorporating that into his existence."[44] In contrast, echoing Spitzer's claim that the informing theme is "the problem of the reality of literature" ("Linguistic Perspectivism," 51), Marthe Robert argues that the entire novel revolves around "Quixotism," which she sees as essentially "a literary matter, an endeavor to portray the struggle of the writer with writing and through this the problematic relationship between books and life."[45] Her notion of quixotism as a self-referentially literary phenomenon linked to the act of writing is unusual, as most commentators derive their definitions of quixotism from their views of Cervantes's hero. Miguel de Unamuno construed the "essence" or "root" of *quijotismo* as the knight's "inextinguishable longing to survive,"[46] while Joaquín Casalduero defines it as "an attempt to achieve a noble ideal, without, however, having the adequate means for doing so."[47] And Carlos Fuentes, complementing Robert's association of quixotism with writing, describes the *Quixote*'s "essence" as a five-stage "critique of reading that projects itself from the book towards the outer world, . . . and for the first time in literature, a critique of creation contained within the created work itself."[48]

Perhaps the most helpful terms for construing the *Quixote*'s theme in its bearing on later literature are those by which Levin (borrowing a line from André Gide) defines the quixotic principle: "the rivalry between the real world and the representation that we make of it for ourselves" ("Quixotic Principle," 236). The result of this rivalry is "quixotic confusion," or the propensity "to confuse the true with the fabulous."[49] In this conflict the voices of the real world, as epitomized by Sancho, rely on reason, experience, and common sense, and are motivated by materialistic concerns. In contrast, the quixotic

44. "Incarnation in 'Don Quixote,'" in *Cervantes Across the Centuries: A Quadricentennial Volume*, ed. Angel Flores and M. J. Benardete (1947; repr. New York: Gordian, 1969), 146–88; here 149.

45. *The Old and the New: From Quixote to Kafka* (Berkeley: University of California Press, 1977), 50.

46. "Glosses on 'Don Quixote,'" in *Our Lord Don Quixote: The Life of Don Quixote and Sancho with Related Essays*, trans. Anthony Kerrigan (Princeton: Princeton University Press, 1976), 356–67; here 359.

47. "Cervantes Saavedra, Miguel de," *New Catholic Encyclopedia*, 17 vols., 1967 ed., 3:314–17; here 315.

48. *Don Quixote, or the Critique of Reading* (Austin: University of Texas Press, 1976), 12.

49. Harry Levin, *The Gates of Horn: A Study of Five French Realists* (New York: Oxford University Press, 1963), 49.

modus vivendi defines itself through the individual's formulation of a non-empirical, idealistic representation of the world, and through his or her effort to think, speak, act, and live in accordance with that representation. Based on a faith in transcendant ideals, dreams, illusions, and other products of fantasy and the imagination, the quixotic worldview tends to be literary in nature because it is most often drawn from literary sources.

Defined abstractly, the thematic rivalry of fantasy and reality in the *Quixote* might seem to entail a static dichotomy. However, the opposed spheres of the real world (windmills) and what the knight's imagination makes of it (giants) enter into a fluid, dynamic relationship through certain developments in character and theme. Don Quixote and Sancho have been seen to influence each other in such a way that the knight's spirit gradually descends from illusion to reality, as he loses his enthusiasm for chivalry, while the squire's spirit ascends from reality to illusion. As a result of these accommodations, or the so-called quixotization (*quijotización*) of the squire and sanchification (*sanchificación*) of the knight, the rivalry of fantasy and reality evolves as a dynamic dialectic through the spiritual and psychological modifications that the two protagonists effect in each other.[50]

In concentrating on Don Quixote's bibliophilic insanity as the cause of his chivalric illusions, scholars and critics of the *Quixote* often overlook the crucialness of his *belief* in those illusions, and the diminishment of that belief in the course of the narrative. To be sure, his confusion of fantasy with reality begins with his excessive reading and lapse into madness in the opening chapter. But the problem of his madness per se leads to and is ultimately eclipsed by a more complex issue: his trying to sustain his faith in his illusions once he starts to be confronted and thwarted by the harsh contingencies of reality. This problem is inherent in the quixotic principle. While the real world is a given, the ideals, dreams, and illusions that conflict with it are produced by the imagination. In order to prevail they must be believed in by the individual imagining them, regardless of how mad or sane he or she may be. Don Quixote's gradual loss of faith in his illusions is caused not only by his companionship with an unchivalric squire and by numerous discouraging defeats and humiliations, but also by his own increasing awareness of the ambiguity that haunts the boundaries of appearances and reality.

50. See Salvador de Madariaga, *Don Quixote: An Introductory Essay in Psychology* (London: Oxford University Press, 1935; rev. 1961), 137–56. Cf. Hipólito R. Romero Flores, *Biografía de Sancho Panza, filósofo de la sensatez* (Barcelona: Aedos, 1952), 135–66.

Don Quixote's Loss of Faith

One of the *Quixote*'s most salient motifs is the anachronicity of the knight. Though an abundance of knights-errant had inhabited Spain in the previous century, the chivalric spirit had waned before Cervantes's time. Don Quixote appears as "a living relic."[51] The spectacle of him dressed in his ancestors' old-fashioned armor, combined with his habit of speaking in an antiquated, quasi-medieval form of Castilian drawn from chivalry books, understandably elicits laughter, astonishment, or both, from everyone he meets on the road.

However, Don Quixote's enthusiasm for chivalry seems to decline in part 1, especially toward the end. As Howard Mancing has shown, this decline is detectable in the decreasing frequency of chivalric archaisms in his speech (e.g., "Non fuyan las vuestras mercedes" ["Flee not, your ladyships," 1:2, 31]), and in the lessening of his references to certain clichés, formulas, and topics that typify his rhetoric of chivalry (e.g., allusions to his fame, mission, strength, and the knightly order; citations of the names of chivalric heroes; and speeches in praise of his beloved Dulcinea). In part 2 the archaisms all but disappear, and the decline in chivalric rhetoric is so dramatic that it seems Don Quixote "hardly exists as a knight-errant at all."[52]

Aside from his companionship with an unchivalric squire whose realism, practicality, and humor tend to counteract his master's chivalric enthusiasm, the most crucial factors abetting the decline of Don Quixote's fantasy are his experiences on the road. The *Quixote* has always been notorious for the cruelty its hero is forced to suffer.[53] It seems possible that his sufferings and his constant interaction with his squire take a toll on his enthusiasm for chivalry by the end of part 1. In its closing chapters his humiliation at being locked in a cage and carted homeward by the village priest and barber, and his

51. Martín de Riquer, "Cervantes and the Romances of Chivalry," in the critical appendix of the Norton ed. of *Quixote*, 895–913; here 910.

52. Howard Mancing, *The Chivalric World of "Don Quijote": Style, Structure, and Narrative Technique* (Columbia: University of Missouri Press, 1982), 133.

53. For example, R. G. Collingwood finds malice in Cervantes "raised to the level of art proper" (*The Principles of Art* [Oxford: Clarendon, 1938], 87). For Vladimir Nabokov the *Quixote* is "a veritable encyclopedia of cruelty," and "one of the most bitter and barbarous books ever penned" (*Lectures on Don Quixote*, ed. Fredson Bowers [New York: Harcourt, 1983], 52). Cervantes himself was aware of this dimension of his art. In the *Quixote*, 2:3, 439, Sansón Carrasco informs Don Quixote that "some who have read [pt. 1 of] the history say they would have been glad if the author had left out some of the countless beatings that were inflicted on Señor Don Quixote in various encounters."

desperate attempt to construe his predicament as the work of enchanters, suggest a straining of his faith in his chivalric fantasy.

Of course Don Quixote began his career as a knight with complete faith in his fantasy. This was demonstrated on his first sally when he demanded of the Toledan merchants that in order to avoid a battle with him, they must confess the supremeness of Dulcinea's beauty without seeing her: "If I were to show her to you, what merit would ye have in confessing a truth so manifest? The essential point is that without seeing her ye must believe, confess, affirm, swear, and defend it" (1:4, 42). The difference between the merchants—who refuse to comply with his demand—and Don Quixote is essentially epistemological, based on the dichotomy of sanity (*cordura*) and madness (*locura*) that separates the knight from all other characters he meets, with the possible exception of Cardenio (1:24). For the "sane," nothing is true unless it can be seen: *seeing is believing.* This attitude is epitomized by Sancho's assertion that "the only thing that has any existence is what we see before us" (2:5, 452)—an ironic claim, given Sancho's own belief in the nonexistent "island" promised to him by his master. In contrast, for Don Quixote *believing is seeing.* If one need not see "truth" (*verdad*) in order to "believe" (*creer*) it, then whatever objects one sees may be transformed in accordance with one's fantasy. From this tendency result all of the knight's famous misperceptions in part 1: prostitutes for damsels, inns for castles, windmills for giants. When he expounds to the canon of Toledo his belief that everything recorded in chivalry books is true (*verdadera*) (1:49), he is arguing not simply for a theory of aesthetics, but also for an epistemology. In Don Quixote's opinion, as Alban Forcione infers, "belief depends on what the reader will accept as true," and "truth is always a function of belief."[54]

The viability of this epistemology breaks down in part 2, where the thematic focus is no longer on the fantasy-reality rivalry itself, so much as on Don Quixote's struggle to sustain his belief in his fantasy in spite of reality. Among the most prominent causes behind his decline is Sansón Carrasco, the sly student of theology. When Don Quixote sallies forth for the third time (2:7), he does so not out of his own chivalric enthusiasm, but rather, at Sansón's prompting. The bachelor's scheme is to disguise himself as a knight, pursue Don Quixote, defeat him in battle, and thereby make him swear to abandon knight-errantry. When this plan, which failed miserably on its first attempt

---

54. *Cervantes, Aristotle, and the "Persiles"* (Princeton: Princeton University Press, 1970), 108, 109.

(2:14–15), succeeds on its second (2:64), the defeated madman pronounces himself "the most unfortunate knight on earth" (787), and never recovers: he falls ill with melancholy (2:65); resolves briefly to become a shepherd (2:67); returns to his village (2:73); falls sick, regains sanity, renounces chivalry books, and dies (2:74).

While the defeat by Sansón catalyzes Don Quixote's final collapse, the decline of his faith in his fantasy can be traced much further back, and is found to be constantly abetted by his relationship with Sancho. According to Salvador de Madariaga, Sancho's gradual ascent from reality to illusion under his master's influence began with the latter's promise of the governorship of an island to him (1:7). That incentive instilled an ambition in Sancho, who later became inflated by vanity and pride upon discovering (at the outset of pt. 2) that the two of them had become famous in a book. While the "quixotized" squire ascends from reality to illusion, Don Quixote descends from illusion to reality under Sancho's influence, and the spiritual depletion to which this process eventually leads is foreboded by his humiliation at the end of part 1. The two "curves" of Sancho's quixotization and Don Quixote's sanchification are thought to intersect when the squire tricks his master into believing that a certain rugged country girl is the enchanted Dulcinea (2:10).[55] From then on, Don Quixote's "quiet humour born of disillusionment," and Sancho's "Vanity, self-importance, [and] belief in himself" (Madariaga, *Introductory Essay,* 153, 166), become increasingly apparent.

After the enchanted Dulcinea episode, perhaps no adventure has such negative and far-reaching effects on Don Quixote's struggle to sustain his chivalric belief as his descent into the cave of Montesinos (2:22–23). Upon emerging from the cave, he tells of the fantastic things he "saw" therein, only to be confronted by this objection raised by his skeptical squire:

> "O señor, señor, for God's sake, consider yourself, look out for your reputation, and don't believe this silly stuff that has left you weak and short of wits."
>
> "You talk in this way because you love me, Sancho," said Don

55. Madariaga, *Introductory Essay,* 145. According to Juan Bautista Avalle-Arce the knight's decline does not begin until after the adventure of the lions in 2:17 of the novel (*Don Quijote como forma de vida* [Madrid: Juan March/Castalia, 1976], 55). In contrast, Mancing finds Don Quixote's "retreat" from his chivalric dedication occurring already in part 1 (*Chivalric World,* chap. 3 ["Knighthood Defeated"], 85–126).

Quixote. "Since you lack experience in worldly matters, everything that offers some difficulty seems impossible to you. But time will pass, as I said before, and I will relate some of the things I saw down there which will make you believe what I have just told you, and the truth of which allows neither reply nor question." (557)

At first glance, Don Quixote's claim for the irrefutability of his visions might seem to reaffirm his faith in his fantasy. However, in his encounter with Master Pedro and the divining ape (2:25), he contradicts his claim that the truth of what he saw admits "neither reply nor question" when, at Sancho's urging, he agrees to submit the question of the veracity of his visions to the ape's judgment. His agreeing to do this betrays two things: first, that he now tolerates his squire's skepticism and audacity in a way he never did before; second, that he now distrusts his own visions, whose truth he is willing to test not only because he longs for Sancho to believe them, but also because he himself has lost his former certainty.

Don Quixote never recovers that certainty. It diminishes further while he and Sancho stay as guests of the duke and duchess who amuse themselves by encouraging the fantasies of the knight and squire while duping them through a series of elaborate pranks (2:30-57). To be sure, we are told upon Don Quixote's first entry into the ducal castle that "this was the first time that he thoroughly felt and believed himself to be a real knight-errant and not an imaginary one" (2:31, 595). But the reader must not be gulled by Cervantes's notoriously unreliable narrator into assuming that the knight's stay at the castle will rekindle his faith in chivalry. On the contrary, he can no longer sustain his own illusions; he needs other characters to sustain them for him. This will become clear shortly after he and Sancho leave the castle and arrive at an inn, where the narrator notes: "I say an inn, because Don Quixote called it so, contrary to his usual practice of calling all inns castles" (2:59, 751). Having stayed at a real castle, Don Quixote will have lost his imaginative capacity to transform an inn into a castle.

While still at the duke's castle, Don Quixote betrays his uncertainty at the close of the episode of the wooden horse Clavileño (2:41). In this pseudo-adventure concocted by the ducal couple, the knight and squire are blindfolded and, through some elaborate devices operated by the duke's flunkies, made to believe that they are being flown on the horse through the fiery spheres of heaven. After a crash-landing, Sancho reports to the duke and duchess—who have been watching all along, greatly amused—that during the "flight" he not only uncovered his eyes and perceived the earth "by enchantment" as being no bigger than a mustard seed with tiny men upon it, but also visited the Pleiades. Overhearing this tale, Don Quixote undoubtedly realizes that some of his own skills at fabricating visions have rubbed off on his squire, including the use of the enchantment motif. After remarking to his hosts that "either Sancho is lying [*miente*] or Sancho is dreaming [*sueña*]" (652), he whispers in his squire's ear: "Sancho, as you would have us believe what you saw in heaven, I require you to believe me as to what I saw in the cave of Montesinos. I say no more" (653).

These words amount to a confession by Don Quixote that he doubts the veracity of his own visions, since he knows that all that Sancho claims to have seen in heaven is fabrication. The knight's willingness to place his own visions on the same level as Sancho's betrays his awareness that both sets of visions were fabricated. What Don Quixote whispers to Sancho might thus be restated: "As you would have me believe what I know is untrue, I require you to believe what you know is untrue." At this point, Don Quixote's notion of truth as the function of belief is strained to its limit. Much later, shortly before his defeat by the Knight of the White Moon, Don Quixote again submits the question of the veracity of his visions to the judgment of a third party; only this time he does so without Sancho's prompting. Upon being introduced to an "enchanted head" known for the wisdom of its utterances, the knight asks it:

> "Tell me, you who answer, was that which I describe as having happened to me in the cave of Montesinos the truth or a dream? . . . "
>
> "As to the question of the cave," was the reply, "there is much to be said; there is something of both in it. . . . " (2:62, 773)

This response, with its ambiguous implication that the visions contain both *verdad* and *sueño*, recalls the enigmatic answer the knight received earlier when he posed the same question to Master Pedro's prophetic ape:

> "The ape," Master Pedro declared at once, "says that the things you saw or that happened to you in the cave are false in part and true in part. He only knows this and no more about the matter." (2:25, 569)

These two responses reveal the crux of the thematic conflict between fantasy and reality. The *Quixote* as a whole seems to argue that the distinction between reality and the imagination cannot be known by mortal beings. Therefore the question of whether one's visions are "likely" (*verisímiles*) or "false" (*falsas*), composed of "truth" or of "dream," must remain a mystery. Somewhat consistent with Lukács's assessment of the *Quixote's* world as godforsaken, a more recent critic suggests that above all dialectical polarities in common human life, the *Quixote* presents "a higher synthesis, a higher dialectic," in the idea of a God who is infinitely removed from human beings.[56] Noteworthily, it is to God's "mercies" (*misericordias*) that the moribund Alonso Quixano the Good attributes the "revelation" (*desengaño,* literally "disillusion") through which he suddenly regains his "reason" (*juicio*) in the last chapter. At last, we realize that the conflict of his fantasy with reality had a deeply religious implication all along.

Cervantes, the Quixote, *and Religion*

That the problem of faith and reason is often raised in *Quixote* criticism seems natural, given the novel's time and place. During the reign of Philip II, as the force of faith held sway over the force of reason through the ongoing triumph of the Counter-Reformation, Spain was, in Walter Nigg's words, "a land totally permeated by the ecclesiastical spirit, and all its manifestations of life were filled with religiosity, even those things that seemingly had little to do with [religion]."[57] Spaniards of that age would have found it impossible to separate "religious" concerns from other matters of life. To them, as Castro puts it, "the supernatural and the natural, the religious and the profane, the spiritual and the physical, the abstract and the concrete, coexisted in one and the same unit of consciousness" ("Incarnation," 153).

There are many different opinions about what Cervantes's views toward religion may have been. Judging from the more than 160 quotations and paraphrases of the Old and New Testaments in the *Quixote,* it would seem a

56. Wilson Currin Snipes, "Teleological Criticism and Cervantes' *Quijote,*" in *Studies in the Spanish Golden Age: Cervantes and Lope de Vega,* ed. Dana Drake and Jose A. Madrigal (Miami: Universal, 1978), 33–45; here 39.

57. *Der christliche Narr* (Zurich: Artemis, 1956), 266.

safe guess that Cervantes knew well and loved the Bible.[58] Those who call him a faithful Christian or a good Catholic[59] are merely echoing the time-honored consensus, supported by claims such as Spitzer's that "the artist Cervantes never denies God, or His institutions" ("Linguistic Perspectivism," 61). Taken to an extreme, this opinion leads to the view of Cervantes as a religious "reactionary" whose work conforms to the dogmatic pronounce-ments of the Council of Trent.[60] However, this view is complicated by speculations about the possible influence of Erasmus on Cervantes's thought,[61] as well as by Américo Castro's contention that the *Quixote's* author was a skilled dissembler who professed allegiance to the Catholic faith and its institutions while disguising constant barbs against the church and the tradi-tional order under the foolishness of the knight's antics. Castro compares Cervantes's "hypocrisy" (*hipocresía*) or "dissemblance" (*disimulo*) to that of other writers and thinkers of the Counter-Reformation period, most notably Bruno, Campanella, Montaigne, Tasso, Descartes, and Galileo (*El pensamiento,* 245–328). Though he never denies that Cervantes was a good Catholic, his notion of him as a "hypocrite" (*hipócrita*) critical of the church has led some to view Cervantes as a secret spokesman for "free thought." From this perspective the *Quixote* is seen as a satirical "transposition"[62] of Cervantes's ideas regarding the theological dispute between Catholic orthodoxy and freethinking, so that "chivalric" can in all instances be read as "theological" or "sacred," and the knight's antics and ideals—such as his penance for Dulcinea and his longing for martyrdom—can be viewed as a continuous parody of certain saints, particularly Ignatius and Teresa.

58. See Juan Antonio Monroy, *La Biblia en el Quijote* (Madrid: Suarez, 1963).

59. E.g., Lukács, *Theory,* 104; Maurice Legendre, *Littérature Espagnole* (Paris: Bloud, 1930), 62–68.

60. See Cesare de Lollis, *Cervantes reazionario* (Rome: Treves, 1924). Cf. Paul Marcel Descouzis, *Cervantes, a nueva Luz: el "Quijote" y el Concilio de Trento* (Frankfurt: Klostermann, 1966).

61. In addition to the intermittent remarks on this topic throughout Castro's *El pensamiento de Cervantes* (new ed., Barcelona: Noguer, 1972), see his "Erasmo en tiempo de Cervantes," in *Hacia Cervantes* (Madrid: Taurus, 1957; 3d ed., rev. 1967), 222–61; Marcel Bataillon, "Cervantes penseur, d'après le livre d'A. Castro," *Revue de Littérature Comparée* 8 (1928):318–38; Marcel Bataillon, *Érasme et l'Espagne: Recherches sur l'histoire spirituelle du XVIe siècle* (Paris: Droz, 1937), 819–49; Antonio Vilanova, *Erasmo y Cervantes,* Publications of the Instituto Miguel de Cervantes de Filológia Hispánica, vol. 10 (Barcelona: CSIC, 1949); August Rüegg, "Lo erásmico en el *Don Quijote* de Cervantes," *Anales Cervantinos* 4 (1954):1–40.

62. L.-P. May, *Cervantes, un fondateur de la libre-pensée: Essai de déchiffrement de "Don Quichotte"* (Paris: Michel, 1947). See also Robert, *Old and the New,* 56–70.

If fully adopted, either of the two extreme views is misleading. To regard Cervantes as an orthodox, reactionary spokesman for Tridentine didacticism is to overlook his novel's aforementioned ambiguity. To regard him as an iconoclastic freethinker parodying the Ignatian or Teresian piety allegedly embodied in the knight, is to overlook the gradual shift in attitude that the narrative encourages us to hold toward the hero, from ridicule and derision in the early portions, to pity, respect, and identification in the later portions.[63] The hallmark of Cervantes's religious consciousness is that it is "profoundly undoctrinaire," being "alive with a complex ferment of spiritual and secular tendencies."[64]

The threat of Inquisitional censorship most likely had a considerable bearing on Cervantes's writing. While his contemporary lay readers would have taken little if any interest in the routine notes of approbation signed by ecclesiastical censors in the front of the *Quixote*'s second part (410–12), he himself must have been greatly relieved by them. In Castro's judgment, Cervantes took "meticulous, sometimes comical, care" to conform to orthodoxy, probably fearing that "his irrepressible tendency to divide all life into the sublime and the low might lead him to upset religion (at least, the visible and ecclesiastical aspects of it) in an inadmissible and dangerous way" ("Incarnation," 166). A perusal of the original versions of his works (e.g., the *Exemplary Novels*) reveals that the published text contains numerous emendations of churchly or moral character. A striking alteration of this sort occurred in part 1, chapter 26 of the *Quixote*. In the first published edition, Cervantes audaciously had his hero recite a million Ave Marias and use as a rosary a strip of his shirt-tail, which presumably was none too clean. This jibe was emended in the second edition of 1605 (see Castro, "Incarnation," 167; *El pensamiento,* 262).

The threat of censorship or chastisement undoubtedly weighed on Cervantes's mind as he wrote part 2. Perhaps he is trying to exert the power of suggestion over his censors when he has Sansón praise part 1 for being thoroughly "Catholic" (*católico*). The lauds of the censors mentioned above seem to echo Sansón's assertion that "this history is the most delightful and least harmful entertainment that has been hitherto seen, for there is not to be found in the whole of it even the semblance of an immodest word or a thought that is other

---

63. See John J. Allen, *Don Quixote: Hero or Fool? A Study in Narrative Technique* (Gainesville: University of Florida Press, 1969). Cf. Krutch, *Five Masters,* 76–77; Herman Meyer, *The Poetics of Quotation in the European Novel,* trans. Theodore Ziolkowski and Yetta Ziolkowski (Princeton: Princeton University Press, 1968), 56–57.

64. Alban K. Forcione, *Cervantes and the Humanist Vision: A Study of Four "Exemplary Novels"* (Princeton: Princeton University Press, 1982), 354.

than Catholic" (2:3, 441–42). One of Cervantes's most humorous efforts to remain within the bounds of ecclesiastical propriety is apparent in the account of the duke's preparations for the duel between Don Quixote and the lackey Tosilos. The duke orders the points to be removed from the lances because "Christian charity, on which he prided himself, could not suffer the battle to be fought with so much risk and danger to life" (2:56, 734).

Nevertheless, part 2 contains a number of minor irreverences that the censors overlooked or were willing to let pass. Among these are the narrator's observation that Don Quixote destroyed Master Pedro's puppet-show "in less time than it takes to say two Creeds" (2:26, 573), and Sancho's exclamation to the duke and duchess that "the way of washing they have here is worse than doing penance" (2:32, 610). Only one line from the *Quixote* was ever officially expunged. In his *Indice expurgatorio,* published at Seville in 1632, Cardinal Zapeta ordered the removal of the duchess's statement to Sancho that "works of charity done in a lukewarm and half-hearted way are without merit and of no avail" (2:36, 628). What the pedantic Zapeta apparently deemed dangerous in this passage is its Erasmian emphasis on the inner human as opposed to the outer.[65] Curiously, the same censor said nothing about the praise Don Quixote utters during his visit to the book-printing shop (2:62) for Felipe de Meneses's *Luz del alma* (1554), a book in which the strong influence of Erasmus's church reform doctrine is unmistakable. Perhaps the *Quixote*'s best assurance against censorship was the fact that "no other writer's work in Inquisitional Spain is so saturated in ironic ambiguity as Cervantes', so elaborately encoded in the intellectual cryptography of the time" (Byron, *Cervantes,* 27). Few scholars would deny the irony—undoubtedly intended by Cervantes—in Sansón's remark to Don Quixote that part 1 of his "history" is "so plain that there is nothing in it to puzzle over" (2:3, 441). Regardless of whether one agrees with Castro that Cervantes protected himself through hypocrisy and dissemblance, it seems plausible that the *Quixote*'s ambiguity reflects what Leo Strauss calls "writing between the lines," the intentional technique of semantic elusiveness typically employed by authors under the threat of persecution.[66]

This is not to gainsay that Cervantes was audaciously open in his occasional jibes at the Inquisition. He evidently deplored that institution's most horrifying ritual, the auto-da-fé, at least one of which he probably witnessed at Seville

65. See Castro, "Cervantes y la Inquisición," in *Hacia Cervantes,* 213–21.
66. *Persecution and the Art of Writing* (Glencoe, Ill.: Free Press, 1952), 7–37.

as a youth (see Byron, *Cervantes,* 60). The burning of heretics is parodied in the *Quixote* where the priest and the barber "try" Don Quixote's books and consign to the flames the ones they condemn (1:6). When the same pair threatens to burn some volumes belonging to an innkeeper, the latter asks, "Are my books heretics or phlegmatics [*herejes o flemáticos*] that you want to burn them?" He is then corrected by the barber for mistaking the word "phlegmatics" for "schismatics" (*cismáticos,* 1:32, 246).

Such jibes do not end with part 1. The stupidity of the Inquisition's officers is mocked as they are shown to be no less credulous than the common people when Don Antonio de Moreno must explain to them the mechanism of his "enchanted head" in order to avoid the possible consequences of a report filed against him (2:62). Similarly, the adventure of Altisadora's funeral (2:68–69) has been read as an elaborate allegorical satire of an auto-da-fé, depicting the arrest of the culprits (Don Quixote and Sancho), the entry of the prisoners with their escort into the court (the duke's castle), the fatuity of the judges (the duke's cronies), and numerous other details of the ritual.[67] Cervantes's jeering may again be sensed when Sancho, having been forced to wear the painted tunic and pointed cap (*coroza*), the *sanbenito* of the Inquisition's convicts, places those garments on his ass (2:73).

Cervantes's low regard for the Inquisition must not, however, be confused with his view of the faith which that institution was originally designed to protect. A. Morel-Fatio, who calls Cervantes "the most orthodox of Christian novelists" and denies that he was an opponent of fanaticism and the Inquisition, differentiates between the Church's dogma and doctrine on the one hand, and, on the other, its large body of representatives such as the priest and his acolytes, the Inquisition, the monastic orders, and the pious associations: "These accessories of worship, especially the lower clergy, were . . . despised in the Spain of Cervantes."[68] Cervantes shows himself "quite noncommittal" regarding the clergy in the *Quixote* (i.e., in his portrayal of the village priest, a hermit, and various monks and other ecclesiastics), but textual evidence suggests that he was not so "respectfully submissive" to church doctrine as Morel-Fatio claims he was.

---

67. See D. Antonio Puigblanch, *The Inquisition Unmasked,* 2 vols., trans. William Walton (London: Baldwin, 1816), 1:339n.–350n. Puigblanch's interpretation is rejected by Castro, who denies that Cervantes anywhere attacks the Inquisition (*El pensamiento,* 291, 325 n.171).

68. "Social and Historical Background," in *Cervantes Across the Centuries,* 101–27; here 101, 102.

How might this point be illustrated? Cervantes, who had studied grammar with the Jesuits at Seville and attended lectures by Father Pedro Pablo de Acevedo in the Colegio de Santa Catelina, would have been keenly sensitive to the current of thought and spirituality emanating from the legacy of Ignatius of Loyola, the canonized founder of the Society of Jesus. Even before the Council of Trent instituted its stringent ex cathedra policies, St. Ignatius had expressed his solidarity with the ecclesiastical hierarchy by suggesting, among the other rules in his *Spiritual Exercises* (composed 1521–41), that rather than to search for truth and reality on one's own, the adherent should conform his own perception of appearances with the church's dictates. In order not to err, "we should always be ready to accept this principle: I will believe that the white that I see is black [*que lo blanco que yo veo, creer que es negro*], if the hierarchical Church so defines it."[69]

This rule demonstrates the bearing of the conflict of faith and reason on the appearance-reality dichotomy: Ignatius asserts the primacy of obedience to the church, and hence the primacy of Roman Catholic faith, over the use of human reason, which, were it to operate freely, would hold that white is white, and black, black. The *Quixote* seems to satirize this Ignatian rule by having the knight invoke those same terms to argue that the basin which he has stolen from a barber is really a helmet: "this piece . . . not only is no barber's basin, but is as far from being one as white is from black [*como está lejos lo blanco de lo negro*] and truth from falsehood" (1:45, 355–56). The Ignatian principle is again recalled in Sancho's soliloquy as he schemes to trick his master into believing that a certain country wench is Dulcinea. The squire concludes that Don Quixote suffers from "a madness that mostly takes one thing for another, white for black and black for white [*lo blanco por negro y lo negro por blanco*]" (2:10, 473). While the phrase "white for black [etc.]" employs the same terms as a proverb Sancho later utters about the relativity of human judgment,[70] it also recalls the Ignatian principle about obedience to the church. Indeed, the affinity between that principle and the method that Sancho perceives in his master's madness is striking. Transposed into quixotic terms, Ignatius's injunction might read: "I will believe that windmills are giants, the monks' mules dromedaries, etc., if my chivalric fantasy so defines them." (Another scholar

69. *The Spiritual Exercises of St. Ignatius,* trans. Anthony Mottola (Garden City, N.Y.: Doubleday, 1963), 140–41.

70. In a letter to his wife, Sancho updates her on news about himself and Don Quixote, advising her: "Say nothing of this to anyone: 'put your business in the public light, and some will say it's black and others will say it's white' " (*Quixote*, 2:36, 629).

finds the *Quixote* in certain places satirizing the pedantic distinctions and minutiae drawn by certain Jesuit theologians concerning *concienca.*[71])

As will later be seen, the affinity between Ignatian faith and Don Quixote's madness has been remarked by numerous readers over the centuries, from Voltaire, by way of Unamuno, to one of the characters in *Monsignor Quixote.* What should be noted is the ease with which the knight, as a madman striving to sustain his faith in his illusions while contending with reality's harsh contingencies, can be linked, satirically or seriously, to such a classic embodiment of Western religious faith as Ignatius.

No work of modern fiction has elicited so many different responses as the *Quixote,* and no literary hero has been viewed in such widely contrasting lights. Because opinions about the *Quixote* are so varied, it is virtually impossible to distinguish the text from what has been said about or read into it by readers.[72] As Castro observes, "There always remains a doubt as to whether we are truly re-expressing what is expressed in the *Quijote;* the anxieties and aspirations that were lived by its author, by its characters, and also by those who read it before us."[73] No responsible interpreter can ignore the quandary articulated by Guy Davenport regarding Vladimir Nabokov's lectures on the *Quixote:* "The book Nabokov took apart so deftly at Harvard was a book evolved from Cervantes's text, so that when one brings up *Don Quixote* in any discussion, the problem of whose Quixote arises. Michelet's? Miguel de Unamuno's? Joseph Wood Krutch's?"[74]

This problem has a special bearing on the present study. While Don Quixote, "like Hamlet, Sherlock Holmes, and Robinson Crusoe, began to stray from his book almost as soon as he was invented," and while the aim of much *Quixote* criticism over the last several decades has been—as Davenport recapitulates Nabokov's aim—"to put Cervantes's hero back into Cervantes's text" (xiv), I shall work in the opposite direction. I intend to follow Don Quixote along one of the many courses he took over four centuries in straying from his text, that is, the religious course. What has yet to be investigated is how and why he was viewed by certain readers over the centuries as a figure of positive religious import, and adapted by Fielding, Dostoevsky, and Greene as a vehicle for religious expression.

71. See Ernest A. Siciliano, *The Jesuits in the Quijote and Other Essays* (Barcelona: Hisapam, 1974), 7–31.

72. This point is made by Paul Hazard, *"Don Quichotte" de Cervantes: Étude et analyse* (Paris: Mellottée, 1931; repr. with new impression, 1970), 291–92.

73. "An Introduction to the 'Quijote,'" in *Idea of History,* 77–139; here 83.

74. Foreword to Nabokov, *Lectures on Don Quixote,* xiv.

Part One

Abraham Adams:
Eighteenth-Century Quixotic Parson

*"Your worship would make a better preacher than knight-errant," said
Sancho. (Quixote,* Ormsby translation, 1:18, 124)

*"God bless me!" said the niece, "that you should know so much,
uncle—enough, if need be, to get up into a pulpit and go preach in the
streets." (2:6, 455)*

Parson Adams, the first country clergyman to figure as a main protagonist in
an English novel, has elicited remarkable praise since the late eighteenth
century. Citing lauds bestowed on him by James Beattie, Sir Walter Scott,
William Hazlitt, John Ruskin, and Oliver Elton, all of whom considered him
Fielding's greatest character, one biographer ranks Adams "among the immortals of English fiction."[1] As such, Adams inspired the creation of several
notable heroes in later eighteenth-century novels; shades of him are detectable
in Fielding's Dr. Harrison, Laurence Sterne's Uncle Toby, Oliver Goldsmith's
Dr. Primrose, and William Thackeray's Colonel Newcome, all of whom, with
Adams, find a common ancestor in Don Quixote.[2]

1. F. Homes Dudden, *Henry Fielding: His Life, Works, and Times,* 2 vols. (Oxford:
Clarendon Press, 1952), 1:354 n.6. Cf. George E. B. Saintsbury, *The Peace of the Augustans: A
Survey of Eighteenth-Century Literature as a Place of Rest and Refreshment* (London: G. Bell
and Sons, 1916), 120–21.
2. See Alexander Welsh, *Reflections on the Hero as Quixote* (Princeton: Princeton University Press, 1981). Cf. William Hazlitt, "On the English Novelists" (1819), in *The Collected*

Today, no one who reads *The History of the Adventures of Joseph Andrews, and of his Friend, Mr. Abraham Adams* in the light of its subtitle, "Written in Imitation of the Manner of Cervantes, Author of *Don Quixote,*" is likely to dispute Wilbur Cross's claim that "the character of Don Quixote, undergoing a sea-change, reappeared in Parson Adams."[3] Nor is one apt to question Stuart M. Tave's view of Adams as one of the preeminent eighteenth-century "amiable humorists" whose "great progenitor" was the Manchegan knight.[4] The novel's subtitle is Fielding's putative acknowledgment of debt to Cervantes for, among other things, some of Adams's more salient traits: his honorableness, high-mindedness, simple-heartedness, and devotion to ideals that are unintelligible to the commonplace people around him; his study of ancient books, and his habit of interpreting the world in the light of a bygone age while failing to see contemporary persons and things as they really are; his vulnerability to the worldly-wise; his abounding charity, and championing of the weak and oppressed; his indomitable bravery, and the delight he takes in fighting (physically) for a good cause; his toughness and ability to stand drubbings; his love for adventure; even his age (fifty), his long legs and physical wiriness, and his weak-kneed horse (which matches Rocinante).[5]

While bearing such a remarkable resemblance to Don Quixote, however, Adams's character finds another source not in fiction, but in Christian religion. He is a classic example of the eighteenth-century "good man": "a combination of heroism and saintliness" suggestive of an "original impression received from Christ Himself."[6] In Sheldon Sacks's view of Adams, Christianity is "an area in which perhaps no other fictional character ever created has more right to act as paragon."[7]

Considered together, these two sides of Fielding's hero form a curious duality: Adams the Christian paragon, reminiscent of Christ and viewed as a

---

Works of William Hazlitt, 12 vols., ed. A. R. Waller and Arnold Glover (London: Dent, 1902–4), 8:106–32; here 115; Dudden, *Fielding,* 1:354.

3. *The History of Henry Fielding,* 3 vols. (New Haven: Yale University Press, 1918), 1:323.

4. *The Amiable Humorist: A Study in the Comic Theory and Criticism of the Eighteenth and Early Nineteenth Centuries* (Chicago: University of Chicago Press, 1960), 151.

5. See Dudden, *Henry Fielding,* 1:338. See also Maurice Johnson, *Fielding's Art of Fiction* (Philadelphia: University of Pennsylvania Press, 1961), 48–49. These two fail to mention that Adams also inherits from Don Quixote his prolixity, and his insatiable curiosity and enthusiasm for listening to other people's tales.

6. Charles Whittuck, *The "Good Man" of the XVIIIth Century: A Monograph on XVIIIth Century Didactic Literature* (London: Allen, 1901), 74, 91.

7. *Fiction and the Shape of Belief: A Study of Henry Fielding* (Chicago: University of Chicago Press, 1964), 75.

moral or religious type ("good man"), is set next to Adams the English Quixote, a figure derived from the Spanish knight and viewed as a literary type ("amiable humorist"). This duality, which also accounts for the different approaches of Homer Goldberg and Martin Battestin in their studies on the art of *Joseph Andrews*, raises certain important questions. What is the relationship between the "essential formula" of the *Quixote* that Goldberg discerns in Adams ("a character set off from the other inhabitants of his fictional world by a persistent tendency to misconstrue that world in a certain way, yet exhibiting, for all his error and oddity, moral and intellectual qualities that earn the reader's affection and admiration"),[8] and those qualities such as good nature and charity that make him a moral paragon for Battestin?[9] Why would Fielding seek to create an edifying Christian example on the model of a figure traditionally viewed as a mad buffoon? Should Adams's journey be considered as "a planned progression . . . of comic actions" (Goldberg, *Art,* 101) that find their formal precedents in the *Quixote* and several Continental romances? Or should it instead be viewed as an allegorical "pilgrimage" of the good man wayfaring through hostile lands to his true home (Battestin, *Moral Basis,* 88–89), a theme that originates in Hebrew and classical traditions, and recurs frequently in the sermons of such Low Church divines as Isaac Barrow, John Tillotson, Samuel Clarke, and Benjamin Hoadly?

To address these questions, one must take into consideration that Fielding modeled his ideal clergyman after Don Quixote, whom he perceived as a figure of positive moral and religious significance. For Fielding the knight was not the ridiculous fool or "enthusiast" he still was for most mideighteenth-century readers. Rather, he seemed an admirable yet amusing embodiment of "good nature" who epitomized the most essential Christian virtues, including innocence, simplicity, compassion, benevolence, and charity. It is in the light of this innovative religious view of Don Quixote that his transformation in Adams should be considered.

Neither Adams's kinship to Don Quixote nor his role as Christian paragon was obvious to readers of 1742, the year *Joseph Andrews* appeared (see Tave, *Amiable Humorist,* 151). Such oversights reflected the general misapprehension and abuse of Fielding and his works by his contemporaries,[10] for whom

8. *The Art of "Joseph Andrews"* (Chicago: University of Chicago Press, 1969), 74.

9. *The Moral Basis of Fielding's Art: A Study of "Joseph Andrews"* (Middletown, Conn.: Wesleyan University Press, 1959), 104–13.

10. See Frederic T. Blanchard, *Fielding the Novelist: A Study in Historical Criticism* (New Haven: Yale University Press, 1926), 1, 4, 20.

Adams was evidently the "crux" of *Joseph Andrews*'s critical problems: "Was Adams ridiculed? And was ridicule a legitimate tool for a sensitive writer?"[11] Undoubtedly those early readers had trouble grasping how Adams could embody both a paragon and an object of ridicule. During the first ten years of the novel's public circulation, there was a marked disagreement between those who praised the whole novel and Adams's character, and others who attacked both as immoral and unnatural.[12] Despite this divergence of admirers and detractors, however, the general response to Adams among the novel's initial readers was laughter.[13]

The first recorded comparisons of Adams and Don Quixote were not drawn until *Joseph Andrews* had been out for twelve years and *Tom Jones* (1749) for five, by which time more than one critic had remarked enough formal and stylistic affinities between those two novels and the *Quixote* to call Fielding the "English Cervantes."[14] Others had elevated him to a status as "humourist" on a level with Lucian, Cervantes, Samuel Butler, and Jonathan Swift.[15] Because Fielding was putatively the first English novelist to transform Don Quixote into a noble figure, it seems no mere coincidence that readers did not begin to appreciate Adams's nobler qualities until they discerned comparable ones in Don Quixote and realized the kinship between the two characters. This conclusion is warranted by the glaring contrast between the first two recorded comparisons of Don Quixote and Adams, drawn in 1754 by the critic Arthur Murphy and Fielding's sister, Sarah. In adhering to the description of Adams in

11. Ronald Paulson and Thomas Lockwood, eds., Introduction to *Henry Fielding: The Critical Heritage* (London: Routledge, 1969), 8. (Cited hereafter as *Critical Heritage.*)

12. For the former opinion, see the remarks of Thomas Gray, letter, [8] April [1742], *Critical Heritage,* 119; Elizabeth Carter, letter, 1 January 1742-43, *Critical Heritage,* 123; William Shenstone, letter, 22 March 1748-49, *Critical Heritage,* 159; [anon.], in *The Student, or, The Oxford and Cambridge Monthly Miscellany,* 20 January 1750, *Critical Heritage,* 217-18. For the latter opinion, see the remarks of Dr. George Cheyne, letter, 9 March 1741-42, *Critical Heritage,* 118; Shenstone, letter, [1742], *Critical Heritage,* 121; "Porcupine Pelagius" [pseud.] *Old England,* 5 March 1748, 1-2, and the anonymous journalist of *The London Evening-Post,* No. 3236 (1748); quoted by Blanchard, *Fielding the Novelist,* 22, 23.

13. In the prologue to Fielding's comedy *The Wedding Day,* which premiered in February 1743, Charles Macklin addresses the playwright: "Ah! thou foolish Follower of the ragged Nine, / You'd better stuck [*sic*] to honest *Abram Adams,* by half. / He, in spite of *Critics,* can make your Readers laugh" (*Critical Heritage,* 125).

14. E.g., [Francis Coventry], *An Essay on the New Species of Writing Founded by Mr. Fielding* (1751), *Critical Heritage,* 269; Arthur Murphy, "An Essay on the Life and Genius of Henry Fielding, Esq." (1762), *Critical Heritage,* 428.

15. E.g., [Christopher Smart], *The Hilliad* (1753), 44, *Critical Heritage,* 358; [Arthur Murphy], in *The Gray's-Inn Journal,* no. 39, 22 June 1754, *Critical Heritage,* 373. Cf. Blanchard, *Fielding the Novelist,* 114.

Allan Ramsay's *Essay on Ridicule* (1753) as a character filled with "strokes of argumentative Ridicule" (quoted in *Critical Heritage,* 8), and Mark Akenside's theory of ridicule as "gay Contempt,"[16] Murphy in an article for *The Gray's-Inn Journal* compares the parson and the knight as characters who furnish "true Instances of the *Ridiculous*" and deserve our "Laughter" and "Contempt."[17] It was this attitude that Sarah Fielding sought to correct in her "New Dramatic Fable," *The Cry* (1754), which appeared some six months prior to Murphy's article. Presumably responding to Ramsay's *Essay* and William Whitehead's *On Ridicule* (1743), she argues:

> [T]hat strong and beautiful representation of human nature, exhibited in Don Quixote's madness in one point, and extraordinary good sense in every other, is indeed very much thrown away on such readers as consider him only as the object of their mirth. Nor less understood is the character of parson *Adams* in *Joseph Andrews* by those persons, who, fixing their thoughts on the hounds trailing the bacon in his pocket (with some oddnesses in his behaviour, and peculiarities in his dress) think proper to overlook the noble simplicity of his mind, with other innumerable beauties in his character. (*Critical Heritage,* 368–69)

In contrast to Murphy's comparison, this one calls sympathetic attention to the praiseworthy qualities of both Don Quixote and Adams. In contending that both characters should be admired and respected no less than laughed at, Fielding's sister introduced a view that would spread toward the end of the eighteenth century,[18] and crystallize early in the nineteenth.[19]

16. Cited by Arthur Murphy, entry in *The Gray's-Inn Journal,* no. 49, 31 August 1754, *Critical Heritage,* 375.

17. In *Gray's-Inn Journal,* no. 50, 6 September 1754, *Critical Heritage,* 378.

18. For example, Murphy in his "Fielding" essay of 1762 reverses his earlier view of Adams and praises the "endearing" qualities—"benevolence of affection," "humanity," "goodness of heart," "zeal for virtue," "excellent talents," "erudition," "real acquirements of knowledge," and "honesty" —that counterbalance the "ridiculous" in him. These virtues

> "command our esteem and respect; while his simplicity and innocence . . . provoke our smiles by the contrast they bear to his real intellectual character, and conduce to make him in the highest manner the object of mirth, without degrading him in our estimation . . . ; and to crown the whole, that habitual absence of mind, which is his predominant foible, . . . makes the honest clergyman almost a rival of the renowned *Don Quixote.*" (*Critical Heritage,* 421)

19. William Combe, *Doctor Syntax* (1812), 98: "He'll furnish laughter for a week: / But still I

That no comparison of this sort was recorded before Sarah Fielding's attests how far ahead of his contemporaries her brother had been in his appreciation of the *Quixote's* hero and its special use of ridicule. Fielding was the first English novelist to relish Cervantes's "manner" as a means by which to depict a protagonist as both noble and amusing. That it took readers twelve years to discern Adams's admirable qualities and his kinship to Don Quixote indicates not only their misunderstanding of Adams, but also their failure to share Fielding's view of the knight as a suitable model for a Christian paragon.

---

say, and tell you true, / You'll love him for his merit too. / You'll see, my Lord, in this Divine, / Quixote and Parson Adams shine" (quoted by Tave, *Amiable Humorist,* 272 n.8). Cf. Mrs. [Anna L.] Barbauld, *The British Novelists* (1810), 18:xiv, *Critical Heritage,* 9; Hazlitt, "English Novelists," 8:115.

1

Fielding
and the
Sympathetic View
of
Don Quixote

The reception of *Don Quixote* in eighteenth-century England brought about an important transition in the criticism of that novel. During the first years of that century Cervantes's readers began to divide into two opposed schools, the "hard" and the "soft," depending on their views of the knight.[1] If English critics expressed a "perplexing diversity of attitudes" toward Don Quixote, including "derisive laughter, identification, pity, and admiration" (Allen, *Hero or Fool?*, 5), the first of these attitudes characterizes the hard view, while the latter three tend toward the soft. All three soft attitudes were held by Fielding, whose creation of Adams stands as a landmark in the reaction against the derisive laughter of hard readers.

By the time Fielding wrote *Joseph Andrews* he had equated good nature in humans with quixotism, and regarded Don Quixote as a spokesman for virtue,

1. This distinction was introduced by Oscar Mandel, "The Function of the Norm in *Don Quixote*," *Modern Philology* 55 (1958): 154–63. See also Susan Staves, "Don Quixote in Eighteenth-Century England," *Comparative Literature* 24 (1972): 193–215.

a foil to hypocrisy, and an embodiment of the good-natured man. But before we consider the development of Fielding's view, we should take into account one of the knight's traits which Fielding ignored, but which most of the latter's contemporaries would have censured on religious grounds: enthusiasm. Eighteenth-century readers, except perhaps for the sentimentalists, were prone to dissociate the good man from the enthusiast. Had Fielding joined in the common tendency of viewing Don Quixote as a crazed enthusiast, he would not have become the first reader to see him as a figure of positive moral and religious significance.

Quixotism, Enthusiasm, and The Spiritual Quixote

"Enthusiasts," according to the conventional religious definition, are "certain teachers of religion, who have believed themselves to be directly inspired by God to impart new truth."[2] In R. A. Knox's classic study of the subject, enthusiasm connotes "a recurrent situation in Church history . . . where an excess of charity threatens unity."[3] Etymologically the word stems from the Greek verb *enthousiazein,* which, as used by Xenophon and Plato, means to be inspired, rapt in ecstasy, or possessed by the god. A canonic source for the modern pejorative connotations is Robert Burton's *The Anatomy of Melancholy* (1621), whose section on "Religious Melancholy" indicates that Guianerius and Felix Plater "put too much devotion, blind zeal, fear of eternal punishment, and that last judgment, for a cause of those Enthusiasticks and desperate persons."[4] For Burton, enthusiasts are persons under demonic influence: certain "prophesies, and Monks' revelations, Nuns' dreams, which they suppose come from God, do proceed wholly *ab instinctu daemonum,* by the Devil's means: and so do those Enthusiasts, Anabaptists, pseudo-Prophets from the same cause" (3:395). Enthusiasm thus seems heretical. If the Devil causes clergymen to become vainly conceited and scornful of the world, they

---

2. *Encyclopaedia of Religion and Ethics,* ed. James Hastings, 12 vols. (New York: Scribner, 1908–22), s.v. "Enthusiasts (Religious)," by W. T. Whitley, 5:317–21; here 317.

3. *Enthusiasm: A Chapter in the History of Religion, with Special Reference to the XVII and XVIII Centuries* (Oxford: Clarendon, 1950; repr. 1951), 1.

4. *The Anatomy of Melancholy,* 3 vols. (London: G. Bell and Sons, 1923), 3:358.

"thereupon turn hereticks, schismaticks, broach new doctrines, . . . or out of presumption of their holiness and good gifts, inspirations, become Prophets, *Enthusiasts,* and what not?" (3:391).

The association of Don Quixote with a pejorative notion of enthusiasm began during the midseventeenth century, when the knight's character struck some readers as analogous to the disposition of contemporary religious fanatics. Enthusiasm was at that time equated with fanaticism, particularly in its Puritan form, and was suspect throughout England.[5] A linking of Don Quixote with enthusiasm is implicit in John Cleveland's angry condemnation of Puritans as "Godly Quixots [*sic*]"[6] prior to the Restoration of 1660. Even more suggestive is Samuel Butler's *Hudibras,* which appeared in installments over the next two decades, and whose satiric takeoff of a Presbyterian fanatic was so clearly influenced by Cervantes's knight that it came to be known as "the English *Quixote.*"[7] The enthusiasm-quixotism equation implicit in this poem becomes explicit for the first time in one of William Melmoth's "Fitzosborne" *Letters* (1749). Deeming "enthusiasm in all other points but that of religion, to be a very necessary turn of mind," Melmoth explains: "There is indeed a certain heightening faculty which universally prevails thro' our species; and we are all of us, perhaps, in our several favourite pursuits, pretty much in the circumstances of the renowned knight of La Mancha, when he attacked the barber's brazen bason [*sic*], for Mambrino's golden helmet."[8]

Though the nineteenth-century Romantic exaltation of enthusiasm finds early anticipation in Joseph Warton's poem "The Enthusiast; or, the Love of

5. See Gerald R. Cragg, *The Church and the Age of Reason 1648–1789* (Middlesex: Penguin, 1960; 2d ed., rev. 1970), 15, 70, 117.

6. In *Mercurius,* no. 1 [no date given], 1, quoted by Edwin B. Knowles, Jr., "*Don Quixote* in England Before 1660," in the published selections from his New York University doctoral dissertation (1939), *Four Articles on "Don Quixote" in England* (New York, 1941), 3–12; here 10.

7. See Tave, *Amiable Humorist,* 153; Edwin B. Knowles, "Cervantes and English Literature," in *Cervantes Across the Centuries,* 277–303; here 284–85.

8. Letter no. 44, September 1719, "To Clytander: Concerning enthusiasms," *Letters on Several Subjects, by the Late Sir Thomas Fitzosborne [pseud.],* 2 vols. (London: Dodsley, 1749; repr. New York: Garland, 1971), 2:1–2. (This letter is not included in the 1st ed. of 1748.) Melmoth extends the equation in the next paragraph: "What is Tully's *aliquid immensum infinitumque,* which he professes to aspire after in oratory, but a piece of true rhetorical Quixotism? Yet never . . . would he have glowed with so much eloquence, had he been warmed with less enthusiasm" (2:2–3).

Nature" (1740),[9] the general contempt for enthusiasm qua fanaticism in religion prevailed as a hallmark of the vogue for reason and formalism through most of the eighteenth century. Dr. Johnson, an admirer of Burton's *Anatomy,* defines "enthusiasm" in his *Dictionary* (1755) as "vain belief of private revelation; a vain confidence of divine favour or communication." To elaborate, he paraphrases Locke, who denied both the rational and religious legitimacy of enthusiasm: "*Enthusiasm* is founded neither on reason nor divine revelation, but rises from the conceits of a warmed or overweening brain."[10] Likewise Voltaire, the antireligious rationalist par excellence of that age, held enthusiasm in low regard, particularly as it pertained to religion. His *Questions sur l'encyclopédie* (1770-72), an enlargement of his *Dictionnaire philosophique* (1764), contains an entry on *enthousiasme* that defines it as a catchall term for various "nuances in our affections" ranging from *approbation* and *sensibilité* to *fureur* and *rage.*[11] After citing a number of hypothetical and historical cases to illustrate how enthusiasm can develop into a *maladie* or *demence* (e.g., Sappho's "enthusiasm of love," which "cost her her life"), Voltaire discusses St. Ignatius and the Jesuits as exemplifying enthusiasm that "has arrived at its utmost degree, which is fanaticism [*fanatisme*]; and this fanaticism became rage" (18:553).

Voltaire's portrayal of Ignatius as an enthusiast is noteworthy because he elsewhere compares the founder of the Jesuits mockingly to Don Quixote (*Dictionnaire philosophique III, Oeuvres,* 19:416-17). However, he is not the first to do so. At the Hague in 1738, Pierre Quesnel, a Frenchman writing under the pseudonym Hercule Rasiel de Selva, had published a two-volume history of Ignatius and his order in which a number of analogies between the *extravagences* and *folies* of that saint and those of Don Quixote are drawn for a satiric purpose.[12] This book anticipated the exploitation of the Don Quixote-enthusiasm association as a means for attacking certain religious movements in Germany and England during the second half of the century.

9. See Edmund Gosse, "Two Pioneers of Romanticism: Joseph and Thomas Warton," *Proceedings of the British Academy* 7 (1915-16): 145-63.

10. *Samuel Johnson's Dictionary: A Modern Selection,* ed. E. L. McAdam, Jr., and George Milne (New York: Pantheon, 1963), s.v. "enthusiasm." Cf. "enthusiast." The paraphrase is from John Locke, *An Essay Concerning Human Understanding* (Oxford: Clarendon, 1975), bk. 4, chap. 19, sec. 7.

11. *Dictionnaire philosophique II, Oeuvres complètes de Voltaire,* new ed., 52 vols. (Paris: Garnier, 1877-85), 18:552.

12. *Histoire de l'admirable Dom Inigo de Guispuscoa, chevalier de la Vierge, et fondateur de la monarchie des Inighistes,* 2 vols. (The Hague: La Veuve de Charles le Vier, 1738).

In attaining its greatest popularity among Germans between 1750 and 1800, the *Quixote* was read by them as "an attack on everything illusory, fantastic, and not in accord with reason or experience."[13] During the *Aufklärung* it was typically viewed as a satire against *Schwärmerei,* or enthusiasm, which, having been associated with the nonconformist sects of the Radical Reformation (mockingly called *Schwärmgeister*), and later with the Pietist movement of the eighteenth century, was deemed unhealthy for religion. For example, the poet Christoph Martin Wieland recalled that in disengaging himself from his Pietist upbringing, he had found reading the *Quixote* to be the most effective antidote against "fevers" of the soul. Accordingly, the first edition (1764) of his novel *The Adventures of Don Silvio von Rosalva,* perhaps the most important German adaptation of the *Quixote* from this period, appeared under the title *Der Sieg der Natur über die Schwärmerei* (The triumph of nature [i.e., reason] over enthusiasm).[14]

In Johnson's England, where a translation of Quesnel's satirical history appeared under the title *The Spiritual Quixote; or the Entertaining History of Ignatius Loyola, Founder of the Order of the Jesuits* (1755),[15] the Society of Jesus had never posed a threat, and Methodism had replaced Puritanism as the most despised form of religious enthusiasm. With the exception of Smollett, the classic English novelists of the eighteenth century say little about Methodism. But in the few places in Fielding's novels where that movement is attacked, the hostility is undisguised; based on principles of practical social amelioration, his latitudinarian morality and benevolist ethic are fundamentally opposed to the antinomian doctrine of the evangelists.[16] In *Joseph Andrews* Adams speaks out against George Whitefield, asserting that "when he began to call nonsense and enthusiasm to his aid, and set up the detestable doctrine of faith against

13. Lienhard Bergel, "Cervantes in Germany," in *Cervantes Across the Centuries,* 315-52; here 319.

14. As Bergel points out, Wieland's view of the knight was shared by J. Bodmer, J. G. Herder (who compared Kant to Don Quixote as a *Schwärmer!*), and F. J. Bertuch ("Cervantes in Germany," 323-27).

15.This two-volume translation, published in London by J. Bouquet and dated 1755, is a reprint of another English edition, entitled *The History of the Wonderful Don Ignatius Loyola de Guispuscoa, Founder of the Order of the Jesuits,* 2 vols. (London: J. Bouquet, 1754). There is reason to suspect that the edition entitled *The Spiritual Quixote* was dated ahead, as a review of it had appeared already in the *Monthly Review* 11 (December 1754):445-53.

16. See Battestin, *Moral Basis,* 81-84; T. B. Shepherd, *Methodism and the Literature of the Eighteenth Century* (1940; New York: Haskell, 1966), 224-25.

good works, I was his friend no longer."[17] Because enthusiasm and fanaticism
were practically synonymous it is not surprising to discover John Wesley's face
represented atop the body of the preacher misleading his flock from the pulpit
in William Hogarth's twin allegories "Enthusiasm Delineated" (c. 1761) and
"Credulity, Superstition, and Fanaticism" (1762).[18] Nor is it shocking to find
Adam Smith fourteen years later denigrating "dissenters" and "methodists" as
"popular and bold, though perhaps stupid and ignorant enthusiasts."[19]

Given the Methodists' reputation as enthusiasts and the association of
enthusiasm with Don Quixote, it was almost to be expected that Methodism
would be satirized as a form of quixotism, just as Presbyterian fanaticism had
been burlesqued as a quixotic enterprise in *Hudibras,* and as Pietism was
ridiculed in Germany. In 1773 an Anglican clergyman and former rector of
Claverton named Richard Graves published anonymously *The Spiritual Quixote;
or the Summer's Ramble of Mr. Geoffry Wildgoose,* a "comic romance" about
an itinerant Methodist preacher (named in the title), and his Sancho-like
cohort, a cobbler named Jerry Tugwell. This novel, which went through so
many editions during its first forty years that it was generally ranked among
English classics, still stands as the paramount literary expression of anti-
Methodism. While Graves's motive for attacking Methodism is known to have
arisen from his own experience,[20] the idea governing his satire is the analogy
between quixotism and Methodist enthusiasm as embodied in Wildgoose, the
Spiritual Quixote. This analogy was perhaps suggested to him by William
Warburton's *The Doctrine of Grace* (1762), which assails Wesley and his
movement, and draws Sancho Pancho [*sic*] and, by implication, Don Quixote
into the discussion by comparing Methodist preachers to them.[21]

17. Henry Fielding, *Joseph Andrews and Shamela,* ed. Martin C. Battestin (Boston: Houghton,
1961), 1:17, 67. The colon separates the book and chapter numbers, followed by the page. All
quotations of *Joseph Andrews* are from this edition.

18. Reproduced in Ronald Paulson, *Hogarth's Graphic Works,* 2 vols. (New Haven: Yale
University Press, 1965), vol. 2, plates 231 and 232 (cat. nos. 209 and 210).

19. *An Inquiry into the Nature and Causes of the Wealth of Nations* (1776), 2 vols. [bound in
1 vol.], ed. Edwin Cannan (Chicago: University of Chicago Press, 1976), 2:310.

20. See Charles Jarvis Hill, *The Literary Career of Richard Graves: Author of "The Spiritual
Quixote",* Smith College Studies in Modern Languages 16, nos. 1–3 (October 1934–April
1935):18, 23–24; Clarence Tracy, Introduction to his edition of Richard Graves, *The Spiritual
Quixote; or the Summer's Ramble of Mr. Geoffry Wildgoose* (London: Oxford University Press,
1967), xv.

21. See *The Doctrine of Grace; or, the Office and Operations of the Holy Spirit Vindicated
from the Insults of Infidelity, and the Abuses of Fanaticism* (1762; 2d ed., London: Millar, 1763),
bk. 2, chap. 3, 91; chap. 12, 166 n.3.

If Graves's novel serves as any indication of his view of the *Quixote,* whose influence on the character and plot of *The Spiritual Quixote* is patent,[22] he undoubtedly saw the knight as the ridiculous butt of Cervantes's satire. In his prefatory "Apology" he asserts that a literary model like Don Quixote "will furnish more hints for correcting the follies and regulating the morals of young persons, and impress them more forcibly on their minds, than volumes of severe precepts." The satirical depiction of Wildgoose is obviously intended to be of use for the correction of enthusiasm. Yet the author wishes not to negate Methodism simply by ridiculing it, but rather to "expose" it as "a species of folly, which has frequently disturbed the tranquillity of this nation," and "to prevent Religion [from] becoming ridiculous, by the absurd conduct of such irregular Teachers of it" (3).[23] His "Essay on Quixotism" (2:4) explicates the analogy between Don Quixote and Methodist preachers, pointing out that although Cervantes ridiculed chivalry, originally chivalry had not been ridiculous. Rather, the "absurdity" we laugh at in the mad knight is "his attempting to revive that profession, when the more perfect regulations of civil society had rendered it, not only unnecessary, but unlawful" (39).

Graves goes on to suggest that Wildgoose and preachers like him are motivated by notions no less anachronistic and absurd than Don Quixote's. Though there was a time when "Patriarchs and Prophets, Apostles and Evangelists, and even St. Paul himself" were truly commissioned by providence to become "Spiritual Knights-errant," the case is different with "our modern itinerant reformers," who "by the mere force of the imagination, have conjured up the powers of darkness in an enlightened age" (40). Moreover, Methodists cause harm to the legitate forms of religion. This criticism is voiced near the end through one of the characters, who argues that "as a true rational system of Religion contributes to the happiness of society, and of every individual; so Enthusiasm not only tends to the confusion of society, but to undermine the foundation of all Religion, and to introduce . . . scepticism of opinion, and licentiousness of practice" (12:16, 468).

Graves's condemnation of enthusiasm through his satirical portrayal of Wildgoose alerts us to an important distinction between his reading of the *Quixote,* and Fielding's: Graves viewed the knight unsympathetically, con-

---

22. See Havelock Ellis, "Richard Graves and 'The Spiritual Quixote,'" *Nineteenth Century* 77 (1915):848-60; see 853; Hill, *Richard Graves,* 44-45.

23. All quotations are from the 1967 Oxford edition. Where included, the colon separates the book and chapter numbers, followed by the page.

demning his enthusiasm and folly (reflected in Wildgoose), whereas Fielding regarded him sympathetically, admiring his nobler qualities while not denying his follies (reflected in Adams). Fielding's innovative view of Don Quixote as a good-natured man introduced the possibility of perceiving him as a Christian paragon. As a familiar eighteenth-century type, the good man was easily distinguishable from the enthusiast.[24] For Fielding good nature was a religious category connoting such essential Christian virtues as innocence, benevolence, and charity, all of which may seem to characterize Don Quixote, but had been obscured by the readers' tendency to dwell on his enthusiasm.

Emergence of the Sympathetic View

The emergence of readings that diverged from the virtually monolithic seventeenth-century view of the *Quixote* as a mere burlesque, and of its hero as merely a ridiculous fool, began with some remarks by Peter Motteux in the preface to his translation of 1700–1703: "Every man has something of Don Quixote in his *Humor,* some darling Dulcinea of his Thoughts, that sets him very often upon mad Adventures. What Quixotes dos [*sic*] not every Age produce in Politics and Religion, who fancying themselves to be in the right of something, which all the World tell 'em is wrong, make very good sport to the Public, and shew that they themselves need the chiefest Amendment."[25] Further on Motteux censures an earlier translator for having "ridicul'd the most serious and moving Passages" in the *Quixote.*

With these suggestions, Motteux planted the critical seeds for an interpretation of the *Quixote* as something other than a mere jestbook. Other critics followed his lead and discerned "serious" or "grave" qualities in the book. To be sure, Pope's reference to "Cervantes' serious air," like Edmund Smith's allusion to "the solemn Air of great *Cervantes,*" should be understood in the light of

---

24. Whittuck, *The "Good Man",* 7: " 'The good man' will, somehow or other, find his way out of every difficulty, and bear up under every trial. And he will do this without asceticism, without 'enthusiasm,' and in some cases, without deriving any assistance from revealed religion."

25. Preface to Miguel de Cervantes, *The Ingenious Gentleman Don Quixote de la Mancha,* trans. Peter Motteux (London, 1700–1703), no page. This preface does not appear in the Modern Library edition (New York: Random, 1950) of John Ozell's revision (1719) of Motteux's translation.

the eighteenth-century commonplace that the serious air is a feature of humor.[26] (Indeed, Pope elsewhere refers to Cervantes's knight as the "true Sublime of Ridicule."[27]) Likewise Sterne's description of Walter Shandy's conversational tone as "Cervantic gravity" in *Tristram Shandy* (1759–67; bk. 3, chap. 10) is probably meant to connote not gravity per se, but humorous gravity. At the same time, whoever penned the unsigned dedication that prefaces Lord Carteret's 1738 Spanish edition of the *Quixote* was surely thinking of seriousness in the literal sense when he described the Spanish author as "one of those inestimable men who, . . . by the fertility of their immortal genius, have produced (albeit through burlesque), the most serious, useful and beneficial effects that can be imagined."[28]

The allusion to these "effects" reflects the common notion that Cervantes had effectually destroyed the reputation of chivalry books through his satire. Directly related to that view was the even graver assumption that the success of Cervantes's satire had caused a decline in the morale of the Spanish nobility. This assumption, expressed by Motteux, was shared by a host of eighteenth-century English critics, and would later be immortalized by Byron in *Don Juan* (canto 13, stanza 11). Hence the *Quixote* was invoked by such authors as Lord Bolingbroke, Addison, and Shaftesbury to support arguments—especially common during the 1720s and 1730s—against the prevalent use of ridicule (see Knowles, "Cervantes and English Literature," 290–91).

Together with their developing sensitivity to the *Quixote*'s "seriousness" and their skepticism about Cervantes's brand of ridicule, some critics began to identify with Don Quixote. Echoing Motteux's claim that "every man has something of Don Quixote in his *Humour,*" Richard Steele observed in *The Tatler,* no. 178 (1710): "As much as the case of this distempered Knight is received by all the readers of his history as the most incurable and ridiculous of all phrensies, it is very certain that we have crowds among us far gone in as visible a madness as his, though they are not observed to be in that condition." Similarly Dr. Johnson asserted in *The Rambler,* no. 2 (1750) that "very few

26. So argues Tave, *Amiable Humorist,* 153–54, quoting Alexander Pope, *Dunciad Variorum,* 1:19, or *Dunciad in Four Books,* 1:21 (ed. J. R. Sutherland [1943], 62, 270); Edmund Smith, *A Poem on the Death of Mr. John Philips* [1710?], 3.

27. Letter, 3 March 1726, to the Earl of Oxford, *The Correspondence of Alexander Pope,* ed. George Sherburn, 5 vols. (Oxford: Clarendon, 1956), 2:370.

28. "A la exma señora, Condessa de Montijo, & c.," Miguel de Cervantes, *Vida y hechos del hidalgo don Quijote de la Mancha,* 4 vols., ed. Lord Carteret (London, 1738), 1:i–iv; here iv.

readers, amidst their mirth or pity, can deny that they have admitted visions of the same kind [as Don Quixote's]. . . . When we pity him, we reflect on our own disappointments; and when we laugh, our hearts inform us that he is not more ridiculous than ourselves, except that he tells what we have only thought" (both statements quoted by Knowles, "Cervantes and English Literature," 291).

Such sympathy for Don Quixote played an essential role in the growing tendency among critics to exalt his positive qualities, such as nobility, humanity, charitableness, and goodness. Though the idealization of Don Quixote before the Romantics was in France and Germany confined to Rousseau and Herder, and in Spain nonexistent, it is already detectable in a letter of 1739 from Pope, who describes a friend as "so very a child in true Simplicity of Heart, that I love him; as He loves Don Quixote, for the Most Moral & Reasoning Madman in the world."[29] This last perception of Don Quixote harbingers Fielding's religiously oriented view.

Fielding: "What is a good-natured man?"

In the development of feelings of identification, pity, and admiration regarding Don Quixote, and in his early idealization, no author played a more crucial role than Fielding,[30] who expressed his sympathetic exegesis in scattered comments on the *Quixote,* and through his creation of Adams.

Exactly when it was that Fielding first encountered the *Quixote* is uncertain. Cross conjectures that he "met with" Motteux's translation "as a boy" (*History,* 1:134), while another biographer (Dudden, *Fielding,* 1:17, and 17 n. 1) speculates that he read Cervantes and Swift some time between his departure from Eton in the summer of 1724 and his writing of his first play, *Love in Several Masques* (1728), which makes allusions to works by those two authors. There is no evidence that Fielding read Cervantes in Spanish; of the four translations available to him when he wrote *Love in Several Masques,* he

29. *Correspondence,* 4:208, cited by Tave, *Amiable Humorist,* 154.
30. Gerhard Buck, "Written in Imitation of the Manner of Cervantes," *Germanisch-romanische Monatsschrift* 29 (1941):53–61; see 60; Tave, *Amiable Humorist,* 155; Anthony Close, *The Romantic Approach to "Don Quixote": A Critical History of the Romantic Tradition in "Quixote" Criticism* (Cambridge: Cambridge University Press, 1978), 13.

probably read Ozell's revised version of the one by Motteux, some of whose phrasings he apparently emulated in another early play, *Don Quixote in England,*[31] which met with considerable success when it opened at the Haymarket in 1734.

In the play's preface Fielding expresses his dissatisfaction with those of its parts "written in my more juvenile years," and recalls his discouragement at trying to keep pace with "the inimitable Cervantes," especially when he realized that an "error" had underlain his original "sketch": "I found it infinitely more difficult than I imagined to vary the scene, and give my knight an opportunity of displaying himself in a different manner from that wherein he appears in the romance. Human nature is every where the same: and the modes and habits of particular nations do not change it enough, sufficiently to distinguish a Quixote in England from a Quixote in Spain."[32] Four years prior to the production of *Don Quixote in England,* and a year after its original draft had been rejected by the managers of Drury Lane, Fielding had already transformed Cervantes's knight into a symbol for all the madness of the world. In *The Coffee-House Politician* (1730) a character named Worthy soliloquizes on the faults of others in this manner:

> The greatest part of mankind labour under one delirium or other: and Don Quixote differed from the rest, not in madness, but the species of it. The covetous, the prodigal, the superstitious, the libertine, and the coffee-house politician, all are Quixotes in their several ways.

> That man alone from madness free, we find,
> Who, by no wild unruly passion blind,
> To reason gives the conduct of his mind.
> (*Coffee-House Politician,* act 2, scene 12, *Works,* 9:108)

This insight, as Tave points out, was not wholly new; Motteux had already suggested that every age produces mad Quixotes in religion and politics, and Steele's Upholsterer in *The Tatler* (No. 178) appears as an eighteenth-century "coffee-house political Quixote" (*Amiable Humorist,* 156). However, if Fielding

31. See Goldberg, *Art,* 29 n.3. Cf. Cross, *History,* 1:314; Ethel M. Thornbury, *Henry Fielding's Theory of the Comic Prose Epic* (1931; repr. New York: Russell and Russell, 1966), 8.
32. *Don Quixote in England, The Complete Works of Henry Fielding, Esq.,* ed. William Ernest Henley, 16 vols. (London: Heinemann, 1903), 11:9.

saw madness as a definitive trait of a Quixote, it was not among those qualities
with which he endowed Adams, who is eccentric but not mad. As characterized in *Joseph Andrews,* Adams embodies good nature. The modeling of him
after Don Quixote is not surprising; Fielding had already equated good nature
and quixotism in another passage of *The Coffee-House Politician.* Two scenes
after Worthy's soliloquy a character named Constant contemplates the predicament he has fallen into: having tried to save a woman from a rapist, he is now
in custody because she accused him of the crime. Voicing his thoughts to the
audience, he says:

> I begin to be of that philosopher's opinion, who said, that whoever
> will entirely consult his own happiness must be little concerned about
> the happiness of others. Good nature is Quixotism, and every Prin-
> cess Micomicona will lead her deliverer into a cage. What had I to do
> to interpose? What harm did the misfortunes of an unknown woman
> bring me, that I should hazard my own happiness and reputation on
> her account? (*Coffee-House Politician,* act 3, scene 2, *Works,* 9:109-10)

The equation of good nature and quixotism here anticipates Fielding's later
conception of Adams as a quixotic hero.

These soliloquies in *The Coffee-House Politician* show that by the time
Fielding composed the final version of *Don Quixote in England,* which
foreshadows *Joseph Andrews,* he associated two universal qualities with
Cervantes's knight: madness, the foremost trait conventionally attributed to
him, and good nature, which Fielding was the first to equate with quixotism.
Don Quixote in England, which adapts the themes of madness and good
nature, is doubly pertinent to the novel. First, the play is an early manifestation
of what Arthur Murphy called Fielding's "love of imitation" ("Fielding,"
Critical Heritage, 412), which later governed the latter's desire to "imitate"
Cervantes in *Joseph Andrews.* Second, the play provides further insight into
Fielding's early perception of the knight.

In *Don Quixote in England* Fielding imports Don Quixote and Sancho to
an English inn in order to satirize the corruption in county politics by
contrasting the "mad" but noble Spanish hidalgo with a group of "sane" but
sordid and hypocritical local citizens; for example, the conniving mayor who
makes Don Quixote a candidate for office in order to ensure a contest, and the

greedy father, Sir Thomas Loveland, who tries to force his daughter to marry the rich but vile Squire Badger. The most salient traits of Fielding's knight and squire are ones with which his audience was well familiar. The knight, depicted with "farcical simplicity" (Knowles, "Cervantes and English Literature," 292), suffers mad illusions on matters relating to chivalry (inns for castles, coachmen for giants, etc.), but otherwise remains an upright gentleman. True to his Cervantine model, he refuses to pay his bill at the inn; he expresses a constant fear of enchantment, which he argues to be the cause of his illusions; and he is constantly mocked by other characters. Sancho for his part does little more than eat, drink, recite proverbs, and sleep.

While he simplifies the characters of the knight and squire, Fielding develops into an extended thesis the notion, first suggested by Worthy in *The Coffee-House Politician,* that madness is something common to all mankind. In the introduction the "author" declares that he has brought Don Quixote and Sancho "over into England, . . . where I believe no one will be surprised that the knight finds several persons as mad as himself."[33] This statement is confirmed in the final scene where the knight, hearing himself called a "madman" by the quack Doctor Drench, reprimands him:

> I have heard thee, thou ignorant wretch, throw that word in my face, with patience. For alas! could it be proved, what were it more than almost all mankind in some degree deserve? Who would doubt the noisy boisterous squire [Badger], who was here just now, to be mad? Must not this noble knight [Loveland] here have been mad, to think of marrying his daughter to such a wretch? You doctor, are mad too, though not so mad as your patients. The lawyer here is mad, or he would not have gone into a scuffle, when it is the business of men of his profession to set other men by the ears, and keep clear themselves. (act 3, scene 15, 69–70)

The play closes with a song, "All mankind are mad, 'tis plain," which, after enumerating various types of madness, concludes:

> Since your madness is so plain,
> Each spectator

33. *Don Quixote in England, Works,* 11:5–71; here 12. All quotations of this play are from this volume.

Of good-nature,
With applause will entertain
His brother of La Mancha:
With applause will entertain
Don Quixote and Squire Sancho. (71)

The suggestion that any good-natured spectator will find a "brother" in Don Quixote prefigures Fielding's claim in his apology for Parson Adams that "the goodness of his heart will recommend him to the good-natured" (*Joseph Andrews*, 12). It also indicates that the response the author wishes his hero to elicit from the audience, like that which he will later hope for Adams to elicit, is not laughter exclusively, but laughter mixed with sympathy and admiration. In this early play Fielding already seems to transcend the standard view of Don Quixote as a mere lunatic and burlesque figure by using him as a mouthpiece for voicing moral insights and denunciations (see Tave, *Amiable Humorist,* 157; Goldberg, *Art,* 28, 280 n. 10. Cf. the discussion of this play in Michael V. DePorte, *Nightmares and Hobbyhorses: Swift, Sterne, and Augustan Ideas of Madness* [San Marino, Calif.: Huntington Library, 1974], 111–12).

Fielding's most innovative use of Don Quixote occurs in the first scene of the second act, where the knight responds to his squire's complaint that they are looked upon as "a couple of madmen" by the other characters. Calling virtue "its own reward" (31), the knight launches into a lengthy speech against hypocrisy and then asks: "What is a good-natured man? Why, one who, seeing the want of his friend, cries, and pities him! . . . Sancho, let them call me mad; I'm not mad enough to court their approbation" (32). It seems wrong to conclude, as one scholar has done, that the ideas expressed by the knight in this passage are discrepant with the rest of the play;[34] on the contrary, he later acts on the very principles of which he spoke by interceding on behalf of the young lovers against the match with Squire Badger, who is preferred by the girl's father (act 3, scene 14).

In that scene Don Quixote appears as an exemplarily good-natured man. His conduct there has been seen to be patterned after his defense of the humble lovers in the episode of Camacho's wedding (2:21–22), where he preaches the identical prescription for marital bliss. Following that episode, which is one of the few from which Don Quixote emerges as a true hero, he is

---

34. Émile Pons, "Fielding, Swift et Cervantes," *Studia Neophilologica* 15 (1942–43): 305–33; see 314–17. Pons also denies Fielding's alleged identification with Adams.

"honour'd" by everyone in town "as a Person of extraordinary Worth and Bravery" (Motteux translation, 2:21, 581), and esteemed as "both a *Cid* in Arms, and a *Cicero* in Arts" (2:22, 581). These expressions of genuine reverence undoubtedly left a strong impression on Fielding. *Don Quixote in England* reflects for the first time his view of the Manchegan knight "as a mixture of folly and wisdom" (Goldberg, *Art,* 28), which recalls the opinion voiced by some of Cervantes's own characters, such as the canon of Toledo (see 1:iv, xxii [49], 416). This duality in the knight's character, which Fielding had evidently grasped by the time he wrote his play, and which his sister articulated in *The Cry* where she alluded to the knight's mixture of "madness" and "extraordinary good sense," is modified in Parson Adams. As the knight oscillates between fits of madness and intervals of lucidity, so Adams can at one moment give moral advice or deliver a sermon with great eloquence and lucidity, while at the next moment he might lapse into absentmindedness.

Critics observe that the depiction of Don Quixote in Fielding's early play is neither so "amiable" (Goldberg, *Art,* 29) as Fielding later conceived him to be, nor so "endearing" (Tave, *Amiable Humorist,* 157) as the portrayal of Adams. These differences may indicate a shift occurring in Fielding's attitude toward the knight during the period between *Don Quixote in England* and *Joseph Andrews.* The transformation of Don Quixote in Adams evinces a much stronger sense of the knight's good nature than does the play's portrayal. Moreover, having subverted in the play the notion of Don Quixote's madness as something unique or peculiar by stressing that "all mankind are mad," Fielding disposed of the insanity theme almost altogether in *Joseph Andrews.* Though Adams is humorously compared to a madman on two occasions,[35] he bears no trace of Don Quixote's violent madness. Madmen were not popular figures in English literature of the eighteenth century, when literary tastes reflected the emerging middle-class morality. In Adams, Don Quixote's madness is replaced by mere absentmindedness.[36]

35. In *Joseph Andrews,* 3:9 we are told that Adams "fought like a madman," and this statement is followed immediately by an allusion to Don Quixote (219). In 4:5 Adams is seen "snapping his fingers, as if he had been mad" (250).

36. Cf. V. S. Pritchett, "Quixote's Translators," in *The Living Novel and Later Appreciations* (New York: Random House, 1964), 439–45; see 441. Fielding personally disdained those among his contemporaries who found sport in laughing at madmen. He was well familiar with Hogarth's *A Rake's Progress* (1735), whose eighth plate presents a chilling scene from Bedlam (reproduced in Paulson, *Hogarth's Graphic Works,* vol. 2, plates 149–50 [cat. no. 139]). Perhaps with that picture of human suffering in mind he states in *The Champion* (13 March 1740) that he cannot "entertain a good opinion of him, who could go to Bedlam, and divert

By the time he wrote *Joseph Andrews* Fielding had presumably concluded that the hero of a comic prose epic should be "amiable" rather than "odious." He articulated this conclusion two years later when he clarified his theory of that genre in the preface (see *Works,* 16:7–13, esp. 11) to Sarah Fielding's *David Simple* (1744). Eight years after that preface appeared with his sister's novel, he elaborated his benevolent notion of Don Quixote's character in a review of Charlotte Lennox's novel *The Female Quixote* (1752). Published in *The Covent-Garden Journal* a month after an article in which he acclaimed Lucian, Cervantes, and Swift as "that great Triumvirate" of satire,[37] this review contains Fielding's final and fullest critical assessment of the *Quixote,* including his explication of the knight as an amiable amalgam of folly and wisdom. According to Fielding, the novel's "Incidents" are "exquisitely ridiculous," and "Don Quixote is ridiculous in performing Feats of Absurdity himself." The reader's "Affection" for him is preserved "in the midst of all the Follies of which [he is] guilty," because he is portrayed as a person "of good Sense, and of great natural Parts, . . . of a very sound Judgement, and what is much more endearing, as [a person] of great Innocence, Integrity and Honour, and of the highest Benevolence" (*Covent-Garden Journal,* no. 24 [24 March 1752], Jensen ed., 1:280). In another article several months later, Fielding formulated a notion of humor that would allow for both the ridiculousness and the nobler qualities of Don Quixote.[38]

Fielding's review of Lennox's novel attests that he regarded ridicule as essential to the *Quixote*'s moral purpose. He evidently accepted the common assumption that Cervantes's intent was simply to render—as the *Quixote*'s narrator puts it—"those fabulous, nonsensical Stories of Knight-errantry, the Object of publick Ridicule" (Motteux translation, 2:74, 936).[39] Hence in his

---

himself with the dreadful frenzies, and monstrous absurdities, of the wretches there" (*Works,* 15:242).

37. No. 10 (4 February 1752), included in Henry Fielding [pseud. Sir Alexander Drawcansir], *Covent-Garden Journal,* 2 vols., ed. Gerard Edward Jensen (New Haven: Yale University Press, 1915), 1:194. All quotations from this journal are from the Jensen edition.

38. *Covent-Garden Journal,* no. 55 (18 July 1752), Jensen ed., 2:59–64; see esp. 62–63. See also Goldberg's discussion of this essay (*Art,* 30–31).

39. All quotations of the *Quixote* in the present part of this study are drawn from the Modern Library edition of Motteux's translation. Because part 1 of this edition is divided into four books, its chapter numbers do not follow a single consecutive sequence; hence in my citations from part 1, a colon separates the part and book numbers, which are followed by the chapter and (where necessary) page numbers, with the chapter number from standard modern editions in brackets. The chapters of part 2 of this edition are numbered in a single consecutive sequence.

Lennox review Fielding considers Cervantes "as an Author who intended not only the Diversion, but the Instruction and Reformation of his Countrymen: With this Intention he levelled his Ridicule at a vicious Folly, which in his Time universally prevailed in Spain, and had almost converted a civilized People in a Nation of Cut-throats" (*Covent-Garden Journal,* Jenson ed., 1:279).

In keeping with this understanding, Fielding may be seen in parts of *Joseph Andrews* to emulate not only Cervantes's comic "Manner" but also what he views as the Spaniard's corrective "Intention," with one obvious difference. The "vicious Folly" that prevailed in Fielding's England, and against which he "levelled his Ridicule" for "the Instruction and Reformation of" his *own* countrymen, was not the outdated ideals and modes represented in books of chivalry, but rather, the hypocritical morality popularized by Richardson's sentimental novel *Pamela, or Virtue Rewarded* (1740–41), which Fielding had already attacked in his *Apology for the Life of Mrs. Shamela Andrews* (1741).

While he admired Cervantes's corrective purpose and was captivated by Don Quixote's amiability, Fielding's Lennox review details his reservations about the structure of the *Quixote*'s narrative, and the likelihood of the knight's adventures. Reformulating an opinion he had expressed elsewhere,[40] he suggests that the *Quixote* lacks "that Epic Regularity which would give it the Name of an Action," and he says of its "loose and unconnected Adventures" that "you may transverse the Order as you please, without any Injury to the whole" (281). Though this negative appraisal of the novel's structure has been justly refuted by at least one modern scholar,[41] Fielding's doubts about the story's verisimilitude would be difficult to contest. Finding it hard to concede that the head of a "very sensible" gentleman might be "entirely subverted by reading Romances," he considers Don Quixote's illusions "extravagant and incredible" (281–82).

This last reservation leads Cross to conclude that by the time Fielding reviewed Lennox's novel, his "interest in Cervantes . . . had considerably declined" (*History,* 2:433–34; cf. 414), and hence that had *Joseph Andrews* been written in 1752, the *Quixote*'s impact upon it would have been much smaller. It has also been conjectured that by the time Fielding wrote *Tom Jones,*

---

40. According to Fielding in his preface to *David Simple,* the "fable" in that novel, like the ones in *Hudibras* and the *Quixote,* "consists of a series of separate adventures, detached from and independent on [*sic*] each other, yet all tending to one great end" (*Works,* 16:11).

41. See A. A. Parker, "Fielding and the Structure of *Don Quixote,*" *Bulletin of Hispanic Studies* 33 (1956): 1–16.

which appeared three years before the review, he had grown "independent"[42] of the influence of Cervantes's comic technique. Though such speculations have no bearing on *Joseph Andrews,* we should note that they ignore Fielding's reverent invocation of Cervantes's muse to "fill my pages with humour" in *Tom Jones,*[43] as well as his proud assertion in *The Journal of a Voyage to Lisbon,* composed the year before his death and published posthumously (1755), that one of his themes "seems (in the stile [*sic*] of Don Quixote) a task reserved for my pen alone."[44]

The Bearing of the
Quixote *on Fielding's Latitudinarian Ethic*

Fielding's innovative equation of quixotism with good nature allowed him to perceive Don Quixote as a character of positive religious significance, and therefore as a worthy model for his ideal clergyman. This perception was supported by Fielding's view of good nature as an active predisposition to charity, the completion of Christian morality. In demonstrating its essentialness as a category in Fielding's Pelagian ethic, and as the ballast for his optimism regarding the possibilities for social amelioration, Battestin finds good nature to be embodied more fully in Adams than in any of the novelist's other heroes. Citing the equation of good nature and quixotism in *The Coffee-House Politician,* he notes: "It was only natural that Fielding should fashion Parson Adams, the incarnation of good nature, after the model of Don Quixote" (*Moral Basis,* 181 n. 47). However, Battestin fails to pursue the idea that Fielding must have esteemed the Manchegan knight as a Christian paragon. The *Quixote*'s bearing on Fielding's thought was not, as most previous scholarship suggests, strictly artistic or literary in nature. Fielding's view of the novel and its hero also pertained directly to his religious, moral, and ethical thinking.

   For Fielding, as Battestin has shown, good nature has four main characteristics that correspond to the cardinal features of the benevolist ethic espoused by

42. Thornbury, *Fielding's Theory,* 123–24. Cf. Knowles, "Cervantes and English Literature," 293–94.

43. *The History of Tom Jones, a Foundling,* bk. 13, chap. 1, *Works,* 5:33.

44. *The Journal of a Voyage to Lisbon* (New York: Nardon, 1963), 47.

latitudinarian divines such as Barrow, Tillotson, Clarke, and Hoadly: its expression is an active, universal benevolence; its motivation is in the sympathetic emotions of compassion and pity; its source is the heart's natural goodness; and its personal recompense is the delight the good man takes in performing labors for others.[45] Located in the benevolist tradition, Fielding's concept of good nature reflects his strong opposition to the negative appraisal of human nature found in Hobbes and Calvinism, and to the philosophy of the Stoics, whose contempt for the affections he deemed contrary to Christian love.

Though good nature per se is a natural virtue, Fielding placed it in a distinctly Christian context, describing it in various places as a godlike, Christlike, and essential Christian virtue.[46] That he had already identified this virtue with Don Quixote and quixotism suggests the plausibility that he viewed the Manchegan knight as a Christian paragon, though he made no explicit reference to him as such. What elements in the *Quixote* might have led Fielding to adopt such a view?

Fielding's stated admiration of Don Quixote's "highest Benevolence" alerts us to the particular aspect of the *Quixote* that has the greatest bearing on his ethics and religious thought: the characterization of its hero as a man dedicated to doing good works on behalf of others. At the novel's outset, where the mad gentleman resolves to set forth as a knight "as the Service of the Publick," and for the purpose of "redressing all manner of Grievances" (1:i, i[1], 4), Fielding would have admired the hero's impulse toward altruistic action. In his strong disapproval of the Methodist emphasis on faith alone, he would have delighted in the knight's assertion that "Faith without good Works is dead" (1:iv, xxiii[50], 423), which paraphrases a biblical passage cited in countless sermons by Fielding's favorite latitudinarian churchmen.[47]

Don Quixote's disposition shares certain natural affinities with the benevolist ethic espoused by those liberal divines. If Fielding happened to contemplate Cervantes's hero in the light of their sermons, he must have recognized a set of

45. Battestin's analysis is based on R. S. Crane, "Suggestions Toward a Genealogy of the 'Man of Feeling,' " *Journal of English Literary History* 1 (1934): 205-30. For a challenging critique of this famous essay, see Donald Greene, "Latitudinarianism and Sensibility: The Genealogy of the 'Man of Feeling' Reconsidered," *Modern Philology* (1977): 159-83.

46. See Fielding's entry in *Champion* (27 March 1740), *Works*, 15:256-60, esp. 260; "Of Good-Nature" (verse-essay), in *Miscellanies* (1743), *Works*, 12:258-61; *An Essay on the Knowledge of the Characters of Men* (1752), *Works*, 14:281-305, esp. 286.

47. On the use of James 2:26 in the latitudinarians' sermons see Battestin, *Moral Basis*, 18.

the knight's prominent traits that correspond to the four principal features of the latitudinarian ethic.

First, Don Quixote expresses the same active, universal benevolence. The climax of *Don Quixote in England,* where the knight lends his support to the oppressed lovers, reflects the deep impression made on Fielding by the former's benevolent action at Camacho's wedding. Certainly Fielding would have been no less struck by some of Don Quixote's other benevolent actions, such as his intervention on behalf of the farm-boy Andrés or his freeing of the galley-slaves. The knight repeatedly asserts that his performance of these actions is mandated by his chivalric calling, such as when he learns that the galley-slaves are being taken involuntarily to row in the king's galleys: "If it be so, said Don *Quixote,* they come within the Verge of My Office, which is to hinder Violence and Oppression, and succour all People in Misery" (1:iii, viii[22], 152). On numerous other occasions he is equally assertive about his desire to perform deeds beneficial to mankind. For example, at the duke's castle, one of the duchess's duennas enters the knight's bedroom at night wearing a white veil and holding a candle. When she drops the candle, leaving them both in the dark, he mistakes her for a distressed phantom and offers to aid her in whatever way he can:

> ["]If thou art a Soul in Torment, tell me, and I will endeavour thy Ease to the utmost of my Power; for I am a Catholick Christian, and love to do good to all Mankind; for which Reason I took upon me the Order of Knight-Errantry, whose extensive Duties engage me to relieve the Souls in Purgatory.["] (2:48, 758)

Fielding probably would have had a twofold response to this passage. Like most readers he would have found ridiculous Don Quixote's misperception of the duenna as a "Soul in Torment." As an enlightened Anglican, he would have also laughed at (what he would have viewed as) the knight's Catholic superstitiousness, which is betrayed in the reference to "Souls in Purgatory." At the same time, however, Fielding would have admired the knight's desire "to do good to all Mankind" and his sense of obligation "to relieve" anyone in distress. Fielding himself once defined good nature as "that benevolent and amiable temper of mind, which disposes us to feel the misfortunes, and enjoy the happiness of others; and, consequently, pushes us on to promote the latter, and prevent the former" (*Characters of Men, Works,* 14:285).

With his eye on the *Quixote*'s ethical implications, Fielding must have noticed that the knight's ridiculous actions are counterbalanced by his good intentions. This balance is especially clear in the episode of Master Pedro's puppet-show. After realizing that the group of fleeing Christians whom he tried to rescue, and the band of pursuing Moors whom he attacked with his sword, were actually marionettes, and that he himself, in violently intervening in the theatrical action, has destroyed the stage and all the puppets, Don Quixote tries to justify his action to the dismayed puppeteer and everyone else present: "I could not contain my Fury, and acted according to the Duties of my Function, which obliges me [to] take the injured Side. Now, tho' what I have done proves to be quite contrary to my good Design, the Fault ought not to be imputed to Me, but to my persecuting Foes" (2:26, 617). He later instructs Sancho to base his actions on "Uprightness of Intention," "just Grounds," and "good Desires" (2:43, 727).

The second trait of the latitudinarian ethic that Don Quixote shares is his compassion and pity. These emotions are reflected in his benevolent actions, and explicated in his sympathetic injunctions to Sancho about how to govern the "island" granted him by the duke: for example, "Let the Tears of the Poor find more Compassion, though not more Justice, than the Informations of the Rich"; "When the Severity of the Law is to be softned [*sic*], let Pity, not Bribes, be the Motive"; and

> ["]In the Trial of Criminals, consider as much as thou canst without Prejudice to the Plaintiff, how defenceless and open the miserable are to the Temptations of our corrupt and deprav'd Nature, and so far shew [*sic*] thy self full of Pity and Clemency; for though God's Attributes are equal, yet his Mercy is more attractive and pleasing in our Eyes, than his Justice.["] (2:42, 721)[48]

48. During Sancho's governorship of Barataria it becomes clear that he has retained his master's lesson on judicial compassion. Called on to settle a certain court case about which the law is ambiguous as to whether the defendant should be executed or set free, Sancho commands that he be set free. He explains:

> " '[T]is always more commendable to do Good than Hurt. . . . Nor do I speak this of my own Head; but I remember one Precept, among many others, that my Master Don *Quixote* gave me . . . , which was, that when the Scale of Justice is even, or a Case is

Highly conscious of his own sympathetic emotions, Don Quixote has already told Sancho: "I am not sorry to have Charity and Compassion bear so great a Part in my Commendation, since my Nature has always dispos'd me to do good to all Men, and hurt to none" (2:25, 609). The knight's reference to his own charitable and compassionate "Nature" is one of many indicators that may have alerted Fielding to the quality in Don Quixote that corresponds to the third essential trait of the benevolist ethic: his heart's natural goodness. As Sancho testifies to the squire of the Knight of the Grove, Don Quixote "has not one Grain of Knavery in him; he's as dull as an old crack'd Pitcher, hurts no Body, does all the Good he can to every Body; a Child may persuade him it is Night at Noon-Day, and he is so simple, that I can't help loving him" (2:13, 522).

Fielding would have also appreciated that Don Quixote, in accordance with the fourth hallmark of the latitudinarian ethic, finds recompense in the delight he takes in performing his benevolent labors. The knight expresses such delight very early on. Upon hearing cries coming from behind a thicket at the start of the Andrés adventure, he thanks heaven "for favouring me so soon with an Opportunity to perform the Duty of my Profession, and reap the Fruit of my Desires!" (1:i, iv[4], 20). This passage evidently caught Fielding's interest; the allusion to reaping "the Fruit of my desires" is echoed in *Don Quixote in England* where the knight, after helping the young lovers finally win consent to marry, expresses satisfaction at the sight of their joy: "Here are the fruits of knight-errantry for you. This is an instance of what admirable service we are to mankind. —I find some adventures are reserved for Don Quixote of la Mancha" (act 3, scene 14, 67). The same passage from the *Quixote* will later inform the scene of Adams's rescue of Fanny in *Joseph Andrews* (2:9).

The passages we have discussed suggest a natural affinity between Don Quixote's character and the latitudinarian ethic, showing why Fielding was prone to see him as an embodiment of good nature. Another pertinent aspect of Fielding's concept of good nature was his awareness that the good man's simplicity, compassion, and charity leave him vulnerable to the schemes of hypocrites and self-seeking men (see Battestin, *Moral Basis,* 72). Fielding's early recognition of such vulnerability in Don Quixote was evidenced by

---

doubtful, we should prefer Mercy before Rigour' " (*Quixote,* Motteux translation, 2:51, 785–86).

Constant's assertion in *The Coffee-House Politician* that "Good nature is Quixotism" because "every Princess Micomicona will lead her deliverer into a cage."

Most scholarship on the sources for *Joseph Andrews* approaches Fielding's imitation of the *Quixote,* and his affinities with the religious values and social ethics of the Low Church divines, as separate matters. This procedure gives rise to the impression that Cervantes's novel and the latitudinarian sermons presented Fielding with totally disparate ingredients that he merely mixed and served up in his novel. I suspect, however, that Fielding recognized some of the affinities between Don Quixote and the benevolist ethic. It even seems plausible that in preparing to compose that novel "in Imitation of" Cervantes, he may have reread the *Quixote* with some of those sermons in mind. I shall elaborate briefly on why I believe this the case.

In Battestin's view the homilies of the latitudinarian moralists decisively influenced Fielding's conception of Parson Adams and Joseph Andrews, and the importance of Barrow's sermon "Of Being Imitators of Christ" in its connection to the meaning and structure of Fielding's novel is "unrivaled" by *Pamela* and the *Quixote:* "The sermons present four points of special significance: (1) the depiction of the good man as hero; (2) the notion that the sum of his goodness is *chastity* (or virtue or temperance . . .) with respect to himself, and *charity* with respect to society; (3) the choice of Joseph and his rejection of Potiphar's wife to exemplify the former, and of the pilgrim patriarch Abraham, the epitome of human faith expressed in works, to represent the latter; and (4) the analogy of the good man's life in a world of vanity and vexation to a pilgrimage through strange lands to his true home" (*Moral Basis,* 26–27). While Battestin demonstrates the correspondence between *Joseph Andrews* and the sermons on these four points, it remains to be considered how Fielding's imitation of Cervantes might be linked with his adaptation of those sermons.

As we have seen, the *Quixote* presents a hero whom Fielding viewed as a good man. In this respect the novel corresponds to the first significant point in the latitudinarians' sermons. In correspondence to the second point, Don Quixote is exemplarily chaste and charitable. We have already discussed his predisposition to charity and good works. His chastity is a motif closely connected to his self-image as a knight and his fidelity to Dulcinea. If the biblical Joseph rejects the amorous advances of his master's wife, Don Quixote on several occasions withstands what he (wrongly) perceives to be assaults on his chastity, as in his nocturnal encounter with the whore Maritornes in the stable of an inn (1:iii, ii [16]). The chastity motif crops up again during Don Quixote's stay at the duke's castle. In his lengthy reply to the humorless ecclesiastic who reproves him there for his chivalric fantasies, Don Quixote lists among his own virtues as a knight the fact that he is "none of this Age's vicious Lovers, but a chaste Platonick" (2:32, 651). Later he becomes convinced that one of the duchess's duennas (Altisidora) wants "to make an Attempt on his Chastity" (2:48, 757), so he launches into an eloquent speech on his resolve to remain faithful to Dulcinea.

Don Quixote is chaste not only in the sexual sense, but also in the more general sense of temperance. He exemplifies this virtue most extremely in his penance in the Sierra Morena, where his behavior borders on the ascetic (1:iii, ix-x[23-24]). The classical ideal of temperance later finds expression in his second set of counsels to Sancho on proper government (2:43).

The *Quixote* cannot be said to correspond explicitly to the third hallmark of the Low Church sermons because nowhere in it is the knight compared to Joseph or Abraham. However, Fielding may well have drawn such comparisons himself, given the *Quixote's* dual emphasis on the knight's chastity and charity, and given Fielding's preoccupation with a tradition of sermons in which the identification of that pair of virtues with those two biblical figures is commonplace. Indeed, it has been suggested that by naming his quixotic hero Abraham Adams he "invited the comparison" (Welsh, *Reflections,* 189) of Don Quixote to the biblical Abraham.

Fielding had to be aware of the *Quixote's* correspondence to the fourth distinctive point in the latitudinarian sermons: the analogy, both scriptural and classical, between the good man's life in a vain and vexing world, and a pilgrimage through alien and hostile lands to one's true home. This analogy, which had been popular among Puritan preachers of the seventeenth century and provided the basis for Bunyan's *The Pilgrim's Progress* (pt. 1, 1678; pt. 2, 1684), was often employed by the latitudinarian sermonizers (see Battestin, *Moral Basis,* 41-43). Thus, in "Of Being Imitators of Christ," Barrow cites Abraham as his primary *exemplum* of faith, in whose life

> we may see the father of the faithful . . . deserting his home and fixed habitation, his estate and patrimony, his kindred and acquaintance, to wander he knew not where in unknown lands, . . . leading an uncer-

tain and ambulatory life in tents, sojourning and shifting among strange people, devoid of piety and civility, (among Canaanites and Egyptians;) upon a bare confidence in the Divine protection and guidance.[49]

This passage could almost be used to describe Don Quixote's journeys and adventures if only the "Canaanites and Egyptians" encountered by the biblical patriarch were replaced by the monsters, enchanters, and hostile knights that haunt the madman's imagination. Years before Fielding read Barrow's sermon, his notion of Cervantes's hero as a good man wandering in an alien and unfriendly realm had provided the conceptual basis for *Don Quixote in England,* which removes the knight from his native Spain and places him in a strange country whose citizens prove to be none too friendly. When asked near the end what brought him to England, Don Quixote replies: "A search of adventures, Sir; no place abounds more with them. I was told there was plenteous stock of monsters; nor have I found one less that I expected" (act 3, scene 14, 67).

This passage's pertinence to *Joseph Andrews* should not be overlooked. Prefigured in Barrow's account of Abraham's journey among Canaanites and Egyptians, the image of Don Quixote among "monsters" in eighteenth-century England anticipates the predicament of Parson Adams, whose experience of so much hostility on the road leads him almost "to suspect that he was sojourning in a country inhabited only by Jews and Turks" (2:16, 151). These correspondences suggest that when Fielding wrote his novel, he viewed Don Quixote and the biblical Abraham not as disparate figures, but as analogous pilgrims and moral paragons.

49. *The Works of Isaac Barrow,* 3 vols. (London: Nelson, 1847), 1:337–46; here 339.

2

Don Quixote's Religious Transformation in Joseph Andrews

Parson Adams is the first quixotic hero in any novel after Cervantes to be used as a vehicle for religious expression. Though modeled after Don Quixote, he embodies Fielding's own latitudinarian ideal of the good-natured man. In analyzing the transformation of the knight in *Joseph Andrews,* we should keep in mind this novel's religiohistorical context.

We have already compared Don Quixote's effort to sustain his chivalric fantasy against reality and reason to the struggle of religious faith to sustain itself against secularity and skepticism in the modern age. Among the symptoms of secularization in England from the Restoration on was the widespread public contempt for the Christian religion and its clergy—a development recorded and lamented by such witnesses as Edward Chamberlayne, Robert South, Daniel Defoe, Swift, Steele, and Thomas Secker.[1]

---

1. Remarks by these men on the contempt for the clergy are cited by Battestin, *Moral Basis,* 130–31. Cf. Bishop [Joseph] Butler's "Advertisement," *The Analogy of Religion Natural and Revealed to the Constitution and Course of Nature,* in *The Works of Bishop Butler,* 3 vols., ed. J.

Various theories blaming the clergy itself were proposed to account for this contempt,[2] which had reduced the priestly order to a lowly social position and impoverished many of its members. Fielding, as we know from his four-part "Apology for the Clergy" in *The Champion* (29 March, and 5, 12, 19 April 1740), held corrupt clerics responsible for the scorn directed against their order. When, some seven months later, Richardson's *Pamela* appeared (in November) and became an immediate best-seller, Fielding must have been offended by the reports that clergymen were lauding from their pulpits what he regarded as a silly and immoral book. He composed *Shamela* not only to burlesque Richardson's tale of "Virtue Rewarded," but also to reprimand the clergy for publicly praising it, and for stupidly regarding one of its characters, Parson Williams, whom Fielding deemed an asinine meddler, as a compliment to their order. *Joseph Andrews,* insofar as it too expresses Fielding's reaction against *Pamela,* offers a portrayal of true virtue, truly rewarded, as an ethical alternative to a tale of false virtue, falsely rewarded, and presents what his preface calls a "comic epic-poem in prose" as a stylistic alternative to *Pamela's* epistolary form. But Fielding's novel also expresses his reaction against the contempt for the clergy, presenting as its central protagonist an ideal parson who embodies the reverse of Parson Williams.[3]

What has escaped scholarly notice is the crucial bearing that Fielding's concern with the scorn for the clergy must have had on his conception of Parson Adams as quixotic. The Manchegan knight was the perfect model for Adams because his predicament was analogous to that of any good clergyman in eighteenth-century England. Like Don Quixote, who is ridiculed as a knight in an unchivalric age, the true clergyman whom Fielding's "Apology for the Clergy" defines as humble, charitable, and poor, would have been derided in a society that scorned the priestly order. As the representative of a widely despised religion, any minister exemplifying its faith and moral ideals would naturally seem quixotic. Fielding's image of some "successor of Christ's disciples" being derided by "boys and beaus, and madmen, and rakes, and fools, and villains" ("Apology for the Clergy," *Works,* 15:283), could not find a more

---

H. Bernhard (London: Macmillan, 1900), 2:xvii, which Battestin does not mention. Also, in n. 1 on that page, the editor cites another pertinent statement by Butler (1751), and similar ones by Bishop G. Burnet (1713) and Robert Southey (1820).

2. See Battestin, *Moral Basis,* 132–35. Cf. Smith, *Wealth,* 2:309–10; Cragg, *Church,* 127–28.

3. Charles B. Woods, "Fielding and the Authorship of *Shamela,*" *Philological Quarterly* 25 (1946): 248–72; see 271–72.

fitting moral explication than the one the knight offers for his own humiliating entrapment in a cage near the end of the *Quixote*'s first part: "Virtue is more zealously persecuted by Ill Men, than 'tis belov'd by the Good" (1:iv, xx[47], 403).

Analysis of the Text

Like the *Quixote*, which opens as a parody of chivalry books but evolves into a satire of life, *Joseph Andrews* starts out as a satire of *Pamela*, but becomes something very different after its tenth chapter: a satirical critique of Christendom in eighteenth-century England. Fielding's imitation of Cervantes is manifest in the facetious chapter headings and introductory chapters; lengthy interpolated tales; general drollery of style; epic narrative of a journey-of-the-road featuring curious adventures; contrast of actual and illusory evils; focus on a pair of contrasting protagonists; and characterization of Adams.[4]

The following analysis of *Joseph Andrews* traces the religious transformation of Don Quixote in Adams, dividing the text into four sections that correspond to what I regard as the four main stages of development in Fielding's imitation of Cervantes. Informed by the novel's subtitle, Fielding's implied reader should watch throughout the narrative for derivations from the *Quixote*. The author's prefatory apology for Adams alerts us to Don Quixote's transformation. The allusions to the parson's "perfect simplicity," "the goodness of his heart," "worthy inclinations," and engagement in "low adventures" (12) disclose his essential likeness to the knight, and we recall that Cervantes closed his own prologue similarly with words of praise for Don Quixote.

---

4. Cf. the parallels drawn by Cross, *History,* 1:322–23; Dudden, *Fielding,* 1:337–39; Johnson, *Fielding's Art,* 48–49. The fullest analysis of the *Quixote*'s formal influences on *Joseph Andrews* remains Goldberg's *Art.* See also Homer Goldberg, "The Interpolated Stories in *Joseph Andrews* or 'The History of the World in General' Satirically Revised," *Modern Philology* 63 (1966):295–310; Leon V. Driskell, "Interpolated Tales in *Joseph Andrews* and *Don Quixote:* The Dramatic Method as Instruction," *South Atlantic Bulletin* 33 (1968):5–8.

1:1–10: "The best man in the world"

The first ten chapters of *Joseph Andrews* satirize *Pamela* by inverting the sexual scenario. Whereas in Richardson's novel a beautiful young waiting-maid has to defend herself against the indecent advances of her employer's son, in Fielding's novel her handsome, strapping young brother must resist the attempts at seduction by his mistress, Lady Booby (1:5 and 8), and by her waiting-gentlewoman, Mrs. Slipslop (1:6). Adding spice to this satire, whose theme of male chastity would have seemed inherently funny to English readers at the time, the author parodies the epistolary format of *Pamela* by including two letters written by the sexually harassed young man to his sister (1:6 and 10).

Parson Adams first appears in a role strictly subsidiary to Joseph's story. Most of the attributes that he shares with Don Quixote are established in his formal introduction in the third chapter: erudition (though the hidalgo does not know all the languages the parson knows), "good sense, good parts, and good nature" (17), innocence, generosity, friendship, courage, and above all, simplicity, a childlike ignorance of worldly ways and therefore a vulnerability to deception.[5] Further in the same profile two more parallels become evident: like the Manchegan gentleman, the parson lives in the country, and is fifty years of age. Besides his Anglicanism and clerical profession, the main factor distinguishing Adams from the hidalgo is his familial situation: while the hidalgo is unmarried and lives with his niece and housekeeper, Adams is "a little encumbered with a wife and six children" (17).

Adams's initial entry into the action occurs in the cameo scene in Sir Thomas Booby's kitchen (1:3), where he questions Joseph on religious matters, and is pleased by the boy's extraordinary devotion. Their mentor-pupil relation-

---

5. Given Fielding's association of good nature with quixotism, and the *Quixote's* bearing on his benevolist ethic, it seems natural that this portrait of Adams as the incarnation of good nature should lend itself to comparisons with the knight. Thus, as the Manchegan hidalgo spends his days and nights reading before he becomes a knight, and later impresses almost everyone he meets with his erudition, so Adams is "an excellent scholar" who, through "the most severe study," acquired a remarkable "fund of learning." As Fielding describes Don Quixote as a person "of good Sense, and of great natural Parts, and . . . of a very sound Judgement" (*Covent-Garden Journal,* no. 24 [24 March 1752], Jensen ed., 1:280), so Adams is "a man of good sense, good parts, and good nature." As Sancho claims that his master "has not one Grain of Knavery in him; . . . a Child may persuade him it is Night at Noon-Day" (*Quixote,* Motteux trans. 2:13, 522), so the narrator of *Joseph Andrews* compares Adams to "an infant" and observes that because "he had never any intention to deceive, so he never suspected such a design in others." And, as Sancho says in that same passage of the *Quixote* that Don Quixote "is so simple, that I can't help loving him" (522), so we are told that Adams's "simplicity was his characteristic."

ship is established here, but is not yet comparable to the knight-squire relation-ship of Don Quixote and Sancho. Adams's offer to instruct Joseph in Latin is hardly analogous to Don Quixote's promise of an island to Sancho; while the knight's promise is enough to entice the peasant to join him as squire, Adams's offer is scoffed at by Slipslop and proves ineffectual a few days later when Lady Booby takes the boy to London as her footman.

While Joseph is in London, we hear of Adams indirectly through the boy's two letters to Pamela, both of which cite him as a paragon of virtue. In one (1:6), which Joseph writes after Lady Booby's first attempt to seduce him, he relates his desire to return home to see Adams, whom he calls "the best man in the world" (24). Between this and the second letter, Joseph resists an onslaught by the libidinous Slipslop and a second overture from Lady Booby, whose frustration and wrath culminate in her command for him to be thrown out of the house (1:9). In his second letter (1:10), which he writes before learning of his dismissal, Joseph reaffirms his resolve to resist his mistress's advances, citing Pamela, Adams, and the biblical Joseph as the three "examples" he keeps in mind to fortify his chastity. In emphasizing Adams's chastity the novel's author might have in mind Don Quixote, who is, according to Cervantes's description, "the most chaste Lover."[6] Especially significant is the linking of Adams with Pamela through Joseph's claim that he has found their examples equally edifying. Once Adams arrives at the Dragon Inn (1:14), where he begins to emerge as the "most glaring" of all the characters, he will appear as a moral and religious alternative to what Fielding viewed as the shallow piety and hypocritical "virtue" of Richardson's heroine.

The satire of *Pamela* ends with Joseph's banishment from Lady Booby's London home. As soon as he steps out of her house, his situation ceases to be a parodic inversion of Pamela's predicament in the home of the aggressive Mr. B., and a satirical counterpart to the biblical Joseph's predicament in the bedroom of Potiphar's wife. In what remains of book 1, the *Quixote* replaces *Pamela* and the Bible as the author's primary source of paradigms for characters and incidents.

6. This phrase occurs in the last paragraph of Cervantes's "Author's Preface" in the *Quixote*, Motteux trans., n.p.

1:11–18: The Theme of Charity and the Dragon Inn

From chapter 11 on, the author imitates a series of characters and incidents from the *Quixote*. Though chosen eclectically, these all pertain to the themes of charity and the clergy. However, the idea of sustainedly modeling Adams after the knight is not apparent at first. When the author first draws on the *Quixote* to characterize Adams, he adapts as his model not the knight, but a certain minor figure from one of that novel's interpolated tales. I base this claim on the one allusion to Adams in chapter 11. Joseph, upon departing from London, sets out to return to his country parish where there lives a certain "young girl" (Fanny) whom he longs to see:

> They had been acquainted from their infancy, and had conceived a very early liking for each other; which had grown to such a degree of affection, that Mr. Adams had with much ado prevented them from marrying, and persuaded them to wait till a few years' service and thrift had improved their experience, and enabled them to live comfortably together.
>
> They followed this good man's advice, as indeed his word was little less than a law in his parish; for as he had shown his parishioners, by a uniform behaviour of thirty-five years' duration, that he had their good entirely at heart, so they consulted him on every occasion, and very seldom acted contrary to his opinion. (39)

This portrait bears an uncanny resemblance to a passage from the goatherd's tale in the *Quixote* describing Marcela's uncle, the curate, in whose charge that extraordinarily beautiful girl was left after the deaths of her parents:

> But though he'd have been glad to have got fairly rid of her, as soon as she was fit for a Husband, yet wou'd not he advise or marry her against her Will; for he's a good Man, I'll say that for him, and a true Christian every Inch of him, and scorns to keep her from marry [*sic*] to make a Benefit of her Estate; and, to his Praise be it spoken, he has been mainly commended for't more than once, when the People of our Parish meet together. For . . . the Parson must have been a good Body indeed, who cou'd bring his whole Parish to give him a good Word, especially in the Country. (1:ii, iv[12], 70)

Adams and Marcela's uncle are strikingly similar. Each is a country parson,[7] the one Roman Catholic, the other Anglican. Each is a "good man" who has earned the favor of all his parishioners through service and example. And each has demonstrated great prudence by discouraging some youth(s) from marrying prematurely. These similarities, together with the notable resemblance between Fanny and Marcela, both of whom are parentless[8] and described as exceptionally beautiful, suggest that the above portrait of Adams is based on Cervantes's characterization of Marcela's uncle. Why Fielding would view the uncle as a paradigm is easy to imagine. Though only a minor character in the goatherd's tale about the tragic love of the youth Chrysostom for Marcela, the uncle is, of all the clergymen in the *Quixote,* the only one presented in an unqualifiably positive light. As an ideal country parson, a "good man," and "a true Christian every Inch of him," he embodies the sort of clerical paragon that Adams is meant to be.

At this point in *Joseph Andrews* the author has yet to tap Don Quixote's full potential as a model for Adams, who remains a subsidiary character in the background of the main action. Aside from a passing allusion in chapter 12, he is not mentioned for three chapters. And the next time the knight is called to our mind, it is in connection with Joseph, not Adams.

This occurs in the account of Joseph's first adventure on the road (1:12). His encounter with two ruffians who beat him with sticks, rob him, strip him naked and leave him lying in a ditch, and the uncharitable reaction of the coach-riders who come across him in that condition, recall not only the biblical story of the Good Samaritan, but also the *Quixote'*s fourth chapter, where the knight falls from his horse and is left sprawled on the ground after a pair of muleteers beat and throw sticks at him. The coach-riders who make jokes at Joseph's misfortune thus appear as counterparts to the Toledan merchants who are amused by the knight's beating.[9]

By this point the author clearly views the *Quixote* as a fruitful source for

7. The term "Parson" is Motteux's rendering of *clérigo.* Earlier Marcela's uncle was introduced by the goatherd as "the Parson of our Parish" (Motteux trans., 69), which is Motteux's translation of "saceredote y beneficiado en nuestro lugar" (Porrúa edition, 60). Motteux's rendering of both *clérigo* and *sacerdote* as "Parson" may have drawn Fielding's attention to Marcela's uncle as a model for his own good parson, Adams. Motteux consistently translates *cura* as "Curate," for example, in reference to Don Quixote's village priest. For distinctions between the English connotations of "Rector," "Parson," and "Curate," see the Modern Library edition, 3 n.1.

8. Only at the end of *Joseph Andrews* do Fanny and the other characters (and the reader) learn that she is the daughter of Gaffar and Gammar Andrews, who are alive and well.

9. These parallels are noted by Johnson, *Fielding's Art,* 51–52.

characters and incidents to imitate in developing his theme of Christian charity and benevolence. Previous scholarship has failed to show how often he appeals to Cervantes's novel for that purpose in the remainder of book 1. There can be no doubt that the depiction of Joseph's recovery at Mr. Tow-wouse's inn (1:13-18) is inspired by the episode in the *Quixote* where the knight, following his brutal beating by the Yangüesans, recovers at an inn he mistakes for a castle. To begin with, not only is an inn a quintessentially Cervantine setting,[10] but the two episodes open similarly. When Don Quixote and Sancho show up at the inn's front door, the knight is "lying quite a-thwart the Ass" led by his squire (1:iii, ii[16], 95). The wounded Joseph likewise must be transported to Tow-wouse's inn in a carriage. In the *Quixote,* after an initial inquiry by the innkeeper who asks Sancho "what ail'd" his master, we are told:

> The Inn-keeper had a Wife, very different from the common sort of Hostesses, for she was of a charitable Nature, and very compassionate of her Neighbour's Affliction; which made her immediately take care of Don *Quixote,* and call her Daughter (a good handsome Girl) to set her helping-hand to his Cure. One of the Servants in the Inn was an *Asturian* Wench.... This charming Original likewise assisted the Mistress and the Daughter; and with the latter, help'd to make the Knight's Bed, and a sorry one it was....
>
> In this ungracious Bed was the Knight laid to rest his belabour'd Carcase, and presently the Hostess and her Daughter anointed and plaister'd him all over, while *Maritornes* (for that was the Name of the *Asturian* Wench) held the Candle. (95-96)

From this amusing yet exemplary scene of Christian charity Fielding adapts several elements for his own purposes. The unforgettable description of Maritornes's physical appearance (which I deleted from the above-quoted passage for the sake not of delicacy but of space), furnished the model for Fielding's earlier description of Mrs. Slipslop (1:6).[11] But as Joseph now assumes the role of the bedridden knight, the combined images of the hostess's

10. Fielding was particularly impressed by the comic adventures that take place at inns in the *Quixote. Don Quixote in England* is set almost entirely at one. No fewer than six inns and alehouses are depicted in *Joseph Andrews,* and several such establishments figure importantly in *Tom Jones.*

11. On the similarity between Maritornes and Slipslop, see Goldberg, *Art,* 232-34.

"good handsome Girl" and the "*Asturian* Wench" who helps "to make the Knight's Bed" furnish models for Betty the chambermaid. Upon Joseph's arrival at the inn, this "good-natured wench" (Betty) promptly "made his bed" and "soon got Joseph to bed" (1:12, 45), and then runs about doing whatever else she can to bring comfort to him: preparing him a fire, finding clothing for him, and summoning a surgeon to his aid. Don Quixote's need for a "Surgeon" is mentioned at one point during his recovery at the inn (1:iii, iii[17], 105), but no physician is summoned.

At the same time, the "charitable Nature" of Cervantes's hostess is inverted in the character of Mrs. Tow-wouse, who personifies the name of her husband's inn, the Dragon. On learning that a penniless, naked, bloody moribund (Joseph) has been admitted to their establishment, she becomes enraged and announces that she will "send him packing." When her husband meekly suggests that they accommodate the "poor wretch" for the sake of "common charity," she is anything but receptive to the idea: " 'Common charity, a f--t!' says she, 'common charity teaches us to provide for ourselves, and our families; and I and mine won't be ruined by your charity, I assure you' " (46).

Fielding's later portrait of Mrs. Tow-wouse's grotesque physical appearance (1:14) may find its source in Hogarth's illustration[12] for the passage quoted from the *Quixote* above. The picture shows the ailing knight reclined in a ramshackle attic inn as the kind hostess anoints him in the presence of her daughter, Maritornes, and Sancho. The hostess, whose physical appearance is not described in Cervantes's text, is endowed by Hogarth with a grotesque physiognomy and physique. Under the apparent conviction that such grotesqueness more befits an uncharitable character than a charitable one, Fielding seems to have copied this depiction meticulously in his portrayal of Mrs. Tow-wouse, of whose "countenance" his narrator notes: "Hogarth himself never gave more expression to a picture" (50).

Serving as a foil to Mrs. Tow-wouse, whose ugly face and figure reflect the hideousness of her soul, the chambermaid appears as an exemplar of charity based on Cervantes's portrayal of Maritornes. After the infamous scene of Sancho's "blanketing" in the inn's backyard, we are informed:

---

12. Reproduced in Paulson, *Hogarth's Graphic Works*, vol. 2, plate 159 (Cat. no. 147). Sean Shesgreen, *Literary Portraits in the Novels of Henry Fielding* (DeKalb: Northern Illinois University Press, 1972), 100, remarks upon the Hogarthian quality of Mrs. Tow-wouse's portrait, but fails to link it with a specific print by the artist.

> But *Maritornes's* tender Soul made her pity a male Creature in such
> Tribulation; and thinking he had danc'd and tumbled enough to be
> a-dry, she was so generous as to help him to a Draught of Water. . . . [H]e
> lifted up the Jug to his Nose, but finding it to be meer [*sic*] Element, he
> spirted out again the little he had tasted, and desir'd the Wench to help
> him to some better Liquor: So she went and fetch'd him Wine to make
> him Amends, and paid for't too out of her own Pocket; for . . . 'twas
> said of her, that tho' she was somewhat too free of her Favours, yet she
> had something of Christianity in her. (1:iii, iii[17], 110–11)

Maritornes's compassion and charity toward Sancho prefigures Betty's treatment of Joseph during his recovery in bed at the Dragon Inn. When "Joseph
complained he was dry, and desired a little tea" (1:13, 49), his request is
refused by Mrs. Tow-wouse, who orders Betty to take him "some small beer"
instead.

> Betty obeyed her mistress's commands; but Joseph, as soon as he had
> tasted it, said, he feared it would increase his fever, and that he longed
> very much for tea; to which the good-natured Betty answered, he
> should have tea, if there was any in the land; she accordingly went and
> bought him some herself, and attended him with it. (50)

A comparison of this passage with its counterpart in the *Quixote* reveals
how Fielding imitated Cervantes to illustrate the virtues of Christian charity
and good works. The two scenes are structurally identical: in each, the sufferer
(Sancho, Joseph) is found to be "a-dry" or "dry"; the servant (Maritornes,
Betty) takes him a beverage (water, beer) which he rejects; the sufferer then
requests another drink (wine, tea), which the servant accordingly purchases
with her own money and takes to him. The two servants display the same
religious quality: Maritornes's charitable deed shows that "she had something
of Christianity in her," just as Betty's shows that she is "good-natured," which
in Fielding's terms is synonymous with being a good Christian.[13]

---

13. Another affinity between Betty and Maritornes is their sexual promiscuity. Betty is
discovered in bed with Mr. Tow-wouse (*Joseph Andrews*, 1:17), allows various male employees
and guests at the inn "to share her favours" (1:18, 70), and tries unsuccessfully to seduce Joseph
(1:18). The narrator explains: "Betty . . . had some good qualities," including "good-nature,
generosity, and compassion, but unfortunately, her constitution was composed of those warm

The next Cervantine scene is Joseph's interview with Parson Barnabas
(1:13), who exemplifies the same bad qualities as the unnamed curate at
Camacho's wedding in the *Quixote* (2:21). A comparison of the Joseph–
Barnabas interview and the exchange between Basilio and the curate following
Basilio's apparent suicide attempt shows Fielding again to be adapting material
from the *Quixote* for his own moral and religious purpose. Both scenes
present an apparently dying youth (Basilio, Joseph) who is unable to detach his
thoughts from his beloved (Quiteria, Fanny), and an unsympathetic clergyman
(the curate, Parson Barnabas) who exhorts the youth to forsake all such
worldly attachments and to concentrate on reconciling his soul with heaven.
Just as the minor figure of Marcela's uncle served as Fielding's model for the
good Parson Adams, so this equally minor curate becomes the model for the
bad Parson Barnabas. What would tarnish this curate's image in Fielding's view
is his lack of pity for an apparently dying man; though he is described as
"tenderhearted" (571), the only concern he shows the seemingly moribund
Basilio is with trying to elicit a confession from him. Barnabas likewise lacks
compassion; after interviewing Joseph, whom he gives no hope for survival, he
rushes his prayers for the sick youth's soul so as not to miss out on the punch
being served downstairs.

Our foregoing analysis reveals an interesting pattern in book 1, chapters
11–13 of *Joseph Andrews*. In these chapters no fewer than six scenes, all of
them involving Joseph and his relationships or encounters with other characters,
find analogies in the *Quixote:* the analogies between Joseph and Fanny being
discouraged by Adams from marrying prematurely, and Marcela being discouraged by her uncle; Joseph's assault by two ruffians, and Don Quixote's beating
by two muleteers; his uncharitable reception by the coach-riders, and the
uncaring response of the Toledan merchants to the knight's beating; his
coldhearted treatment by Mrs. Tow-wouse, and inversely, the compassionate

ingredients which . . . were by no means able to endure the ticklish situation of a chambermaid at
an inn, who is daily liable to the solicitations of lovers of all complexions" (70). Similarly, the
observation by Cervantes's narrator that Maritornes "had something of Christianity in her," is
preceded by the humorous qualification: "'tho she was somewhat too free of her Favours"
(Motteux trans., 1:iii, iii[17], 111). Maritornes's prostitution revealed itself in her comically
ill-fated tryst with a muleteer in the previous chapter. The moral lesson that Fielding evidently
drew from Cervantes's portrayal of Maritornes and illustrates in his own characterization of Betty,
is first, that the humblest servant can epitomize the highest Christian virtues ("good nature,
generosity, and compassion"); and second, that those virtues do not preclude, nor are precluded by,
the all-too-human quality of concupiscence.

nursing of Don Quixote by the hostess; his charitable treatment by Betty, and the similar treatment of Sancho by Maritornes; and the lack of compassion shown to Joseph by Barnabas, and the lack of that same emotion shown to Basilio by the curate. These analogies all show Fielding to be adapting characters and scenes from the *Quixote* to illustrate goodness, charity, compassion, pity, or qualities opposed to those virtues, and the first and the sixth analogy show him adapting models for depicting a good clergyman and a bad one respectively.

This pattern in Fielding's imitation of Cervantes helps explain his idea of introducing Adams into the main action as a quixotic hero. While the most essential traits Adams shares with Don Quixote were disclosed in his formal introduction in chapter 3, his quixotism does not really manifest itself until chapter 14. The author, having drawn characters and scenes eclectically from the *Quixote* to develop the Christian themes of charity, compassion, and the clergy in the last three chapters, now realizes that the best way to combine and develop those themes is to make his ideal parson the central protagonist, and to fashion him sustainedly after that most entertaining exemplar of charity and compassion, the Manchegan knight.

Adams's quixotism reveals itself at once upon his arrival at the Dragon Inn, where he is introduced anonymously as "a grave person" (1:14, 50). Having gone directly to the kitchen, he overhears several persons discussing the robbery that took place the previous night, and "the poor wretch" (Joseph) who lies above them in a "dreadful condition." Like the Manchegan knight, who feels called upon to aid anyone in distress, the unnamed newcomer instinctively feels "a great deal of emotion at the distress of this poor creature" (50) whom he has not yet seen. Driven by "compassion," he begs the surgeon who is present to do whatever he can to heal the sick man, adding that it is "the duty of men of all professions to apply their skills *gratis* for the relief of the poor and necessitous" (51). However, in accordance with Fielding's view of good nature and quixotism as qualities vulnerable to exploitation, this compassionate man—who, sharing Don Quixote's bibliophilia, admits that "the little I know I have from books" (51)—is derided by the surgeon and laughed at by the others there.

Between his reunion with Joseph (1:14) and their departure from the inn, Adams proves to be as naïve as Don Quixote about financial affairs. Almost out of money, he requests a loan from the landlord, offering to leave his sermons (which he does not yet realize he left at home) as a pawn (1:16). When the landlord does not comply, we are reminded of Don Quixote's financial incompetence; the latter, who does not carry money, irritates inn-keepers by refusing to pay his bills on the grounds that the knights of old were never known to do so.[14]

Adams's likeness to Don Quixote develops further in his initial encounter with Parson Barnabas (1:16), and in his discourse with both Barnabas and the bookseller who arrives at the inn (1:17). Like the knight, who defends chivalry books against the criticism advanced by the priest and the canon of Toledo that such literature is false and foolish, Adams defends the value of publishing religious sermons against the arguments of Barnabas and the bookseller that sermons are not worth spending the money to print because no one reads them. Curiously, it is while serving as a foil to Barnabas, the bad clergyman, that Adams first betrays his only consistent flaw, which he shares with Don Quixote: vanity. Though not nearly so vain as Don Quixote, who speaks of himself as one of the greatest knights that ever lived, Adams boasts to Barnabas about his own skill as a writer of sermons.

Adams again resembles Don Quixote when he responds to Barnabas's criticism of Whitefield's attack on clerical corruption. In his ensuing harangue, Adams's protest against "the detestable doctrine of faith against good works" (1:17, 67) accords with the knight's claim that "Faith without good Works is dead." Adams praises Hoadly's *A Plain Account of the Nature and End of the Sacrament* (1735) as a book "calculated to restore the true use of Christianity, and of that sacred institution" (68). By lauding the book in these terms, Adams suggests his own role as Fielding's symbol of Christian and clerical reform, and, as such, recalls Don Quixote's self-image as the restorer of the Age of Gold.

Adams will next be seen as he sets out on a journey patterned intermittently after episodes from Don Quixote's chivalric career.

2:1-17; 3:1-13: A Cervantine Journey

The two middle books of *Joseph Andrews* imitate the Cervantine narrative of a journey-of-the-road, and in them Adams truly emerges as the novel's "most glaring" character, assuming the role of a quixotic, clerical knight-errant. Though there are obvious contrasts between Adams and Don Quixote,[15]

14. E.g., *Quixote,* 1:i, iii[3] and 1:iii, iii[17]. Fielding adapted this motif in *Don Quixote in England,* where the knight's refusal to pay his bill to the English innkeeper is a recurrent issue.

15. As Dudden observes, in addition to their contrasts in familial and religious status, Don

their ongoing similarities are now completed by Adams's partnership with a contrasting character. Although there are differences between Sancho and Joseph in their relation to their companions,[16] the two share the function of foil: as the squire's reason and common sense counterbalance the knight's illusions, so the footman's alertness, practicality, and worldly knowledge counterbalance the parson's naïveté, impracticality, and absentmindedness.

Aside from Adams's likeness to Don Quixote, two aspects of books 2 and 3 are of special interest: the modeling of five episodes (all involving Adams) after ones from the *Quixote,* and the satirical critique of English Christendom revolving around the depiction of Adams as a quixotic misfit in a hostile world. Let us examine both aspects.

Quixotic Episodes   The narrative recommences with Adams's discovery that he forgot his sermons at home (2:2), which necessitates his return with Joseph to their parish. In the account of that journey, Fielding's narrator twice refers to Don Quixote by name (2:16, 145; 3:9, 219), and no fewer than five episodes involving Adams find counterparts in Cervantes's novel.

The first is the parson's fight with an innkeeper who threatens to harm Joseph (2:5). When Adams appears "all over covered with blood" (100) after the innkeeper's wife has dumped a pan of hogs puddings on him, we are reminded of Don Quixote's battle with the wine-skins, during which Sancho "saw his Blood run all about the House" (1:iv, viii[35], 304). The next quixotic incident is Adams's rescue of Fanny from an attempted ravisher (2:9).

Quixote and Adams differ in the readings on which their worldviews are based (chivalry books vs. Homer and the classical poets); in temperament (madness, melancholy, asceticism vs. absent-mindedness, cheeriness, proclivity for eating, drinking, smoking); and in the sources of their pride (knightly prowess vs. learning and preaching) (*Fielding,* 1:338–39). Also, as Goldberg points out, while the knight's chivalric obsession causes him to misperceive all aspects of reality, the parson's misperceptions are, with few exceptions, confined to his misassessments of the characters of other persons (*Art,* 74–76).

16. As A. R. Penner points out, Sancho views Don Quixote as "master," while Joseph regards Adams as his mentor and "friend." And in the *Quixote* the middle-aged, unmarried knight, not the younger, married squire, is the one who pursues love, whereas in *Joseph Andrews* the young single footman, not the middle-aged married parson, is the one in love ("Fielding's Adaptation of Cervantes' Knight and Squire," *Revue de Littérature Comparée* 41 [1967]:508–14; see 510). There is disagreement over whether the characters of Adams and Joseph and their relationship ever change in the course of their novel as do those of Don Quixote and Sancho. According to Dick Taylor, Jr., Joseph undergoes a "noticeable and sympathetic change and development of character into maturity" ("Joseph as Hero of *Joseph Andrews,*" *Tulane Studies in English* 7 [1957]:91–109; here 109). For Goldberg's objection to this view, see *Art,* 90–91 n.19.

After an account of the parson's stroll and conversation with a man who makes excessive boasts of courage, we are told:

> Night overtook them much about the same time as they arrived near some bushes; whence, on a sudden, they heard the most violent shrieks imaginable, in a female voice. Adams offered to snatch the gun out of his companion's hand. "What are you doing?" said he. "Doing!" said Adams; "I am hastening to the assistance of the poor creature whom some villains are murdering." "You are not mad enough, I hope," says the gentleman, trembling: " . . . This is no business of ours; let us make as much haste as possible out of the way, or we may fall into their hands ourselves." The shrieks now increasing, Adams made no answer, but snapt his fingers, and, brandishing his crabstick, made directly to the place whence the voice issued; and the man of courage made as much expedition towards his own home. (115)

Compare this passage with the one that opens the account of Don Quixote's adventure with Andrés:

> The Knight had not travell'd far, when he fansy'd he heard an effeminate Voice complaining in a Thicket on his right Hand. "I thank Heaven (said he when he heard the Cries) for favouring me so soon with an Opportunity to perform the Duty of my Profession, and reap the Fruit of my Desires! For these Complaints are certainly the Moans of some distressed Creature who wants my present Help." Then turning to that Side with all the Speed which *Rozinante* could make, he . . . came into the Wood. (1:i, iv[4], 20)

The two scenarios are strikingly similar, despite the fact that Don Quixote is alone on his horse during the day, while Adams is on foot with a companion at night. Several Cervantine elements (from Motteux's translation) are hardly altered by Fielding: "a Thicket" becomes "some bushes"; "an effeminate Voice" (which turns out to be that of the farm-boy) becomes "a female voice"; "Cries" and "Moans" become "shrieks"; and "some distressed Creature who wants my present Help" becomes "the poor creature whom some villains are murdering." Most important, Adams fulfills Don Quixote's heroic role. Undoubtedly impressed by the knight's courage in the Andrés adventure, Fielding exposes the coward-ice of Adams's companion in order to highlight the parson's bravery. While presenting Adams as totally sane, the author hints at his likeness to the insane knight by having the "man of courage" suggest that the parson would be "mad" to intervene in such a dangerous situation. Though the crimes in which the knight and parson intervene differ (Andrés's whipping vs. Fanny's attempted ravishment), both heroes believe their roles as deliverers to be divinely sanctioned: as Don Quixote thanks "Heaven" for giving him this "Opportunity," so Adams tells Fanny "He doubted not but Providence had sent him to her deliverance" (2:9, 117). He even addresses her as "damsel" (121), the chivalric archaism used regularly by Don Quixote to address young women (in Motteux's translation).

Adams's rescue of Fanny demonstrates his good nature as well as his courage, and leads him into a predicament based on the theme introduced in *The Coffee-House Politician:* "Good nature is Quixotism, and every Princess Micomicona will lead her deliverer into a cage." Fanny becomes Adams's unwitting Micomicona when, as the result of his deliverance of her, he is apprehended with her for attempted theft and murder, with the ravisher as their accuser (2:10), and is brought before a judge as a highwayman and robber (2:11).

Adams's third quixotic adventure is the "night scene" (3:2), whose corre-spondences to Don Quixote's nocturnal adventure of the funeral procession include the motif of mysterious lights being mistaken for ghosts; the false anticipation of a physical threat; and the hero's display of courage—that is, Don Quixote's attack on the procession, and Adams's advance "towards the place of combat" (163).

Up through the "night scene," all the Cervantine characters, scenes, and adventures in *Joseph Andrews,* with the exception of Barnabas, are drawn from the *Quixote's* first part. Fielding had at least two reasons for favoring part 1. First, it contains most of the comic inn scenes he loved so much, and *all* the ones he adapts in *Joseph Andrews.* Second, it contains all the interpolated stories, which he greatly admired. One of these stories, the "History of the Curious Impertinent" (*Quixote* 1:iv, vi–viii[33–35]), pro-vides the formal prototype for his own novel's "history of Leonora" (2:4

and 6).[17] However, Fielding certainly did not ignore Cervantes's sequel. Though his preference for the *Quixote's* first part will reassert itself in book 4 of his own novel, the two main episodes in book 3 are inspired by a pair of episodes in the *Quixote's* second part.

Adams's encounters with Mr. Wilson (3:2–4) and "the hunter of men" (3:6–7) are the last two episodes in his journey to reflect the *Quixote's* influence. They recall the knight's encounters with Don Diego de Miranda, the "Gentleman in Green" (2:16–18), and with the duke and duchess (2:30–57, 68–70). These episodes inspired Fielding's idea of having Adams meet successively, and receive opposite treatment from, two antithetical characters: an exemplar of Christian charity and benevolence (Wilson), and an embodiment of devilish cruelty and contempt (the hunter of men).

What Fielding found in the episode of Don Diego and imitates in the Wilson episode is an account of the comic hero's encounter with a character whose person and life-style (for some readers) provide an ethical norm for the whole novel.[18] Alluded to in the heading of part 2, chapter 16 of the *Quixote* as a "Sober Gentleman of La Mancha," Don Diego is introduced as an anonymous "Gentleman in Green" whom Don Quixote and Sancho meet on the road. Like Don Quixote, this "Traveller" is "about Fifty." From his "Mien and Appearance," the knight judges him "to be some Man of Consequence" and "a Man of Quality." Gazing at Don Quixote, the man in green thinks to himself that he "never beheld before such a strange appearance of a Man." Taking in the spectacle of Rocinante's "Lankness" and "the Long-back'd, Raw-bon'd Thing that bestrid him; His wan, meagre Face, his Air, his Gravity, his Arms and Equipage," the gentleman concludes that "such a Figure . . . perhaps had not been seen in that country time out of mind." Don Quixote notes the traveler's look of "Surprize" at his own "new and exotick [*sic*]" figure, and so to allay the man's curiosity he introduces himself as "one of those Knights who go in quest of Adventures," and explains his plan "to give a new Life to Knight-Errantry, that so long has been lost to the World." When Don Quixote boasts of the "many Valorous and Christian-like Atchievements"

17. See Goldberg, "Interpolated Stories," 303–7; *Art,* 189–96. Fielding's great admiration of the *Quixote's* interpolated tales is reflected in *Joseph Andrews,* 3:1, where he cites seven of their protagonists by name as examples of "true history" (157–58).

18. According to Mandel, Don Diego "provides an ethical focus for [Cervantes's] entire novel" ("Function of the Norm," 160). This opinion matches Goldberg's claim that the mature Wilson functions as *Joseph Andrews's* "central norm of sensible humanity" (*Art,* 105). Cf. Battestin, *Moral Basis,* 122–29.

by which he claims to "have merited the Honour of the Press in almost all the Nations of the World" (538), the man in green makes no attempt to hide his skepticism:

> I must confess, . . . I remain no less surpriz'd and amaz'd than ever. For is it possible there should be at this time any Knights-Errant in the World, or that there shou'd be a true History of a living Knight-Errant in Print? I cannot persuade myself there is any body now upon Earth that relieves Widows, protects Damsels, or assists Married Women and Orphans. (539)

This speech, whose emphasis on the knight's anachronicity bears on Fielding's depiction of Adams as a misfit, is followed by an exchange on the subject of chivalry books. When Don Quixote challenges the traveler's suggestion that such literature is "false," the latter suspects that the former is "distracted," and expects Don Quixote's "next Words would confirm him in that Opinion" (539).

Turning now to consider Adams's encounter with Wilson, we notice unmistakable similarities between the two episodes from the moment the parson and his two companions show up at Wilson's house seeking a place to rest. Wilson appears at the door as "a plain kind of man" (3:2, 164), and, like the man in green, he at first remains anonymous. Evidently struck by the way Cervantes's narrator traces the traveler's evolving impressions of Don Quixote, Fielding has his own narrator trace Wilson's developing opinion of Adams. In admitting the three strangers into his house, where his wife readily attends to them, Wilson has "no apprehensions from the civil behaviour of Adams" (164). But he soon has second thoughts. While they sit "cheerfully around the fire," Wilson,

> having surveyed his guests, and conceiving that the cassock, which, having fallen down, appeared under Adams's greatcoat, and the shabby livery on Joseph Andrews, did not well suit with the familiarity between them, began to entertain some suspicions, not much to their advantage. (165)

This line opens a lengthy paragraph patterned roughly after the four stages of development in Don Quixote's initial conversation with the man in green.

First, the "suspicions" which Adams's peculiar attire arouses in his host are analogous to the "Surprize" and "Curiosity" that the knight's "new and exotick" figure elicited in the man in green. Second, as Don Quixote seeks to allay the traveler's curiosity by introducing himself as a knight, so Adams announces to his equally curious host: "I am a clergyman at your service" (165). Third, as Don Quixote's boast about his "Atchievements" leaves the traveler unconvinced that anyone on earth still "relieves Widows, protects Damsels, [etc.]," so, after the parson claims that the two "poor young people" with him are his "parishioners, and I look on them and love them as my children," we are told that Wilson, "notwithstanding the simplicity which discovered itself in Adams, knew too much of the world to give a hasty belief to professions. He was not quite certain that Adams had any more of the clergyman in him than his cassock" (165). And fourth, as Don Quixote eventually launches into a learned and eloquent discourse on poetry, which "struck" the man in green "with so much Admiration, that he began to lose the bad Opinion he had conceiv'd of [Don Quixote's] Understanding" (543), so Adams, responding to his host's attempt to "try him" with a question about poetry, discourses so impressively on Homer that he leaves the gentleman "so far from entertaining any further suspicion of Adams, that he now doubted whether he had not a bishop in his house" (168).

Following his discourse on poetry, Adams satisfies Wilson's expressed "curiosity" (168) about Joseph and Fanny by relating their whole story. Afterwards, having "cured" Wilson of his suspicions, Adams asks Wilson "to return the favour" by telling his own "history," for Wilson's "extraordinary goodness . . . had raised in him more curiosity than he had ever known" (169). This request, which is met by Wilson's narration of the "history of his life" (3:3), matches the request Don Quixote makes to the man in green at the spot in Cervantes's text where we left off: "But before they enter'd into any further Conversation, Don *Quixote* begg'd him to acquaint him who he was, since he had given him some Account of his own Life and Condition" (539). There can be no doubt that Don Diego's ensuing speech figured prominently in Fielding's conception of Adams's encounter with Wilson (see Goldberg, *Art,* 196–200). Both Don Diego and Wilson are presented as perfect Christian gentlemen: Don Diego's account of his life-style epitomizes the Renaissance ideal of discretion (*discreción*), with his reason and sobriety providing a "norm" against which Don Quixote's extravagance and madness may be measured (Mandel, "Function of the Norm," 161), and Wilson embodies Fielding's latitudinarian ideal of good nature, with his worldly experience and knowledge serving as a foil to Adams's simplicity and naïveté.

For Wilson to be presented as so worldly-wise a man, certain aspects of his past must be revealed. This explains the formal difference between Wilson's "history," and Don Diego's account of his own "way of living." Don Diego's account is relatively brief, and focuses exclusively on his present life-style, while disclosing nothing about his past except that he was "born at a village." In contrast, Wilson's "history" comprises the longest chapter of Fielding's novel, and recounts exclusively the character's past. This "history" is followed by "A description of Mr. Wilson's way of living" (3:4), which closely resembles Don Diego's life-style. The idea of having Wilson narrate his own "history" may have been suggested to Fielding by Don Diego's avowal that he himself is "no Saint but a great Sinner" (540). While Cervantes would have viewed Don Diego as a sinner only insofar as he, like all humans, must be linked to Original Sin, the *Quixote* makes no mention of any specific sin committed by him. Fielding, however, provides a rationale for the paradoxical image of the sinner-saint by presenting Wilson as a good man with an immoral past. Wilson's "history" is often viewed as a Hogarthian account of a rake's progress: having lost his father at an early age, and thereby being forced to proceed through life with no source of moral guidance, Wilson lost himself in the world of pleasure and had to pass through a long series of follies (debauchery, promiscuity, prodigality, idleness, vanity, etc.) before repenting, meeting and marrying the perfect woman, and thereby attaining prudence and happiness.

From an ethical perspective, Wilson's two most crucial insights into his unhappy past are, first, that it is to his "early introduction into life, without a guide," that all his "future misfortunes" (170) are imputable, and second, that "vanity is the worst of passions, and more apt to contaminate the mind than any other" (180). These lessons, both of which bear on the novel's ethical meaning, accord with specific notions espoused by Don Quixote and Don Diego in their conversation. As illustrated by Adams's fatherly guidance of Joseph, Wilson's belief that a paternal "guide" is essential to the proper moral upbringing of a youth finds paradigmatic expression in Don Quixote's advice to Don Diego about the latter's relation to his son: "'Tis the duty of a Father to train [his Children] up from their tenderest Years in the Paths of Vertue [*sic*], in good Discipline and Christian Principles" (541). Likewise Wilson's declamation of vanity as "the worst of passions" not only reminds us that *Joseph Andrews* is, in its author's prefatory words, aimed at exposing "vanity or hypocrisy" as the two primal causes of "affectation," or "the true Ridiculous" (10), but also matches Don Diego's description of "Hypocrisy and Vainglory" as "Enemies that too easily possess themselves of the best guarded Hearts" (540).

There are significant parallels between Wilson's "way of living" and Don Diego's. Both men lead happy, retired lives with their families. Like Don Diego, who claims to "pass my time contentedly with my Wife, my Children and my Friends" (540), Wilson claims to be "neither ashamed of conversing with my Wife, nor of playing with my children" (3:4, 191), a statement that is borne out by his guests' observation of "the tenderness which appeared in the behaviour of the husband and wife to each other, and to their children" (192). Like Don Diego, who is "no curious Inquirer into the Lives and Actions of other People," Wilson literally and figuratively cultivates his own "little garden," where he seldom passes "less than six hours of the twenty-four" (190). Both characters are also paragons of unostentatious charity. Don Diego habitually gives "to the Poor, without making a Shew of it, or presuming on my good Deeds" (540). His munificence is manifest when Don Quixote and Sancho stay four days at his house and meet "with a very generous Entertainment" and a "kind Reception" (2:18, 561). Likewise, Adams and his two companions meet with "kind entertainment" (3:4, 193) at Wilson's home, where they pass the night, and the parson is "delighted" by

> an instance or two of [the Wilsons'] charity: for whilst they were at breakfast, the good woman was called for to assist her sick neighbour, which she did with some cordials made for the public use; and the good man went into his garden at the same time to supply another with something which he wanted thence, for they had nothing which those who wanted it were not welcome to. (192)

Before Don Quixote departed from Don Diego's home, the latter likewise "desired him to command whatever their House afforded, assuring him he was sincerely Welcome to do it" (561).

Having reshaped elements from the Don Diego episode for depicting Adams's encounter and visit with Mr. Wilson, Fielding draws on another episode from part 2 of the *Quixote* for depicting the parson's encounter and visit with Wilson's devilish antithesis. While the differences between Adams's experience with the "hunter of men" and Don Quixote's meeting and sojourn with the duke and duchess are too obvious to warrant discussion, several striking similarities should be noted. The latter episode begins with an account of "What Happen'd to Don Quixote with the Fair Huntress" (2:30), who turns out to be the duchess. Similarly the former episode opens with a "hunting adventure" (3:6) in which Adams is mauled by a wicked squire's hounds, much to the squire's amusement.[19] Like Don Quixote, who becomes dupe to a series of "Jests" contrived by his hosts at the ducal mansion, Adams visits the squire's house and is there subjected to a "roasting"—an eighteenth-century English diversion which Fielding condemned[20]—consisting of a string of "jokes" perpetrated by the squire and his cronies (3:7). When Adams, "standing up in the posture of one who intended to make a speech" at the squire's dinner table, rebukes his host and the latter's cronies for having "treat[ed] me with disrespect as a parson" (209), we are reminded of "Don Quixote's Answer to His Reprover" at the duke's dinner table, where the knight "suddenly got up, shaking from Head to Foot for Madness, as if he had Quick-silver in his Bones" (2:32, 650) to reply to the grave ecclesiastic who condemned his chivalric illusions.[21] Finally, as the duke sends horsemen in pursuit of Don Quixote and Sancho after they leave his castle, so the squire sends some cronies in pursuit of Adams and his two companions after they escape from his house.

Perhaps more than any other aspect of Fielding's "Imitation" of Cervantes, his adaptation of the themes of predation, "jokes," and *Schadenfreude* from the ducal episodes to portray the parson-hunting events attests the *Quixote's* crucial bearing on the picture *Joseph Andrews* presents of its contemporary England as a distinctly unchristian world. Let us take a closer look at that picture.

---

19. The mauling of Adams by the hounds is also reminiscent of Don Quixote's combat with a flock of sheep (*Quixote,* 1:iii, iv[18]); his being buffeted by a herd of bulls (2:58); and his being trampled by a pack of pigs (2:68).

20. See his essay on "roasting" in *Champion* (13 March 1740), *Works,* 15:240-43.

21. In his characteristic manner as imitator, Fielding does not simply copy "Don Quixote's Answer to His Reprover," but rather reshapes elements from it for his own purposes. While Don Quixote informs his clerical "Reprover" that "the Presence of these noble Persons, and the Respect I have always had for your Function, check my just Resentment, and tie up my Hands from taking the Satisfaction of a Gentleman" (*Quixote,* 2:32, 650), one of the squire's cronies tells Adams: "If you was [*sic*] not a parson, I would not take these words; but your gown protects you" (*Joseph Andrews,* 3:7, 210). The difference is that while Don Quixote is sincere in his expression of "Respect" toward the clergy's "Function," the squire's crony desists from challenging Adams not out of respect for his clerical "gown," but out of cowardice.

Critique of English Christendom   Books 2 and 3 of *Joseph Andrews* constitute, among other things, a critique of English Christendom. This critique revolves around the portrayal of Adams as a quixotic good man traveling through a hostile world. Battestin's thesis that the parson's innocence and role as a pious pilgrim recall his biblical namesakes, Adam and Abraham, is not to be disputed. However, the most prominent characteristics of the first man and the first patriarch are also comically combined (though surely unwittingly on Cervantes's part) in Don Quixote, who is an innocent man of faith wandering through an environment that conflicts with his ideals.

It is in the discrepancy between Adams's primitive Christian ideals and expectations, and the unchristian society with which he actually comes into contact, that we discern Fielding's modification of the quixotic principle—the conflict of fantasy and reality—as a means for criticizing English Christendom. The central criterion for moral judgment in this critique is charity, which Adams defines as "a generous disposition to relieve the distressed" (3:13, 233), and which he regards as the sine qua non of the Christian: "Whoever, therefore, is void of charity, I make no scruple of pronouncing that he is no Christian" (2:14, 142). In book 1 the charity theme was developed positively by the postilion, Betty, and Adams, and antithetically by some of the coach-riders, Mrs. Tow-wouse, and others at the Dragon Inn. In the course of Adams's journey with Joseph, whose "moral reflections" (3:6) elaborate the parson's definition of charity, almost all the strangers whom they encounter represent the opposite of that ideal.

Aside from Mr. and Mrs. Wilson, the only charitable individuals Adams meets are a peddler who pays a bill for him (2:15), and one friendly innkeeper (2:16). All the other innkeepers are hostile and greedy. The man of courage, Parson Trulliber, and the false promiser in book 2 are all uncharitable hypocrites. The man of courage cowardly refuses to assist Adams to rescue someone in distress. Trulliber, the hog-breeding antithesis of Homer's charitable swine-herd Eumaeus,[22] behaves inhospitably toward his fellow parson and refuses to loan him some much-needed money. And the false promiser makes empty offers of charity to him. In book 3 the "roasting" squire and his henchmen are devilish antitheses of the charitable Wilsons. Finally, Adams's journey is capped off by his abusive ride in the chariot of Lady Booby's steward, Peter Pounce (3:13): after denigrating charity as "a mean parson-like quality" (233),

22. See Douglas Brooks, "Abraham Adams and Parson Trulliber: The Meaning of 'Joseph Andrews,' Book II, Chapter 14," *Modern Language Review* 63 (1968):794–801.

this malicious hypocrite insults Adams so acrimoniously that the latter leaps out of the chariot, preferring to walk the last mile rather than to ride in the company of such a wicked man.

Adams's journey presents the spectacle of a Christian paragon traveling through a country that professes to be Christian, but whose inhabitants prove unworthy of that name through their hostility, uncharitableness, and cruelty toward the parson and his companions. This is a land whose "high" and "low" denizens are "so far from looking on each other as brethren in the Christian language, they seem scarce to regard each other as of the same species" (2:13, 132). At its worst, this land can produce such human "curs" (3:6, 201) as the "roasting" squire and his cronies, one of whom equates "Christians" with "vermin" (205).

Aside from representing the "pilgrimage" of the Christian good man "from the vanity of the town to the relative naturalness and simplicity of the country" (Battestin, *Moral Basis,* 129) Adams's journey has a quixotic resonance. Don Quixote left home under the illusion that he is a knight, only to come into constant conflict with reality. Likewise, Adams left his parish only to find himself in a world that refuses to conform to his primitive Christian ideals and expectations. After failing to obtain a loan from Trulliber or anyone else in that parson's parish, he laments that "it was possible, in a country professing Christianity, for a wretch to starve in the midst of his fellow-creatures" (2:15, 143). On learning later that a man's promises of free lodging and other amenities to him were empty, he cannot hide his dismay: "Good Lord! . . . what wickedness is there in the Christian world! I profess almost equal to what I have read of the heathens" (2:16, 150).

Conceived as someone morally superior to the immoral majority, any eighteenth-century "good man" was bound to appear out of place in most social situations. While Adams epitomizes this type, his role as a social misfit and foil to immorality also derives from Don Quixote. As the knight contrasts the moral perfection of the Golden Age with the corruption of his own "degenerate Age," so Adams—like his author[23]—looks back fondly to what another character calls "the example of the primitive ages," or "the Church in its infancy" (1:17, 67), and observes of his own age: "Good Lord! what wicked

---

23. In his journalism and essays Fielding speaks of the corruption of his own "Gothic leaden age" (*Of True Greatness* [1741], *Works,* 12:249–57; here 254), which he contrasts with the natural simplicity of "the first Ages of the World" (*Covent-Garden Journal,* no. 11 [8 February 1752], Jensen ed., 1:202).

times these are!" (3:3, 171). By their chosen professions, both Don Quixote and Adams serve heaven in a special sense. The Manchegan claims that he and other knights are "the Ministers of Heaven, and the Instruments of its Justice upon Earth" (1:ii, v[13], 75), while Adams, as parson, is an ordained minister of God. Not unlike Don Quixote, who says that the "proper and natural Office of Knights-Errant" is to perform such altruistic tasks as "relieving Widows, protecting Damsels, assisting Marry'd Women and Orphans" (2:16, 538), Adams conceives of his clerical office in the loftiest terms, and tries to convince one innkeeper that

> "there is something more necessary than life itself, which is provided by . . . the learning of the clergy. Who clothes you with piety, meekness, humility, charity, patience, and all the other Christian virtues? Who feeds your souls with the milk of brotherly love, and diets them with all the dainty food of holiness? . . . —Who doth this?" "Ay, who, indeed!" cries the host; "for I do not remember ever to have seen any such clothing or such feeding." (2:17, 156)

The host's reply, which is analogous to Don Diego's skeptical response to Don Quixote's self-characterization as a knight ("I cannot persuade myself there is any body now upon Earth that relieves Widows, protects Damsels" [2:16, 539]), is a reminder that Adams lives in a time when the clergy is scorned. In denying "to have seen any such clothing or such feeding," this kindhearted innkeeper—who told Adams earlier, "I honour the clergy" (1:16, 151)—is not expressing contempt so much as simply observing that clergymen in reality do not live up to Adams's lofty ideals.

This point squares with one of the most crucial elements in Fielding's critique: the implicit argument that corrupt clergymen are themselves responsible for the general contempt for their profession. By the time Adams and that innkeeper meet, the reader should realize that with the exception of Adams, none of the six clergymen met or mentioned in the novel's first two books are of a sort that would be liable to clothe or feed souls with Christian virtues. These "bad" clergymen not only lack all the primitive Christian virtues that Fielding defines as essential to their profession in his "Apology for the Clergy," but also demonstrate the sort of vices that any "good" Christian would abhor: hypocrisy, pride, avarice, etc. (see Battestin, *Moral Basis,* 143–46). Such clergymen bring the ministry into the sort of contempt that is sensed when Slipslop utters to Adams "some reflections on the clergy not decent to repeat" (2:13, 135), or when Peter Pounce mocks the poor parson's "torn cassocks" and "pitiful curacy" (3:13, 234). Such contempt manifests itself in its cruelest form when "parson-hunting" becomes a squire's "sport" (3:6-7).

Like Don Quixote, who travels as a knight through an unchivalric world where chivalry is dead, Adams travels as a primitive Christian through a "wicked" world where the religion of Christianity has all but ceased to exist, largely because the clergymen who are supposed to uphold it have brought themselves into contempt through their corruption. The climactic difference is that Don Quixote in the end sadly gives up his career as a knight, returns to his village, and dies, whereas Adams happily returns to his parish and, in his role as a parson, achieves a sort of triumph by seeing that Joseph and Fanny are joyfully married despite all opposition.

4:1-16: Return and Conclusion

In the fourth and final book, which opens with the return of all the principal characters to the parish, Cervantes's influence on Fielding's narrative diminishes as the focus shifts to the events leading up to the marriage of Joseph and Fanny. Though Adams at times drops out of the reader's view, he remains the "most glaring" character, and some of the scenes that involve him have unmistakably Cervantine resonances.

Fielding's final book begins by paraphrasing the opening words of the *Quixote*'s penultimate chapter, which relates the warm reception of the defeated knight and squire "When they were entering into the Village" (2:73, 925) and exchanged embraces with the priest and the bachelor while a group of boys "ran hooping and hollowing about 'em through the Town" (926). The narrator of *Joseph Andrews* tells of the "affection" Adams received from his parishioners as he "entered the parish": "They flocked around him like dutiful children round an indulgent parent, and vied with each other in demonstrations of duty and love" (4:1, 236). The expressions of annoyance by the wives toward their husbands in the "discourse which happened between Mr. Adams [and] Mrs. Adams" (4:8) and "The Wise and Pleasant Dialogue between Sancho Panza, and Teresa Panza his Wife" (2:5) are too alike to be merely coincidental. The "History of Two Friends" narrated by Adams's young son

(4:10) is akin in theme and plot to Cervantes's "History of the Curious Impertinent" (see Goldberg, *Art,* 192-95), and the interruption of the former narration by Joseph's scuffle with the foppish Beau Didapper (4:11) is structurally similar to the interruption of the latter narration by Don Quixote's combat with the winesacks. The "curious night-adventures" at Booby Hall, where Adams inadvertently winds up in bed with Slipslop, and then with Fanny (4:14), parallel the incident that begins when Don Quixote pulls Maritornes to his bedside after mistaking her for the "Daughter of the Lord of the Castle" (1:iii, ii[16]).[24] Finally, when Adams, in exulting over Joseph's wedding, accidentally "gave spurs to his horse, which the generous beast disdaining . . . immediately ran away full speed, and played so many antic tricks that he tumbled the parson from his back," an accident that "afforded infinite merriment to the servants" (4:16, 294-95), we are reminded of the knight's frequent tumbles with Rocinante.

Despite Adams's kinship to Don Quixote, the two characters' fates are very different: the defeated knight solemnly dies in Cervantes's final chapter, whereas Adams is alive and well at the close of Fielding's novel. Our last glimpse of him is at the joyful wedding feast, where he "demonstrated an appetite surprising, as well as surpassing, everyone present," and, "being well filled with ale and pudding, had given loose to more facetiousness than was usual to him" (4:16, 297). The character whom this bacchanalian image recalls from the *Quixote* is not the ascetic, melancholy knight, but his worldly, voracious squire. Indeed, this image displays a side of Adams's character that differs from his ecclesiastical side as much as Sancho differs from Don Quixote. It has been said that "Adams's easy, *débonnaire* nature" is counterbalanced by his "strict" view of life: his "conduct" is characterized by "his freedom from restraint, his disregard of clerical propriety, his love of social, and especially convivial discourse — in short, his enjoyment of life," whereas in "the sphere of belief" he is distinguished by "the strictness of many of his views, the unworldliness of his disposition, the loftiness of his aims" (Whittuck, *"Good Man, "* 85). This claim holds true with Adams's display of joie de vivre at the wedding feast "When the church rites were over" (297). As he himself puts it, "Mr. Adams at church with his surplice on, and Mr. Adams without that ornament, in any other place, were two very different persons" (296-97).

24. See Goldberg, *Art,* 145-51. Note that by modeling the "night-adventures" in "Booby Hall" after that famous incident in an inn which Don Quixote mistook for a castle, Fielding symbolically transforms the snobbish lady's "Hall" into a bawdy inn.

Adams's "two very different persons" are derived in part from Don Quixote. The manner in which his ecclesiastical person ("at church with his surplice on") is triggered to take precedence over his secular person ("without ornament, in any other place") corresponds to what the canon of Toledo observes of the knight: if Adams loses his usual "submission and deference" only "where the least spice of religion intervened" (296), Don Quixote "in all his Words and Answers display'd an excellent Judgment," and "only rav'd when the Discourse fell upon Knight-Errantry" (1:iv, xxii[49], 416). Though utterly free of his prototype's "unparallel'd Sort of Madness," Adams is controlled as much by "religion" as Don Quixote is by "Knight-Errantry."

Critics have noted that whereas Adams is latitudinarian in his emphasis on charity, he is a high-churchman in his strict obedience to the forms of the church. This is especially clear near the end in his repeated insistence on the publication of banns, and in his rebuke of Pamela and her husband for laughing in church. Both sides of his character are consistent with Don Quixote: the knight is exemplarily charitable, and his scrupulous adherence to the chivalric code corresponds to Adams's obedience to church forms.

Though Fielding evidently delighted in fashioning Adams's "low adventures" in books 2 and 3 after several of Don Quixote's, he was aware that the parson's engagement in such adventures would strike some readers as not befitting a clergyman. Some might even agree with Lady Booby, who tells Adams that it does not "become a man of your character, to run about the country with an idle fellow and wench" (4:2, 240). The depiction of Booby as a vain, spiteful hypocrite who bitterly mocks the parson's poverty (4:9), and who, according to Slipslop, "talks of servants as if they were not born of the Christian *specious* [*sic*]" (4:6, 255), speaks for itself as Fielding's comment on any reader who might share her contempt.[25]

While Adams on one occasion fails to follow his own stoical precepts (4:8), Fielding's estimation reflects itself in Fanny's assessment of him as "the worthiest, best-natured creature" (4:5, 249), and in Joseph's observation that "there is not such another in the universe" (249). As a mixture of nobility and eccentricity, he is as easy to laugh at as Don Quixote. But he is not a "fool," unless we understand that word as Fielding defined it in his facetious *Modern Glossary* (1752): "A complex Idea, compounded of Poverty, Honesty, Piety, and Simplicity" (*Covent-Garden Journal,* no. 4 [14 January 1752], Jensen ed., 1:156).

25. Fielding proved correct in his expectation that some readers, especially Richardsonians, would find Adams's adventures inappropriate for a clergyman. See Dudden, *Fielding,* 1:391-92.

By this definition alone may Adams be deemed foolish, as may also that other great descendant of Don Quixote, Prince Myshkin—whom many have esteemed as a *holy* fool.

Part Two

Prince Myshkin:
Nineteenth-Century Quixotic Saint

*"My meaning is," said Sancho, "let us set out to become saints, and we'll
get the fame we are striving after more quickly." (Quixote, Ormsby
translation, 2:8, 467)*

*There were no more images, so Don Quixote told them to cover them
up again, and said to those who had brought them, "I take it as a happy
omen, brothers, to have seen what I have; for these saints and knights
were of the same profession as myself, which is the calling of arms.
Only there is this difference between them and me, that they were
saints, and fought with divine weapons, and I am a sinner and fight with
human ones." (2:58, 743)*

Substantiated as it is by Dostoevsky's famous letter to his niece Sofia Ivanova,
which discloses his idea of portraying a positively beautiful person on the
models of Christ, Don Quixote, Mr. Pickwick, and Jean Valjean, George
Steiner's description of the hero of *The Idiot* as "a composite figure" in whom
we discern "parts of" those figures "and of the saintly fools from the Orthodox
tradition"[1] expresses the scholarly consensus. Comparisons of Prince Myshkin and Christ, whose followers the holy fools considered themselves to be, and
of Myshkin and Don Quixote, from whom Pickwick is a direct literary descendant,
are commonplace. It is generally agreed that Christ, Don Quixote, and Myshkin
have in common simplicity, innocence, directness, compassion, concern for
victims of injustice, disregard for the claims of law and property, and a special
relationship with women of ill repute; that Myshkin, while lacking Christ's
sternness and clear sense of divine mission as preacher and healer, and while

1. George Steiner, *Tolstoy or Dostoevsky: An Essay in the Old Criticism* (1959; New York:
Random House, 1961), 152.

not embodying a universal *telos* as does Christ, shares the latter's love, humility, gentleness, submissiveness, insight, refusal to judge others, and preference for the company of children; and that the prince, while lacking Don Quixote's militancy, shares the knight's idealism, childlike naïveté, "enthusiast virtue," ignorance of the ways of man, and inability to make effective use of his talents, and appears no less ridiculous as an "idiot" than did the knight as a madman.

Though Don Quixote and Myshkin are "two stellarly distant Christians," the knight being Catholic like Cervantes, and the prince's religious views according with Dostoevsky's Greco-Russian theology, this difference does not make the search for parallels between them a "vain task."[2] Myshkin's kinship to Don Quixote transcends their denominational and doctrinal differences and illuminates their relation to Christ. Much as the world's particularity is dramatized in the *Quixote* through ironic contrasts with the chivalric system, so the world's contingency and the failure of *Heilsgeschichte* are emphasized by certain lacunae in the Christology of Myshkin's story.[3]

The correspondences between the prince and his two primary models invite a pair of questions: why would Dostoevsky juxtapose Christ and Don Quixote as models for a positively beautiful person? And, does Myshkin really appear as such a figure? One's answer to the second question must depend on one's perspective. The exalted view of Myshkin as "a modern kind of saint, a latter-day Christ" and "perfect man," is largely attributable to a group of commentators writing in the 1880s, led by the French critic E.-M. de Vogüé.[4] The development of this "legendary" Myshkin culminated with the German Catholic theologian Romano Guardini, who in 1932 analyzed Myshkin as "ein Christussymbol."[5]

This soft view of Myshkin was opposed by a hard view that evolved early

2. Santiago Montero Díaz, "Cervantes en Turguenief y Dostoyevsky," *Revista de Estudios Políticos* (Madrid) 15 (1946):111-42; here 139.

3. See Michael Holquist, "The Gaps in Christology: *The Idiot*," in *Dostoevsky: New Perspectives,* ed. Robert Louis Jackson (Englewood Cliffs, N.J.: Prentice-Hall, 1984), 126-44, esp. 132-34. This essay originally appeared in Michael Holquist, *Dostoevsky and the Novel* (Princeton: Princeton University Press, 1977).

4. Robert Lord, "An Epileptic Mode of Being," in *Dostoevsky: Essays and Perspectives* (Berkeley: University of California Press, 1970), 81-101; see 81-82.

5. *Religiöse Gestalten in Dostojewskijs Werk* (1932; Munich: Kösel, 1947), chap. 7 ("Ein Christussymbol"), 241-84. Trans. by Francis X. Quinn as "Dostoevsky's Idiot, a Symbol of Christ," *Cross Currents* 6 (1956): 359-82. (Cited hereafter as "Symbol of Christ".)

this century with the Marxist approach to Dostoevsky's works in Russia. In an essay of 1913, Maksim Gorky, who had already branded Dostoevsky a petit bourgeois writer for teaching passivism and faulted him for depicting in all his characters only the dark side of the Russian soul, criticized Myshkin and Alyosha Karamazov as "half dead fatalists."[6] Similarly, in an essay of 1924, seven years after the Russian Revolution, the orthodox Marxist critic Georgy Yefimovich Gorbachov included Myshkin along with Stavrogin and Svidrigailov in a list of "typical degenerate nobles"[7] who in Gorbachov's view exemplify the dangers of individualism.

The hard and soft approaches to Myshkin are not irreconcilable; they merely shed light on two different sides of his character: the divine, spiritual side, and the human, material. The contradiction underlying Dostoevsky's conception of Myshkin as a positively beautiful man is that *since every person is mortal and therefore corruptible, no person except Christ (conceived as God in human form) can be positively beautiful.* This contradiction is implicit in Guardini's claim that Myshkin is neither the God-Man, nor a second Christ, nor wholly human, but rather, the Man-God: "Can the life of the Man-God, as it is given us in the Gospels, . . . be translated into a man's life, and told by it, without ridiculing the man or robbing the Son of God of his divinity? . . . This is the problem which Dostoyevsky is trying to resolve" ("Symbol of Christ," 378).

This "problem" of Myshkin's double nature, which stems from his synthesis of Christ (God-Man) and Don Quixote (madman), has intrigued a number of English and American critics over the last thirty years. Probing beneath Myshkin's "legendary" image, they consider him "a lay or private substitute for God who is blighted in the attempt to do God's work,"[8] or whose "difficulties" arise from his being "only half-saint (or half-'idiot') and half-man, half out of the world but half committed to it."[9] Others attribute his alleged

6. "O Karamazovshchine" (On Karamazovism); first published in *Russkoe slovo* (Russian Word) (St. Petersburg, 22 September 1913); quoted by Vladimir Seduro, *Dostoevsky in Russian Literary Criticism: 1846–1956* (New York: Columbia University Press, 1957), 87.

7. "Sotsial'nye korni propovedi Dostoevskogo" (The social roots of Dostoevsky's teaching), *Bor'ba klassov* (The class struggle) (Leningrad), nos. 1–2 (1924), 172; quoted by Seduro, *Dostoyevski in Russian Literary Criticism,* 161–62.

8. R. P. Blackmur, "*The Idiot*: A Rage of Goodness," in *Eleven Essays in the European Novel* (New York: Harcourt, Brace & World, 1964), 141–62; here 144.

9. Murray Krieger, "Dostoevsky's 'Idiot': The Curse of Saintliness," in *The Tragic Vision: Variations on a Theme in Literary Interpretation* (1960; Chicago: University of Chicago Press, 1966), 209–27; here 216.

saintliness to some underlying psychological quirk, such as an "undeveloped ego" and "unbridled superego,"[10] or "alienation by default,"[11] and arrive at a wholly naturalistic understanding of his "special but deviant kind of human personality" (Lord, "Epileptic Mode of Being," 91).

As compelling as such analyses may be, they do not explain why Dostoevsky would compare two seemingly divergent characters as models for a positively beautiful person. That comparison, and its reflection in Myshkin, represent a monumental step in the interpretation of Cervantes's knight and the understanding of Christ. Most crucially, the analogy implies there is something inherently Christ-like about Don Quixote, and something potentially quixotic about Christ. (This implication was explored by Kierkegaard,[12] who was the first and, aside from Turgenev, the only person before Dostoevsky to compare Christ and Don Quixote.) How that odd coupling of the Messiah and the madman became conceivable must be understood in the context of the *Zeitgeist* that conditioned the perception of them both in Dostoevsky's age: Romanticism.

10. Simon O. Lesser, "Saint and Sinner: Dostoevsky's 'Idiot,' " *Modern Fiction Studies* 4 (1958): 211–24; here 211.

11. Howard Keller, "Prince Myshkin: Success or Failure?," *Journal of Russian Studies* 24 (1972): 17–23; here 22.

12. See Eric J. Ziolkowski, "Don Quixote and Kierkegaard's Understanding of the Single Individual in Society," in *Foundations of Kierkegaard's Vision of Community: Religion, Ethics, and Politics in Kierkegaard,* ed. George B. Connell and C. Stephen Evans (Atlantic Highlands, N.J.: Humanities, 1991), chap. 8.

3

Dostoevsky and the Romantic View of Don Quixote

The Romantic interpretation of *Don Quixote* changed the knight from a comic figure into a noble, idealistic, tragic, and ultimately Christ-like hero, and transformed the book from a mere satire of chivalric literature into a universal satire of all life. This development reversed the seventeenth-century view of the *Quixote* as a funny book about a silly man, and far exceeded the view held by Fielding and other eighteenth-century English readers who had exalted it as a classic humorous satire.[1]

While the Romantic interpretation of the *Quixote* has been judged in different ways for its divergence from the earlier view,[2] our task is historical,

1. See Edwin B. Knowles, "Don Quixote Through English Eyes," *Hispania* 23 (1940): 103–15; here 111–12.

2. For Julio Casares the excessive seriousness of Romantic interpreters such as Hugo, Sainte-Beuve, Heine, and Dostoevsky represents the "adolescence" of *Quixote* criticism, as opposed to the "childhood" implied by the "loud laughter" of the novel's seventeenth-century readers, and the "maturity" achieved by eighteenth-century English readers like Fielding and Sterne through their discernment of the book's "harmonious synthesis of the comic and the

not evaluative. With Oscar Mandel we might ask: "How did the romantic readings, culminating in the identification of Don Quixote with Christ, arise?" Mandel surmises that they arose "because, almost at once, the knight assumed under Cervantes' direction a double, paradoxical role," with the result that he was "split" in two, "half of him an arrant madman and the other half a wise man" ("Function of the Norm," 156). But this answer begs the question. Why was the knight's "wise" half (whose creation Mandel attributes to Cervantes's "didacticism") not appreciated for more than a century after the *Quixote* first appeared? The recognition of Don Quixote as half "mad" and half "wise" does not explain why he was eventually compared to Christ. A more satisfactory answer may be arrived at by considering the Romantic interpretation in the light of the revolutionary changes that Romanticism brought about in readers' religious and literary sensibilities.

Romanticism, Religion, and Don Quixote

In his celebrated study of the poetry and metaphysics of the Romantic Age, M. H. Abrams distinguishes Romantic writers as those who, living "inescapably" after the Enlightenment, "undertook to save the overview of human history and destiny, the experiential paradigms, and the cardinal values of their [Judeo-Christian] religious heritage, by reconstructing them in a way that would make them intellectually acceptable, as well as emotionally pertinent, for the time being."[3] While Novalis, Fichte, Schelling, together with Friedrich and A. W. Schlegel in Germany, and Blake, Coleridge, Wordsworth, Keats, and Shelley in England, assume justifiable prominence in Abrams's study of this Romantic tendency "to naturalize the supernatural and to humanize the divine" (67–68), he surprisingly makes no mention of Friedrich Schleiermacher, whose celebrated apologia (1799) to religion's "cultured despisers" did more than any single work by another author to make religion acceptable to

---

tragic" ("Las tres edades del *Quijote*," *Boletín de la Real Academia Española* 27 [1947–48]: 43–60). While Casares considers the third view more valid than the first two, Ángel del Río sees the Romantic interpretation as the most valid because it recognizes "the transcendent significance of [Don Quixote's] madness," which prior readers failed to discern ("Quijotismo y cervantismo: el devenir de un símbolo," *Revista de Estudios Hispánicos* 1 [1928]:241–67; here 245).

3. *Natural Supernaturalism: Tradition and Revolution in Romantic Literature* (New York: Norton, 1973), 66.

the post-Enlightenment mind. Appearing at a time when its subject seemed superfluous, his volume of speeches created a new understanding of religion by redefining it in the Romantics' own terms.

For Schleiermacher religion is the means by which theoretical knowledge of the deistic type (whether rationalist or supernaturalist) and moral obedience of the Kantian type, both of which presuppose a split between the subject, I, and the object, God, are to be overcome.[4] Adapting Schelling's principle of identity, Schleiermacher construes religion as "feeling" (*Gefühl*), by which he means our experience of the identity between the human subject and the divine object. (It is in the same Romantic spirit that Goethe has Faust describe religion as "Gefühl" in his conversation with Margarete in her garden, and that Friedrich Schlegel would later open a lecture on the philosophy of language by repeating Faust's famous claim: "Gefühl ist alles."[5]) Religion "is to have life and to know life in immediate feeling, only as such an existence in the Infinite and Eternal.... In itself it is an affection, a revelation of the Infinite in the finite, God being seen in it and it in God."[6]

It is in the light of Schleiermacher's view of religion, and Abrams's thesis, that we should consider the interpretation of the *Quixote* by the first generation of German Romantics, of whom Heine would say: "That school was bitten by the very same madness which drove the noble knight of La Mancha to all his follies. Like him, it wishes to restore medieval chivalry, and to revive a dead past."[7] The *Quixote* corresponds to the basic synthesis of opposites essential to the religious thinking of that age—what Abrams calls natural supernaturalism, the experience of the infinite within the finite—insofar as it tells of a man who, through the force of imagination (or illusion), transforms the natural world into a supernatural world by projecting imagery from the former (e.g., castles, giants, knights) onto the objects of the former (e.g., inns, windmills, innkeepers). Viewed from the Romantic perspective as representing the ideal in its struggle with the real, the soul in opposition to the body, or

4. See Paul Tillich, *A History of Christian Thought from Its Judaic and Hellenistic Origins to Existentialism,* ed. Carl E. Braaten (New York: Simon and Schuster, 1967), 392.

5. *Philosophie der Sprache und des Wortes, Sämmtliche Werke,* 15 vols. (Vienna: Klang, 1846), 15:166.

6. *On Religion: Speeches to its Cultured Despisers,* trans. John Oman (New York: Harper & Row, 1958), 36.

7. *The Romantic School* (1836), excerpt in *The Poetry and Prose of Heinrich Heine,* ed. Frederic Ewen, trans. Louis Untermeyer et al. (New York: Citadel, 1948), 611.

poetry in dialogue with prose, Don Quixote seems to symbolize the religious experience of the infinite within the finite.

In accordance with the highly spiritual function that art, poetry, and literature served for them, the Romantics endowed the *Quixote* with religious significance. Schleiermacher argued that there is an affinity between religion and art because art provides humans the means by which to lift themselves above the finite to grasp, even if only momentarily, a "sense" for the infinite (*On Religion,* 138–40). As art became religiously significant, the aesthetic dimension of the religious was brought to the fore. Blake was speaking for most Romantics when he proclaimed the Bible "the Great Code of Art."[8] Given these connections between art and religion, it is fair to presume that if, as Heine observed, *Hamlet, Faust,* and the *Quixote* were the favorite reading of the Romantic school, they were so because they struck harmonious chords with that generation's most basic religio-aesthetic yearnings. If the great enterprise of the Romantics was to create a "new Mythus" (Abrams, *Natural Supernaturalism,* 67) out of the Judeo-Christian religion by transposing biblical myths into the terms and schemes of their own metaphysics, the *Quixote* lent itself perfectly to that purpose. As read by them it embodied a "myth" that anticipated their own speculative view of life as the struggle of the ideal and the real.

The pioneers of this revision in Germany were the Schlegel brothers, in their capacities as aestheticians and literary historians; Schelling and Jean Paul Richter as aestheticians; and Tieck as translator of the *Quixote* and literary critic.[9] These men, who made their most important statements on the *Quixote* during the years 1797–1805, utterly rejected earlier views of the knight as a ridiculous fool or mere object of satire. They discovered in the novel a theme that mirrored a preoccupation central to their movement's metaphysics, aesthetics, and art: the opposition between subject and object, mind and nature, spirit and matter, freedom and necessity. Articulating a view that Tieck and F. Schlegel had already vaguely suggested, Schelling transformed the *Quixote* into a Romantic work by approaching Cervantes as a philosophical "poet" (*Dichter*) who depicted the universal antagonism of the ideal and the real through the "myths" (*Mythen*) of Don Quixote's conflicts

8. *The Laocoön* (1820), *The Complete Poetry and Prose of William Blake,* ed. David V. Erdman (newly rev. ed., Garden City, N.Y.: Doubleday, 1982), 274.

9. See Close's section, "The German Romantics," in *Romantic Approach,* 29–41. The most complete study remains J.-J.A. Bertrand's vast tome, *Cervantès et le romantisme allemand* (Paris: Alcan, 1914).

with society: "Das Thema im Ganzen ist das Reale im Kampfe mit dem Idealen."[10]

This Romantic interpretation had been anticipated by Schiller, whose theory of literary types and literary growth established the foundation for the critical system developed by the Romantics, which attributes such great importance to Cervantes (see Bergel, "Cervantes in Germany," 330). Though Schiller, whose sense of humor was not his most conspicuous trait, wrote little on Cervantes, the *Quixote* figured crucially in the German dramatist's conception of his own first play *The Robbers* (1781). Schiller admits that his hero, Karl Moor, was modeled partly after the good-hearted thief Roque Guinart from the *Quixote*'s second part;[11] in his preface he indicates the correspondence between Moor and Don Quixote:

> The hero's false conception of his abilities and his power, his overabundance of energy which overflows all limits set by law—such qualities must collide inevitably with the established institutions of society and lead to a catastrophe, and if to these enthusiastic dreams [*enthusiastischen Träumen*] of greatness and unbounded activity is added a feeling of bitterness against the world because of its imperfection and its remoteness from ideals, then we possess the complete picture of the strange Don Quixote whom we abhor and love, admire and pity in the robber Karl Moor.[12]

This statement justifies the claim that Schiller originated the Romantic interpretation of Don Quixote. Prior eighteenth-century readers outside England had found little to commend in the knight's dreams. But Schiller "without hesitation represents Don Quixote as the noble idealist who suffers from the imperfections of the world" (Bergel, "Cervantes in Germany," 331). Schiller thus adumbrates the Romantic view and is but one conceptual step away from Dostoevsky's comparison of the knight to that most hallowed idealist who actually did suffer in the imperfect world: Christ.

10. *Philosophie der Kunst*, in *Friedrich Wilhelm Joseph von Schellings sämmtliche Werke*, 14 vols., ed. K. F. A. Schelling (Stuttgart: J. G. Cotta, 1856–61), 5:679.

11. See Friedrich Schiller, *Die Räuber: Erläuterungen und Dokumente*, ed. Christian Grawe (Stuttgart: Reclam, 1976), 118–22.

12. *Sämtliche Werke*, ed. Gerhard Fricke and Herbert G. Göpfert, 5 vols. (Munich: Hanser, 1960), 1:486; quoted by Bergel, "Cervantes in Germany," 331.

The Humanized Savior and the Idealized Knight

Previous scholarship has overlooked that before Dostoevsky's comparison of Christ and Don Quixote could be imaginable, two interpretive developments had to occur. On the one hand, the image of Christ, traditionally regarded as divine or semidivine, had to be humanized and naturalized enough for him to be comparable to a mere mortal such as Don Quixote. On the other hand, the image of Cervantes's knight, who prior to the Romantics had generally been viewed as a burlesque or satirical butt, had to be elevated and idealized to the extent that he could seem worthy of comparison with a religious savior.

Of course, the concern with replacing the "cosmic" Christ with a "human" Jesus had begun long before the Romantic Age; by then that concern had become a venerable tradition expressing two main forces of thought: the rationalist and deistic thought of the Enlightenment, and the attack against orthodox Trinitarian and christological dogmas. The anti-Trinitarian tendencies that had begun with Michael Servetus's *De Trinitatis Erroribus* (1531) developed with the emergence of the Unitarian movement in England during the sixteenth and seventeenth centuries. The "humanizing" effect that Unitarianism had on christological speculation is reflected in the statement of Bartholomew Legate of Essex—who would be burned as a heretic in 1612—that Christ was "a mere man," but "born free from sin."[13] To a large extent Unitarianism became part of the grand legacy of Enlightenment thought. After Newton and Hume, and with the increased conceptual domination of rationalism, deism, and "natural religion," the concept of the Cosmic Christ was rendered untenable; hence, the reigning notion of Jesus in the Age of Reason was that of the Teacher of Common Sense.[14] Even Immanuel Kant remained faithful to this humanistic view of Jesus. His *Religion Within the Limits of Reason Alone* (1793) presents Jesus as "the Teacher of the Gospel" (*der Lehrer des Evangeliums*), a suitable "example [*Beispiel*] conforming to the archetype of a humanity alone pleasing to God."[15]

The continued humanization of Jesus in the nineteenth century was largely the effect of that epochal theological enterprise whose history Albert Schweitzer

13. *Encyclopaedia of Religion and Ethics,* s.v. "Unitarianism," by J. E. Carpenter, 12:520.

14. See Jaroslav Pelikan, *Jesus Through the Centuries: His Place in the History of Culture* (New Haven: Yale University Press, 1985), chap. 15 ("The Teacher of Common Sense"), 182–93.

15. *Religion Within the Limits of Reason Alone,* trans. Theodore M. Greene and Hoyt H. Hudson (1934; 2d ed., La Salle, Ill.: Open Court, 1960), bk. 3, div. 2, 119–20.

traced in his *Geschichte der Leben-Jesu-Forschung* (1906), known in English as *The Quest of the Historical Jesus.* Initiated in the late eighteenth century, the effort to demythologize and establish a historical conception of Jesus' life dominated critical theology throughout the next century, especially in Germany. The steady sharpening of the distinction between the Christ of faith and the Jesus of history effectually "de-Christianized" Jesus, which helps explain the prevalence of the latter's "transfigurations" in later fiction.[16]

At the same time, the continued idealization of Don Quixote throughout Europe during the nineteenth century remained consistent with the German Romantics' views, especially as transmitted through the sections on Cervantes in Friedrich Bouterwek's *Geschichte der Poesie und Beredsamkeit* (8 vols., 1801-9; French, 1812; English, 1823; Spanish, 1829) and J. C. L. Simonde de Sismondi's *De la littérature du midi de l'Europe* (4 vols., 1813; English, 1823; Spanish, 1841-42).[17] Like the "de-Christianized" Jesus, the romanticized knight found himself repeatedly transfigured in fiction. Such memorable characters of nineteenth-century literature as Cyrano de Bergerac, Prince Myshkin, Captain Ahab, and Maxi in Benito Pérez Galdós's *Fortunata y Jacinta* (1887) display the same blend of contrasting qualities that the Romantic interpreters attributed to Don Quixote, including saintliness, chivalry, frenzy, comical ineptness. To the extent that such characters are modeled after the knight, Anthony Close assumes that their creators "would [not] have found *Don Quixote* an inspiring model had they not been able to re-interpret him in this way" (*Romantic Approach,* 54-55).

What remains to be shown is how Jesus' humanization and Don Quixote's idealization prepared the conceptual grounds for Dostoevsky's comparison of them. Both figures were reinterpreted in the distinctly poetic and aesthetic categories of Romanticism, and the resulting perceptions of them share several suggestive affinities.

It was no mere coincidence that just when the quest for the historical Jesus was gaining momentum a distinctly Romantic image of him emerged. Jaroslav Pelikan characterizes as Romantic the effort by such thinkers as Schleiermacher, Coleridge, and Emerson "to go beyond the quest of the Historical Jesus to a Jesus who—(to use [René] Wellek's formula) by identifying subject and object

16. See Theodore Ziolkowski, *Fictional Transfigurations of Jesus* (Princeton: Princeton University Press, 1972), chap. 2 ("De-Christianizing Jesus"), 30-54.

17. See Close, *Romantic Approach,* 41-67; J.-J.A. Bertrand, "Génesis [y desarrollo] de la concepción romántica de *Don Quijote* en Francia," 3 pts., *Anales Cervantinos* [pt. 1] 3 (1953):1-41; [pt. 2] 4 (1954):41-76; [pt. 3] 5 (1955-56):79-142.

and by reconciling man and nature, consciousness and unconsciousness—could be called the Poet of the Spirit" (*Jesus Through the Centuries,* 194). The most innovative aspect of this endeavor of the Romantics was their assumption that aesthetic experience, which they identified with Schleiermacher's concept of "God-consciousness," furnished an understanding of Jesus that should "supersede the dogmatic, the moral, and even the historical" (197–98). Though none of the men mentioned above ever applied the term "poet" to Jesus, that notion of him was conveyed by several other Romantics,[18] and later by Thomas Carlyle, whose eccentric classic *Sartor Resartus* (1833–34) is suffused with Romantic ideas.[19]

One year after *Sartor*'s final serial installment had appeared in a London journal, David Friedrich Strauss published in Germany his epochal *Das Leben Jesu* (1835). Not only was Strauss "the first to distinguish systematically between the Christ of faith and the Jesus of history, who can be reached only by stripping away the 'mythic' additives from the recorded life," but his biography of Jesus "mapped out virtually every important area that New Testament scholarship was to explore in the following century" (T. Ziolkowski, *Fictional Transfigurations,* 36). Especially innovative is his handling of the question of Jesus' "enthusiasm," a quality the Romantics esteemed as a source of poetic inspiration. In discussing Jesus' notion of his preexistence with reference to the Gospel of John 8:58 ("Before Abraham was, I am"), Strauss argues that to suggest that Jesus was speaking "from his own presumed memory of his pre-human and pre-earthly condition" would be "to demolish the healthy human consciousness of Jesus and to accuse him of enthusiasm [*Schwärmerei*], from which he shows himself to be free on all other occasions."[20] If Strauss is unwilling to accuse Jesus of enthusiasm as a rationalist might do, he is equally unwilling to side with the supernaturalist who accepts everything in

18. The identification of the poetic imagination with Jesus, which Abrams finds implicit in bk. 13 of Wordsworth's *The Prelude* (1805), is also implied in Blake's definition of "Imagination" as "the Divine Body of the Lord Jesus" (*Jerusalem* [1804–8], chap. 1, plate 5, lines 58–59, *Complete Poetry,* 148). Expressing a similarly poetic notion of Jesus, Friedrich Hölderlin's rapturous elegy "Brot und Wein" (1799–1801) culminates with a blending of Christ ("son of the Almighty") and Dionysus ("the Syrian"): "Aber indessen kommt als Fackelschwinger des Höchsten / Sohn, der Syrier, unter die Schatten herab" (stanza 9, lines 155–56, *Sämtliche Werke* ["Kleine Stuttgarter Ausgabe"], 6 vols. [Stuttgart: Kohlhammer, 1944–59], 2:99).

19. See *Sartor Resartus,* ed. Charles Frederick Harrold (Indianapolis: Odyssey, 1937), where the hero, Diogenes Teufelsdröckh, characterizes Jesus as the "Highest" of all "religious Symbols," or "those wherein the Artist or Poet has risen into Prophet" (bk. 3, chap. 3, 224), and as "Our highest Orpheus" (chap. 8, 263).

20. *Das Leben Jesu, kritisch bearbeitet,* 2 vols. (Tübingen: Osiander, 1835), 1:484.

the New Testament as the Gospel truth. In characteristic Hegelian manner, Strauss instead opts for the synthetic view.

Elsewhere Strauss suggests that what might appear as enthusiasm in Jesus' attitude toward eschatology actually reflects his accordance with certain deeply ingrained messianic notions of the Palestinian Jews (see 1:494). Strauss skirts both the rationalist explanation, which might reduce Jesus to a politically motivated enthusiast (*Schwärmer*), and the supernaturalist explanation, which would accept uncritically the myth of his divine spirituality; taking a middle path, Strauss contends that while Jesus did not aim to effect through any action of his own or of his followers the eschatological events that he anticipated (restoration of the throne of David, establishment of Jesus' rule over a liberated humanity, etc.), he entrusted the actualization of those events to his heavenly Father.[21]

Strauss's careful qualifications regarding Jesus' enthusiasm were ignored by Ernest Renan, whose critically and theologically unsound but aesthetically alluring *Vie de Jésus* (1863) did more than any work by another author to popularize the humanized conception of Jesus that had been initiated by Strauss and been undergoing modifications through the assiduous labors of his successors for three decades. Renan describes Jesus' belief in his supernatural role as *l'enthousiasme,* because it "removed him almost from the possibility of doubt."[22] (Accordingly, J. R. Seeley's *Ecce Homo* [1865], one of the most widely read of the so-called liberal lives of Jesus spawned by Renan's book over the next thirty years, will devote an entire chapter to Jesus' "Enthusiasm of Humanity."[23]) In addition, Renan presents a blend of Strauss's humanized image of Jesus, and the aesthetic-poetic image that had emerged with Romanticism. While the Romantics conceived of Christ as poetic by making him a metaphor for the "imagination" (Blake) or alluding to him in conjunction with Dionysus (Hölderlin) and Orpheus (Carlyle), Renan attempts to reveal Jesus' poetic nature by analyzing him as a historical figure: "As occurs often in very lofty natures, his tenderness of heart developed into an infinite sweetness, a vague poetry, a universal charm" (34). Though Jesus "had little to add to the doctrine of the synagogue" on ethics and morality, he made ancient

21. This thesis is discussed by Albert Schweitzer, *The Quest of the Historical Jesus: A Critical Study of Its Progress from Reimarus to Wrede,* trans. W. Montgomery (New York: Macmillan, 1959), 92–93.

22. *Vie de Jésus* (28th ed., Paris: Lévy, 1885), 161.

23. *Ecce Homo: A Survey of the Life and Works of Jesus Christ* (1865; London: Dent, 1907), chap. 14.

aphorisms new and more endearing by articulating them in poetic terms: "The poetry of the precept, which makes one love it, is more than the precept itself" (40).

If Jesus was poetic and an enthusiast, he also was in Renan's view an anarchist with a utopian dream. However, "what in effect distinguishes Jesus from the agitators of his time and those of all centuries is his perfect idealism" (69). Unwittingly echoing Emerson, whose essay "Circles" (written in 1840) contrasts Jesus' "idealism" with Bishop Berkeley's,[24] Renan calls Jesus "a perfect idealist [*idéaliste accompli*]" (70) whose "poetic conception of nature" amounts to a "transcendent idealism" [*idéalisme transcendente*] that "prevented him from ever having a very clear notion of his own personality" (155–56). Yet, for all his poetry, enthusiasm, and idealism, Jesus was completely human in Renan's view. Echoing Emerson's description of Jesus as "the perfect man" (letter of 30 July 1835, *Selections,* 20), and anticipating Dostoevsky's view, Renan concludes that he was a "sublime person," one of those "columns" that appear amidst the "uniform vulgarity of mankind" and "rise toward the sky and attest a nobler destiny. Jesus is the loftiest of these columns that show man whence he came and whither he should tend. In him is condensed all that is good and elevated in our nature" (258) (cf. Seeley, *Ecce Homo,* 131–32). The humanized and aesthetic conceptions of Jesus thus coalesce in Renan's *Vie,* which Dostoevsky read shortly before he wrote *The Idiot.*

It is no small irony that in the same period when the life of Jesus was being demythologized, the story of Don Quixote was being elevated to the status of myth. As the quest for the historical Jesus was evaporating the savior's aura of divinity, and as the Romantic exaltation of Don Quixote was removing the knight from the sphere of satire, the two figures were often construed in the same philosophical and aesthetic terms. Thus the knight was associated with poetry, enthusiasm, and idealism no less strongly than was the savior.

Long before Renan perceived his humanized Jesus as a "perfect idealist," Don Quixote had been exalted by the German Romantics as symbolic of their own self-image as idealistic martyrs. While they construed Cervantes's theme metaphysically as the struggle of the ideal and the real, viewing Don Quixote as the tragic idealist, they also interpreted that theme aesthetically as the conflict of poetry and prose, viewing the knight as the epitome of the poetic. In 1800, the same year that Hölderlin composed an elegy combining the images

24. *Selections from Ralph Waldo Emerson,* ed. Stephen E. Whicher (Boston: Houghton, 1960), 172.

of Christ and Dionysus (see note 18), A. W. Schlegel wrote a sonnet entitled "Don Quixote de la Mancha," which opens by suggesting that the knight embodies chivalric poetry in an ongoing dialogue with prose, as incarnated in his squire:

> Auf seinem Pegasus, dem magern Rappen
> Reit't in die Ritterpoesie Quixote,
> Und hält anmuthiglich, in Glück und Nothe,
> Gespräche mit der Prosa seines Knappen.[25]

> (On his Pegasus, the decrepit black nag,
> Quixote rides into chivalric poetry,
> And gracefully converses, in good fortune and bad,
> With the prose of his squire.)

Anticipating Heine's reading of the *Quixote* as an allegory of the human "soul" (*Geist*) in the figure of the knight juxtaposed with the "body" (*Leib*) in the squire (*Romantic School, Poetry and Prose,* 612), the identification of Don Quixote with poetry became a critical commonplace. Sismondi speaks of Don Quixote's "poetic imagination" (*imagination poétique*) by which all vulgar objects are transformed: "The fundamental discovery of *Don Quixote* is the eternal contrast between the poetic and the prosaic spirit."[26] Observing that "imagination, sensibility, and all the generous qualities lead us to exalt Don Quixote" because his "heroism [and] illusions of virtue are . . . the theme of lofty poetry," Sismondi suggests that our laughter at such a noble hero reflects the perspective from which we view him, and the "contrasts" between him and his surrounding reality:

> But the same character who is admirable when seen from an elevated viewpoint, can be ridiculous when seen from the level of the earth, especially because errors are what elicit laughter the most quickly, and the man who sees heroism and chivalry everywhere he looks is bound to err ceaselessly; and because vivid contrasts are, after errors, the

25. *Sämmtliche Werke,* 12 vols., ed. Eduard Bocking, 3d ed. (Leipzig: Weidmann, 1846–47), 1:442.

26. *De la littérature du Midi de l'Europe,* 4 vols. (Paris: Treutel, 1813; 3d ed. rev., 1829), 3:349, 351. Cf. Henry Hallam, *Introduction to the Literature of Europe in the Fifteenth, Sixteenth, and Seventeenth Centuries,* 4 vols. (London: Murray, 1837–39), 3:671.

most potent means for exciting laughter, and nothing contrasts more
than poetry and prose, the overly romantic imagination and the most
trivial details of life. (3:351-52)

Shared by other Romantic interpreters, Sismondi's admiration of Don Quixote's
imagination reflects the general reaction of Romanticism against the Enlightenment. While the great thinkers of that age had scorned excessive imagination
as a flaw, the Romantics cherished it as a virtue. Schleiermacher spoke for all
German Romantics when he called the imagination (*Phantasie*) "the highest
and most original faculty in man" (*On Religion,* 98; cf. 283). The same attitude
flourished in England, where an indigenous Romantic appreciation of the
Quixote evolved, initially independent of German influence, during the first
three decades of the nineteenth century. We not only find Wordsworth alluding with "reverence" to Don Quixote as the avatar of the imagination in *The
Prelude* (bk. 5, lines 140-52), and Lord Byron expressing equal admiration for
him in *Don Juan* (canto 13, stanzas 8-11). We also come across important
comments on the *Quixote* by such leading Romantic spokesmen as Hazlitt,
Coleridge, John Gibson Lockhart, and Charles Lamb, that exalt the imagination,
genius, passion, and sensibility as faculties opposed or superior to reason (see
Close, *Romantic Approach,* 43, 43 n.2, 52-53). Around the time when Blake
identifies "Imagination" with Jesus' "Divine Body," Lockhart heralds Don
Quixote as the "symbol of Imagination, continually struggling and contrasted
with Reality."[27]

The Romantics' elevated, idealized image of Don Quixote corresponded in
one other way to the demythologized, humanized image of Christ that emerged
with the quest for the historical Jesus: as Jesus' alleged "enthusiasm" was
viewed in a neutral light by Strauss and later construed in positive terms
by Renan and Seeley, so did that same quality come to be revered in Don
Quixote. Regarded with suspicion by most Enlightenment thinkers, enthusiasm,
like the imagination and all the affective faculties associated with it, was
reappraised and exalted by the Romantics. In accordance with their primarily
expressive (as opposed to mimetic) theory of art and poetry, they regarded
enthusiasm as the inspirational fount of all great artistic creations. Schleiermacher exhorted religion's "cultured despisers" to appreciate "the power of the
enthusiasm" in the poet Novalis (*On Religion,* 41). Elsewhere he states:

27. Preface to the reedition of Motteux's translation of *Don Quixote* (Edinburgh, 1822), lxii;
quoted by Close, *Romantic Approach,* 57.

"The poetic expression is always based originally upon a moment of exaltation which has come purely from within, a moment of enthusiasm or inspiration [*Begeisterung*]."[28] This notion was elaborated by Schleiermacher's close friend, Friedrich Schlegel, who discussed "longing" (*Sehnsucht*), "love" (*Liebe*), and "enthusiasm" or "inspiration" (*Begeisterung*) as the "three forms of man's higher effort," and "the inner-life springs of true art and higher poetry."[29] For Schlegel enthusiasm is "the animating impulse of all great inventions, creations, and discoveries" (38). As the one emotion in which faith, love, and hope—the three highest "grades of feeling"—are "most perfectly united, blended, and fused together," enthusiasm has "the divine" for its object (479–80).

A notion of enthusiasm no less spiritualized was applied to Don Quixote by Bouterwek, Sismondi, and Lockhart. For example, anticipated by Schiller's reference to the "enthusiastic dreams" of his own ennobled, albeit "strange Don Quixote," Karl Moor, Bouterwek characterizes the knight as "the immortal representative of all men of exalted imagination [*aller Phantasten*], who carry the noblest enthusiasm [*dem herrlichsten Enthusiasmus*] to a pitch of folly."[30] Later interpreters under the sway of Romanticism tended to appraise Don Quixote's enthusiasm in an equally favorable light. It could just as well be Bouterwek speaking when the French poet Alfred de Vigny states that Cervantes's aim was "to express the misfortune of imagination and enthusiasm [*enthousiasme*] misplaced in a vulgar and materialistic society."[31]

Our discussion in this section may be summarized as follows. With the Romantic elevation and idealization of Don Quixote, together with the demythologization and humanization of the historical Jesus, and the Romantic tendency to imagine Jesus in aesthetic terms, the evolving conceptions of the savior and the knight in the early nineteenth century became analogous on three prominent points: both figures were perceived as pure idealists, both were viewed as epitomizing the poetic imagination, and both were admired for their enthusiasm, a quality revered in its association with poetic inspiration. These analogies help account for Dostoevsky's

28. *The Christian Faith,* translation of the 2d German edition, ed. H. R. Mackintosh and J. S. Stewart (Philadelphia: Fortress, 1928; repr. 1976), 78.

29. *The Philosophy of Life and Philosophy of Language in a Course of Lectures,* trans. A. J. W. Morrison (New York: Harper, 1855), 40, 421.

30. *History of Spanish and Portuguese Literature,* 2 vols., trans. Tomasina Ross (London: Boosey, 1823), 1:333.

31. *Journal d'un poète* (February–March 1840), 152; quoted by Close, *Romantic Approach,* 55.

comparison of two figures who once appeared as opposites, the one divine, the other satiric. His view of Christ and Don Quixote as "beautiful" figures seems a logical corollary to Renan's description of the historical Jesus as a "sublime person" and the "loftiest" of men, and Sismondi's perception of Don Quixote as "a perfect man" (*homme accompli*) (*Littérature,* 3:352).

Dostoevsky: "Such is my inference from life"

Dostoevsky's relation to Cervantes is highlighted in part by the uncanny parallels between their lives. Both men were natives of a country where religion and patriotism were inseparable; both came from the city and from socially decadent families; both were sons of surgeons; both, despite their fame as writers, had to struggle with the literary market for remuneration; both came into conflict with other great writers of their respective periods and nations (Cervantes with Lope de Vega, Dostoevsky with Turgenev and Tolstoy); both experienced imprisonment (Cervantes as a slave in Algiers, and later as a prisoner in the jails of Seville and Valladolid, Dostoevsky as a prisoner in the Petropavlovsky Fortress, and later as an exile in Siberia); and, as Cervantes was the first novelist to create an abnormal character as his hero, so Dostoevsky filled his own novels with deviant types.[32]

Notwithstanding these similarities, certain "antitheses" between Cervantes and Dostoevsky should not be overlooked. While both men suffered greatly and possessed exceptional and tortured sensibilities, they reacted in different ways to suffering and injustice: Cervantes with serene dignity, Dostoevsky bafflingly, returning from his Siberian exile with praise for the czar. They were strikingly distinct in their Christian affiliations: Cervantes being a Catholic, Dostoevsky, an adherent to Greco-Russian theology. As novelists, Cervantes signifies "plenitude," while Dostoevsky represents "disintegration." Furthermore,

> There is a perfect psychological antithesis between Cervantes, whose most important creation is a madman who reasons in an impeccable way, and Dostoevsky, in whom the sane are subject to the internal

32. Ludmilla B. Turkevich, *Cervantes in Russia* (New York: Gordian, 1975), 115.

quakes of the subliminal world. For Cervantes the integrity of the human person is an aesthetic-religious dogma presiding over conscious life. In Dostoevsky that harmonious personality—an inheritance from the Greek *phrónesis*—begins to vanish in the mists of a world where, even in conscious states, it recalls the mysterious space of dreams. Cervantes is centered in the intellectualism of Roman theology. Dostoevsky goes beyond the vulgarism of Russian Orthodoxy. (Montero Díaz, "Cervantes en Turguenief y Dostoyevsky," 139)

Regardless of how their biographical and literary relationship is seen, Cervantes's enormous influence on Dostoevsky cannot be denied. Exactly when, where, or in what translation Dostoevsky first encountered *Don Quixote* is not known, though it is certain that by 1873 he had read and admired Louis Viardot's popular French version (1st ed., 1836).[33] Scholars have often remarked that Dostoevsky's view of the novel accords with the Romantic interpretation which had spread to Russia from western Europe. But despite the unmistakable correspondence between Dostoevsky's "ideological and philosophical" approach to the *Quixote,* and that of Bouterwek, Sismondi, and Turgenev (Turkevich, *Cervantes in Russia,* 115), there is no evidence that he read Bouterwek or Sismondi. And from his comments in letters and journal articles about his voracious reading, especially as a youth, we may surmise that his understanding of the *Quixote* as a revelatory commentary on life and the human heart had developed under the sway of a number of other Romantics long before he heard or read Turgenev's controversial lecture "Hamlet and Don Quixote" (1860), and perhaps before he read the novel itself. Who were those Romantics?

Dostoevsky's initial exposure to the Romantic interpretation may have come

33. In one of his journalistic writings Dostoevsky alludes to Viardot's "admirable French version of Don Quixote" ("Apropos of the Exhibition," 1873, *The Diary of a Writer,* trans. Boris Brasol [Salt Lake City, Utah: Peregrine Smith, 1985], 74). His ownership of an undated edition of Viardot's translation is indicated by Leonid Grossman, *Biblioteka Dostoevskogo: Po neizdannym materialam* [Dostoevsky's library, from unpublished materials] (Odessa: Ivasenko, 1919), 139. Segundo Serrano Poncela conjectures that Dostoevsky first read the *Quixote* "en sus años jóvenes, durante ese período esponjoso y devorante de libros del que hallamos abundante constancia en la correspondencia con su hermano Mijail [i.e., 1834–44]" ("Don Quijote en Dostoievski," *Insula* 23 [1968]:19). Yakov Malkiel places the date much later: "When his interest in the Spaniard's works was at length awakened, possibly through the *furore* created by Turgenev's celebrated essay ['Hamlet and Don Quixote'], he avidly read *Don Quixote* and responded to it in a highly personal, passionate way" ("Cervantes in Nineteenth-Century Russia," *Comparative Literature* 3 [1951]: 310–29; here 327).

through his reading of Schiller, who had anticipated the Romantics in viewing the knight as a tragic idealist struggling in an imperfect society. From childhood on, Dostoevsky developed a passion for this poet's works, having been deeply moved by a performance of *The Robbers* at age ten.[34] As we have already seen, Schiller himself likened his hero Karl Moor to Don Quixote.

Even had Dostoevsky failed to recognize the kinship between Karl Moor and the Manchegan knight, he was bound to be impressed by the Romantic reverence with which the *Quixote* was viewed by Lord Byron, in whose poetry he immersed himself as a youth. We will later find Dostoevsky in one instance rehearsing *Don Juan*'s summation of "that too true tale": "Of all tales 'tis the saddest" (canto 13, stanzas 8, 9).

It must also have been at an early age that Dostoevsky first read the well-known Russian ballad "A Poor Knight," to whose subject Aglaya compares Myshkin in *The Idiot.* This ballad is commonly attributed to Pushkin, who himself had been greatly influenced by Byron, and whose works Dostoevsky was citing with familiarity in his letters by the late 1830s. The similarities between Pushkin's knight and Don Quixote are compelling, and the poet's emphasis on the former's fearlessness, extraordinary vision, and purity of love reflects a highly Romantic response to the latter's character.[35]

Another channel through which the young Dostoevsky may have been exposed to the Romantic view of the *Quixote* was his friendship with Vissarion Belinsky, whom he met in 1845, three years before the critic's death. In a letter of 23 June 1837 to Mikhail Bakunin, Belinsky had written: "*Don Quixote* is an extraordinary work. In the literature of Europe the *Quixote* is the unique example of synthesis of the serious and the amusing, the tragic and the comic."[36] This passage is noteworthy because the same "synthesis" in Cervantes's novel was later remarked upon by Dostoevsky. Equally significant is Belinsky's critical appraisal of the *Quixote* in his review of Count Vladimir Sollogub's novella *Tarantas* (1845), which contains a character whom Belinsky

34. See his letter of 18 August 1880, to N. L. Osmidov, *Letters of Fyodor Michailovitch Dostoevsky to His Family and Friends,* trans. Ethel Colburn Mayne (1961; New York: McGraw, 1964), 254.

35. See Turkevich, *Cervantes in Russia,* 42–44. In contrast, Malkiel denies that *Quixote* was "the sole or principal source of Pushkin's inspiration" for the poem ("Cervantes in Nineteenth-Century Russia," 320).

36. Quoted by Z. I. Plavski, "Cervantes v Rossii," in *Miguel de Cervantes Saavedra: bibliografiia russkikh perevodov i kriticheskoi literatury na nerusskom iazyke* (Moscow: Izdatel'stvo vsesoiuznoi knizhnoi palaty, 1959), 9; cited by George Soltys, "Don Quijote en la obra de Dostoyevski" (Ph.D. diss., Middlebury College, 1983), 12.

compares to the knight. If Dostoevsky came to regard Don Quixote as the most beautiful character in Christian literature, Belinsky had already called him "the most excellent and the most noble of men," "a true knight, fearless and irreproachable," and "a veritable sage."[37]

Belinsky's opinion is akin to the insight that led his German contemporary, Heine, to rhapsodize on the *Quixote*'s pervasive "irony." In the fourth volume of his *Travel Pictures,* entitled *Italy: The Town of Lucca (Reisebilder 4—Italien: Die Stadt Lucca,* 1830), Heine recalls the emotions he felt as a child one fine morning in a garden while reading Cervantes's novel for the first time:

> In my childish innocence I took everything in dead earnest; no matter how ridiculously the poor hero of the story was treated by fate, I still thought it had to be so and was all a part of heroism, the ridicule as well as the bodily wounds. The former vexed me as deeply as the blows, which I felt in my own soul.
>
> I was a child and did not know the irony with which the Lord had permeated the world, and which the great poets have reflected in their published microcosms. I would shed bitter tears when the noble knight received only blows of ingratitude for his magnanimity. (*Poetry and Prose,* 382)

It cannot be doubted that Dostoevsky read this passage, and that the Romantic sentiments it expresses informed his understanding of the *Quixote.* Further on, Heine erroneously alludes to Don Quixote's vanquisher, Sansón Carrasco, as "a disguised barber" (*ein verkappter Barbier*) (383), a mistake that is repeated in an article by Dostoevsky to be considered later.

Although it is not known when he read Heine's remarks on the *Quixote,* Dostoevsky's immersion in Schiller, Byron, and Pushkin, as well as his friendship with Belinsky, could have instilled in him a Romantic view of it well before 1860, which was probably when he became familiar with Turgenev's new essay "Hamlet and Don Quixote."[38] Turgenev was not the first to

37. "Tarantas, putevye vpechatleniia soch. Grafa V. A. Solloguba" [no date], *Sochineniia* (Kiev, 1908), 4:11; quoted by Turkevich, *Cervantes in Russia,* 24.

38. Turgenev introduced this essay as a lecture, which he delivered at St. Petersburg in January 1860, several weeks after Dostoevsky's return from penal exile. According to Joseph Frank, who considers it likely that Dostoevsky attended that lecture, "Whether or not Dostoevsky was present in the audience, there is no doubt that he thoroughly absorbed the essay, whose ideas left significant

juxtapose the two masterpieces named in his essay's title.[39] But he was the first to focus on the two heroes' personalities as basic "types" incarnating "the two elementary and opposite manifestations of the human nature, the dual extremes upon which it revolves."[40] Suggesting that "all humanity belongs to one or the other of these two types" (99), he prefers Don Quixote as the self-sacrificing man of faith, over the earthly, egoistic, introspective Hamlet who "incarnates the spirit of negation" (111). The knight epitomizes trust, fearlessness, humility, courage, enthusiasm, steadfast will and service to a lofty ideal, and these qualities make him in moral terms a giant who dwarfs the analytical, skeptical, ironic, and indecisive Danish prince. Whereas the Hamlets of the world tend to be "useless and doomed to practical inaction inasmuch as they are paralyzed by their gifts," the Don Quixotes are "useful to humanity" and become "leaders of men . . . because they know and can see only a single point on the horizon, often even when it is actually not at all what it appears to their eyes" (112). To illustrate this type, Turgenev alludes to Christ's Passion:

> The Don Quixotes are always trampled beneath the feet of swine at the end of their lives. This is the ultimate tribute which they must suffer to uncouth Destiny, to the world's indifference and its supercilious lack of understanding. It is the derisive blow of the Pharisees. Then only may they die in peace. . . . Then, they will have compassed immortality. (116-17)

Prior to Turgenev, the only person who compared Don Quixote to Christ was Kierkegaard, who was not known in Russia. Turgenev's comparison (implied by the allusion to the Pharisees) may have suggested the idea to Dostoevsky. Indeed, Turgenev's essay closes with praise for Don Quixote as "the most splendid Beauty" (120), precisely the criterion on which Dostoevsky's comparison is based.

---

traces on his own thinking" (*Dostoevsky: The Stir of Liberation 1860-1865* [Princeton: Princeton University Press, 1986], 11).

39. Friedrich Schlegel had already argued that *Hamlet* and *Don Quixote*, together with Goethe's *Wilhelm Meister*, were the most complete masterpieces of Romantic art because they embodied a kind of living form that had outgrown the original intentions of their authors. See Schlegel's *Seine prosaischen Jugendschriften* (Vienna, 1906), 2:381; cited by Turkevich, *Cervantes in Russia*, 107-8.

40. "Hamlet and Don Quixote," in *The Anatomy of Don Quixote: A Symposium*, ed. M. J. Benardete and Ángel Flores (Ithaca, N.Y.: Dragon Press, 1932), 98-120; here 99.

Dostoevsky's earliest recorded remark on Don Quixote occurs in the often-quoted letter of 1/13 January 1868, which he wrote at age forty-eight from Geneva to his niece Sofia, several weeks after beginning his final draft of *The Idiot*. This letter discloses his idea of trying to portray a positively beautiful person, and juxtaposes Christ, Don Quixote, Dickens's Mr. Pickwick, and Hugo's Jean Valjean as models:

> The main thought of the novel is to portray a positively beautiful person [*izobrazit' polozhitel'no prekrasnogo cheloveka*]. There is nothing more difficult than this in the world, and especially at this time. . . . The beautiful is an ideal, but an ideal which neither we nor civilized Europe has in the least perfected. On earth there is only one positively beautiful person—Christ, so that the appearance of this immeasurably, infinitely beautiful person is, of course, an infinite miracle in itself. . . . Of the beautiful characters in Christian literature Don Quixote is the most finished. But he is beautiful only because at the same time he is also comic. Pickwick of Dickens (an infinitely weaker idea than Don Quixote, but nevertheless great) is also comic, and by that alone affects us. Compassion appears toward the beauty that is mocked and doesn't know its own worth—and consequently sympathy appears even in the reader. This awakening of compassion is the secret of humor. Jean Valjean is also a powerful attempt, but he excites sympathy by his terrible misfortune and by society's injustice toward him.[41]

Dostoevsky's remarkable stunt in this passage is his comparison of the Christ of St. John's Gospel (see note 41) with Don Quixote. In comparing Don Quixote and Pickwick, he was probably unaware that their link was already well established among English and American readers.[42] Nor, in juxtaposing

41. Quoted by Robin Feuer Miller, *Dostoevsky and "The Idiot": Author, Narrator, and Reader* (Cambridge: Harvard University Press, 1981), 74. A parenthetical sentence replaced by the second ellipsis in Miller's translation reads: "the whole Gospel of St. John is full of this thought: John sees the wonder of the Incarnation, the visible apparition of the Beautiful" (*Letters*, 142).

42. Tave, *Amiable Humorist*, 242: "To the earliest reviewers Mr. Pickwick and Sam [Weller] were the modern Quixote and Sancho of Cockaigne." See, for example, Washington Irving, letter of 26 May 1841, to Dickens, in *The Letters of Charles Dickens*, ed. Madeline House, Graham Storey, et al., 6 vols. (Oxford: Clarendon, 1965–88), 2:269 n. 1; George Cayley, *Las Alforjas; or, The Bridle Roads of Spain*, 2 vols. (London: Bentley, 1853), 2:80–81. Cf. John Forster, *The Life*

those two figures with Valjean, was he apt to be aware of how greatly the *Quixote* had influenced Valjean's creator, Balzac.[43]

Dostoevsky's next two recorded allusions to Don Quixote occur in his notebooks for *The Idiot*. Both allusions are terse, and reflect again his Romantic view of the knight. The first, dated 21 March 1868, occurs as part of his attempt to formulate Myshkin's character in the notes for part 2, and virtually repeats the comparison of Don Quixote and Pickwick from his letter to Sofia. Having posed the question, "How [to] make the hero's personality charming to the reader?" he notes that "Don Quixote and Pickwick as philanthropists are charming . . . because they are comical," whereas Myshkin "is not comical but does have another charming quality: he is *innocent.*"[44] The second allusion, in the notes dated 8 September 1868 for parts 3 and 4, associates Myshkin's "inspired discourse" (236) with Don Quixote's speech to the goatherds on the Golden Age, a speech that helped establish the knight's image as a utopian dreamer for the Romantics.

Dostoevsky's most extensive remarks on the *Quixote* occur in two entries in *The Diary of a Writer,* a compilation of his journalistic writings from 1873, 1876, 1877, 1880, and 1881. These are the comments Walter Nigg has in mind when he suggests that Dostoevsky viewed the *Quixote* from an "apocalyptic perspective" (*Der christliche Narr,* 265); and the ones Bakhtin is thinking of when he says that Dostoevsky evaluated the *Quixote* as a typical "threshold dialogue": that is, a dialogue expressing the situation of an individual human soul, or human life in general, poised at some momentous turning point (*Problems,* 128). In the first entry, dated March 1876, Dostoevsky describes Count Chambord as "a magnanimous and true knight, almost a Don Quixote," adding:

> I know not any greater praise. Who was it—Heine, was it not?—who recounted how, as a boy, he had burst into tears when, reading *Don Quixote,* he had reached the place where the hero was conquered by the despicable and common-sense barber-surgeon Samson Carasco [*sic*]. In the whole world there is no deeper, no mightier literary work.

of Charles Dickens (New York: Doubleday, 1927), 91–92. See also Steven H. Gale, "Cervantes' influence on Dickens, with comparative emphasis on *Don Quijote* and *Pickwick Papers,*" *Anales Cervantinos* 12 (1973):135–56; Welsh, *Reflections,* intermittently throughout.

43. Regarding Cervantes's influence on Hugo, see Bertrand, "Génesis," [pt. 1], 37–41.

44. *The Notebooks for "The Idiot",* ed. Edward Wasiolek, trans. Katherine Strelsky (Chicago: University of Chicago Press, 1967; 2d imprint, 1973), 190–91.

This is, so far, the last and greatest expression of human thought; this is the bitterest irony which man was capable of conceiving. And if the world were to come to an end, and people were asked there, somewhere: "Did you understand your life on earth, and what conclusion have you drawn from it?"—man could silently hand over *Don Quixote:* "Such is my inference from life.—Can you condemn me for it?"[45]

The impact of Heine on Dostoevsky's appraisal in this passage cannot be overestimated. Dostoevsky repeats the German's error of mistaking Sansón Carrasco for the barber from Don Quixote's village (a mistake that suggests Dostoevsky had not read the *Quixote* for a long time). His emphasis on the novel's "bitterest irony" recalls Heine's comment on its reflection of "the irony with which the Lord has permeated the world." It may not be simply by chance that whereas Heine reminisced about Cervantes's novel as "the first book which I read after I reached the age of understanding [*verständiges Knabenalter*] (*Poetry and Prose,* 382), Dostoevsky speculates that the *Quixote* would suffice on Judgment Day as the summary expression of man's "inference from life." Perhaps captivated by the thought that the *genesis* of Heine's "understanding" had coincided with the poet's childhood reading of the novel, Dostoevsky shifts the perspective from individual autobiography to general prophecy, and imagines how that novel might pertain to all mankind's understanding after the *apocalypse.*

The second and much longer allusion to the *Quixote* in *The Diary of a Writer* encompasses an entire entry of September 1877, "A Lie is Saved by a Lie," where the Romanticism of Dostoevsky's view is unrestrained. He exalts Don Quixote as "the most magnanimous of all knights on earth, the simplest in soul and one of the greatest men in heart" (835), and lauds Cervantes as "the great poet and heart-reader [who] discerned one of the deepest and most mysterious traits of the human spirit," and who created one of those great books that "are bequeathed to mankind once in several hundred years" (836). The Romantic tradition in *Quixote* criticism may be said to reach a climax in Dostoevsky's ensuing elaboration on the book's revelatory and apocalyptic significance. Echoing Byron's claim that "Of all tales 'tis the saddest," he argues that

45. "Don Carlos and Sir Watkin. Again, Symptoms of 'the Beginning of the End' " (March 1876), *Diary,* 260.

acquaintance with this the grandest and saddest book conceived by the genius of man would unquestionably ennoble the soul of a youth with a great thought and would plant in his heart momentous queries, helping to divert his mind from the worship of the eternal stupid idol of mediocrity, self-complacent conceit and trivial prudence. This saddest of all books man will not forget to take along with him to the Lord's last judgment. He will point to the very deep and fatal mystery of man and of mankind revealed in it. He will show that the most sublime beauty of man, his loftiest purity, chastity, naïveté, gentleness, courage, and finally, the greatest are often . . . reduced to naught, . . . solely because all these the [*sic*] noblest and richest gifts with which man is frequently endowed have lacked one and the last gift—*genius* in order to administer the wealth of these blessings and all their power,— . . . along a truthful and not fantastic and insane path of action—for the benefit of the human race! (836–37)

In asserting that "man," as epitomized by Don Quixote, lacks the genius by which to apply his blessings truthfully and sanely for the benefit of the race, this passage implies that "man" should not expect to receive any assistance from God, who may be absent. Once again recalling Heine's discussion of the *Quixote*'s "irony" and the "bitter tears" which the poet shed over the knight's sufferings,[46] Dostoevsky warns that

the spectacle of the cruel irony of fate which so often dooms the labors of the noblest men and most ardent friends of mankind to hisses and ridicule, to stoning, solely because they are unable at the fatal moment to discern the true meaning of things and to discover their *new word*, —this spectacle . . . may lead a friend of humanity to despair, . . . stirring him to bitter tears, forever angering his hitherto pure and credulous heart with doubt. (837)

Dostoevsky had already depicted this sort of disheartening "spectacle" in *The Idiot*, whose hero becomes the object of people's bewilderment and amusement because of his seeming moral perfection.

"A Lie is Saved by a Lie" was occasioned by Dostoevsky's fascination with

---

46. Further in the same page of the *Diary*, Dostoevsky repeats Heine's error of mistaking Sansón for the barber, as he did in the March 1876 entry.

the thought that Don Quixote could at one point ponder in "doubt and perplexity" a problem that threatened his "belief" in the truth of chivalry books: how was it possible that the knights of those books could, with but a single arm and sword, defeat whole armies of a hundred thousand men in battle? According to Dostoevsky, Don Quixote preserves this "lie" by concocting an even more fantastic, absurd, and cruder "lie" of his own, concluding that those legendary knights could accomplish such fantastic feats in combat because enchanters had beforehand transformed the bodies of their enemies through magic into soft and illusory "mollusk-bodies" through which the knight's sword could pass much more quickly and effectively than through humans: "Thus *realism* is taken care of, *truth is saved,* and now the first, principal fancy may be believed without any further doubts,—and this, again, owing to the second far more nonsensical vision" (838).

Based on a remarkable misreading of Cervantes's text, that is, a misreading that overlooks Don Quixote's unflagging conviction that the magic enchanters are his persecutors, not his benefactors, Dostoevsky's notion that the knight saves a lie with a still greater lie might be emended as follows: "Don Quixote does not lie: he fictionalizes [*ficciona*]."[47] As it is, Dostoevsky's misinterpretation leads him to entertain the troubling thought that, in fact, we all do the same thing as Don Quixote in our own lives: "Haven't you conceived a new vision, a new lie, perhaps, of the crudest kind, in which you hasten lovingly to believe only because it has solved your initial doubt [regarding some prior lie or fancy]?" (838). Though not posed as a religious problem, this question could be easily transposed to theological terms: have not religious thinkers for centuries continually conceived new theologies ("new visions" or "new lies") to believe in because the new ones resolved their doubts about the older, dated ones?

We must await Unamuno for a full discussion of Don Quixote in his relation to the problem of faith and doubt, as Dostoevsky records no explicit remark on that relation. After "A Lie is Saved by a Lie" his next and last recorded allusion to the *Quixote* occurs in a letter of 18 August 1880 (to N. L. Osmidov, *Letters,* 254), five months before his death, where he includes it in a reading list of classics that he recommends for a friend's daughter.

---

47. F. Maldonado de Guevara, "Dostoievski y el 'Quijote,'" *Anales Cervantinos* 3 (1953): 367–75; here 372.

The Bearing of the Quixote
on Dostoevsky's Religious Thought

The centrality of religion in Dostoevsky's thinking and writing can hardly be disputed. This fact contributes to what Steiner calls "the radical distinction between nineteenth-century fiction in western Europe and in Russia," that is, between the "secular" tradition of Balzac, Dickens, and Flaubert, and the "religious" art of Tolstoy and Dostoevsky (*Tolstoy or Dostoevsky,* 43). It is with no intended hyperbole that Czeslaw Milosz opens a paper on "Dostoevsky and the Religious Imagination of the West" by asserting: "Dostoevsky's religious thought marks a critical moment in the history of the only civilization that has conquered the entire planet Earth."[48] Achieving what no French, English, or German author could do, he "made use of fiction to render the fundamental antinomy facing modern man" (51), namely, "the antinomy between science and the world of values" (55).

In this light the *Quixote*'s considerable bearing on Dostoevsky's religious thought assumes great importance. While his notorious anti–Roman Catholic bias was confirmed for him by the Polish insurrection of 1863, and is reflected in Myshkin's embarrassing harangue at the Yepanchin's party, and in the very premise of "The Legend of the Grand Inquisitor," Dostoevsky ironically found some of his most basic religious notions and beliefs expressed in the *Quixote,* a classic from an ultra-Catholic nation, by a Catholic author, about a Catholic hero. If Cervantes, together with Rabelais, Shakespeare, Grimmelshausen, and others in Bakhtin's view "belongs to that line of development in European literature in which the early buds of polyphony ripened, and whose great culminator, in this respect, Dostoevsky was to become" (*Problems,* 33–34), Dostoevsky must have recognized this kinship. In appreciating the polyphonic nature of Cervantes's art, he may have viewed the many obeisances paid to Roman Catholicism in the *Quixote* as merely an iconic veneer superimposed over a deeper, nondenominational religious meaning. As Arturo Serrano-Plaja observes, the "contact" in the two men's religious thinking "goes beyond that born from a mere coincidence in the Christian conscience of both authors," and only a "superior spirit" like Dostoevsky's "would have been

---

48. *The Land of Ulro,* trans. Louis Iribarne (New York: Farrar, Straus and Giroux, 1984), 50–61; here 50.

capable of seeing and letting us see the profundity of Cervantes's Christian thought."[49]

What elements in the *Quixote* would have struck a harmonious chord in Dostoevsky's religious sensibility? The ethical and moral lessons he derived from that novel would have appealed to what V. V. Zenkovsky calls his "antinomism [which] was rooted in his religious consciousness."[50] When, in the 1877 *Diary* entry quoted earlier, Dostoevsky suggested on the example of Don Quixote that humans are incapable of applying all their gifts for the benefit of their race, he was anticipating Lukács's view of the *Quixote* as a reflection of God's "abandonment" of the world to meaninglessness. Indeed, the *Quixote* bears greatly on Dostoevsky's well-known dread of the concept that "everything is permitted"[51]—a phrase invoked by Ivan Karamazov as the logical corollary to loss of belief in God and immortality. Don Quixote never loses that belief; on the contrary, he repeatedly affirms it. But the spiritual autonomy implicit in his effort to define himself as a knight and to render chivalric meaning from the otherwise meaningless reality around him undoubtedly captivated the religious imagination of Dostoevsky, who "was occupied with the modern 'tragedy of mind' and perceived that the autonomization of the mind must be, in our time, the necessary consequence of the belief that God is dead."[52]

Despite his recognition of our inability as humans to direct the wealth of our gifts toward fruitful action, Dostoevsky never abandoned what Zenkovsky calls his " 'Christian naturalism'—his faith in the goodness of man and human 'nature' " ("Religious and Philosophical Views," 131). Rooted in his Russian Orthodoxy, this faith helps explain his obsession with the myth of the Golden Age that depicts human nature in its morally best and uncorrupted form. Dostoevsky's adaptations of that myth in several works[53] suggest that he must have taken a special interest in its recurrence in the *Quixote*. As noted earlier,

49. *"Magic" Realism in Cervantes: "Don Quixote" as Seen Through "Tom Sawyer" and "The Idiot"*, trans. Robert S. Rudder (Berkeley: University of California Press, 1970), 80.

50. "Dostoevsky's Religious and Philosophical Views," in *Dostoevsky: A Collection of Critical Essays*, ed. René Wellek (Englewood Cliffs, N.J.: Prentice-Hall, 1962), 130–45; here 131.

51. Soltys, who considers this concept in the light of Lukács's view of the novel, suggests that Dostoevsky "inherited" it from Cervantes ("Don Quijote in la obra de Dostoyevski," 30–31).

52. Nathan A. Scott, "Dostoievski: The Costs of Unbelief in the Major Fiction," *Craters of the Spirit: Studies in the Modern Novel* (Washington: Corpus, 1968), 25–44; here 26.

53. See Harry Levin, *Myth of the Golden Age in the Renaissance* (Bloomington: Indiana University Press, 1969), 162–63; Elizabeth W. Trahan, "The Golden Age—Dream of a Ridiculous Man," *Slavic and East European Journal* 17 (1959):348–71.

his notebooks for *The Idiot* contain an entry associating Myshkin's "inspired discourse" with Don Quixote's speech on the Age of Gold.

In noting Don Quixote's self-conceived role as restorer of the Golden Age, Dostoevsky must have recognized in him six traits corresponding to his own notion of true religion: faith, compassion, suffering, a tendency toward humiliation, foolishness, and being childlike. These qualities of Don Quixote figure prominently in Dostoevsky's three most religiously significant heroes, Myshkin, Alyosha, and Father Zossima, and are often discussed in the author's letters and journalistic writings. All six traits, whose pertinence to Dostoevsky's religious thought will be considered below, help account for his perception of Don Quixote as a supremely beautiful character.

For Turgenev, whose view so greatly influenced Dostoevsky's, Don Quixote's primary characteristic is faith, which figures crucially in what Leonid Grossman sees as the central dialectic in Dostoevsky's worldview: the uninterrupted conflict of humanistic skepticism and faith.[54] Amidst the polyphony that Bakhtin calls the artistic and ideological key to Dostoevsky's novels, the voice of faith—or, more specifically, the voice of Christ as translated through such saintly characters as Myshkin, Alyosha, and Zossima—seems to take precedence over all the rest (cf. Bakhtin, *Problems,* 97). A. Boyce Gibson insists that "no account can properly represent [Dostoevsky], even as an artist, which in any way slurs his complete devotion to Christ."[55] Nothing substantiates this point better than Dostoevsky's own stated creed in a letter of March 1854: "If anyone could prove to me that Christ is outside the truth, and if the truth really did exclude Christ, I should prefer to stay with Christ and not with truth" (from Omsk, to N. D. Fonvisin, *Letters,* 71).

This credo underscores in Jean Drouilly's view "the profound irrationalism which is perhaps the dominant mark of Dostoevsky's spirit."[56] Dostoevsky shared such irrationalism with Don Quixote. Reminiscent of the knight's willful belief in his illusions despite the rational arguments of other characters, Dostoevsky's choice of Christ over truth suggests how natural it was for him to read the *Quixote* as a religiously significant book and to sympathize with its hero. Much as the knight insists to the Toledan merchants that one must believe in Dulcinea without seeing her, so Dostoevsky states to his brother Mikhail in a letter: "Nature, the soul, love, and God, one recognizes through

---

54. *Put' Dostoevskogo* (Dostoevsky's path) (Leningrad: Brokgauz-Efron, 1924), 17; cited by Bakhtin, *Problems,* 16.

55. *The Religion of Dostoevsky* (Philadelphia: Westminster, 1973), 5.

56. *La Pensée politique et religieuse de F. M. Dostoievski* (Paris: Cinq Continents, 1971), 12.

the heart, and not through the reason" (31 October 1838, from Saint Petersburg, *Letters,* 6). Directly related to Dostoevsky's emphasis on the heart and faith is his exaltation of Christian compassion, another quality exemplified by Don Quixote. (Earlier we considered the knight's compassion in its bearing on Fielding's latitudinarian ethic.) "Compassion," Dostoevsky has Myshkin conclude in *The Idiot,* "was the chief and, perhaps, the only law of all human existence" (2:5, 248).[57] And "The Dream of a Strange Man," a "fantastic story" and putative apologue expounding Dostoevsky's own beliefs, closes with the narrator echoing Christ: "The main thing is—love thy neighbors as thyself. This is the cardinal point; that's all."[58]

In Dostoevsky, compassion and universal love entail an obsession with suffering, which is the third trait he would have found religiously significant in Don Quixote. Like all Romantic readers, as we have seen, Dostoevsky sympathized with the Knight of the Sad Countenance as a noble sufferer. The *Quixote* is thus pertinent to Dostoevsky's "religion of suffering" (see Gibson, *Religion of Dostoevsky,* 100-101). The intensification of love between Don Quixote and Sancho through their enduring of misfortunes lends support to the following assertion by the narrator of "The Dream of a Strange Man": "On our earth we can truly love only with suffering, only through suffering! We do not know how to love otherwise and we know no other love" (*Diary,* 681). When Don Quixote becomes so depressed that he refuses to eat and asserts that he was "born to live dying" (Ormsby translation, 2:59, 750), he would have won the heart of Dostoevsky, who once wrote: "I believe that the main and most fundamental spiritual quest of the Russian people is their craving for suffering—perpetual and unquenchable suffering—everywhere and in everything" ("Vlas," 1873, *Diary,* 36). The *Quixote*'s closing chapters, where the knight returns home defeated and melancholic only to regain his sanity and reconcile himself with God before dying, might suitably illustrate Dostoevsky's conviction that humans and their ideals are "purified" through suffering.[59] In the words of Nikolai Berdiaev, "The idea that suffering raises man to his highest level is essential in Dostoevsky's anthropology; suffering is the index of man's depth."[60]

---

57. All quotations are drawn from Fyodor Dostoevsky, *The Idiot,* trans. David Magarshack (Middlesex: Penguin, 1955; repr. with new pagination, 1986). The colon separates the part and chapter numbers, followed by the page.

58. Included in the section dated April 1877, *Diary,* 672-90; here 690.

59. E.g., his letter, 17/29 August 1870, from Dresden, to Sofia, *Letters,* 206. Cf. "The Milieu," 1873, *Diary,* 16.

60. *Dostoevsky,* trans. Donald Attwater (New York: Meridian, 1974), 92.

Conditioned to a large extent by his experience in penal servitude, Dostoevsky's reverence for suffering harmonizes with what George P. Fedotov calls "the dominant motif in Russian spirituality": kenoticism, the imitation of Christ's humility.[61] The term *kenosis* derives from Paul's description of the Incarnation as a humiliation or emptying (from the Greek, *kenoûn*) in Philippians 2:7, a verse that refers to Christ as "servant," appealing apparently to the portrait of the Suffering Servant in Isaiah 53. There is a natural affinity between the kenotic ideal and the *Quixote,* which is a virtual epic of humiliation. From being trampled by various herds of farm animals to being transported in a cage on a cart, from being beaten and stoned to being victimized by practical jokesters, Don Quixote is subjected to constant humiliation and hence might appear as a kenotic figure—or a parody of one. That this is the case may not be merely coincidental. In one scholar's opinion, Don Quixote's "development . . . toward humiliation is probably the most disconcerting aspect of the historical and ideological filiation of Cervantes with Saint Paul."[62] Another scholar traces a line of religio-ethical correspondences from St. Paul through Cervantes to Dostoevsky, whose "ultimate conclusion" is that "man ought to humble himself" (Soltys, "Don Quijote en la obra de Dostoyevski," 33–34).

Dostoevsky must have recognized Don Quixote's approximation to the kenotic ideal, and found the knight's foolishness religiously meaningful. Foolishness is the sine qua non of what is defined as that "peculiar kind of religious practice in the Eastern Orthodox church that is characterized by eccentric acts which violate moral precepts and etiquette and are often accompanied by comic effects," and are practiced by "a religious man, generally thought of as a saint and called in Greek *salos* [Russian: *iurodivyi*]: a 'fool for Christ's sake.'"[63] Constituting an order of canonized saints in the Eastern Orthodox church, the holy fools are "a radical manifestation of Christian kenoticism" (Fedotov, *Russian Religious Mind,* 2:316). This kind of life first appeared in Russia in the fourteenth century (e.g., St. Procopius of Ustyug), and developed there through the next two centuries (e.g., St. Isidore of Rostov and St. Basil of Moscow), before the many abuses and impostures that became linked to it led ecclesiastic officials in the seventeenth century to halt the canonization of holy

61. *A Treasure of Russian Spirituality* (1950; New York: Harper & Row, 1965), 14. See also the same author's *The Russian Religious Mind,* 2 vols. (Cambridge: Harvard University Press, 1966), vol. 1, chap. 4 ("Russian Kenoticism"), 63–93.

62. Paul Descouzis, "Cervantes y San Pablo," *Anales Cervantinos* 11 (1972):33–57; here 47.

63. Alexander Y. Syrkin, "On the Behavior of the 'Fool for Christ's Sake,'" *History of Religions* 22 (1982):150–71; here 150.

fools and to interdict their life-style. However, holy foolishness (*salia*) resisted official condemnation, and its practitioners, though no longer eligible for canonization, never ceased to be venerated by the Russian people.

From Greek hagiography Fedotov extracts four principles on which the holy *salia* is based: (1) ascetic repression of vainglory; (2) service to the world in a special mission through the power of the Spirit manifested in clairvoyance and prophecy; (3) living homelessly among people in cities, and walking naked or half-naked; (4) an irrational and disinterested impulse to madness stemming from a religious motivation free from practical and moral concerns (*Russian Religious Mind,* 2:319-22). While the first three principles are "practical, morally religious purposes of *salia,*" they do not account for the paradox inherent in the fourth principle, which is scripturally motivated by St. Paul's remarks on the "foolishness" of the Cross and his injunctions in 1 Corinthians for believers to become "fools" for Christ's sake.

Whether validly or not, some have linked Myshkin's foolishness to that Pauline doctrine,[64] and this link suggests a further correspondence between Cervantes and Dostoevsky. Dostoevsky fits easily in that "irrationalist current of Christian thought" (Fedotov, *Russian Religious Mind,* 2:322) that runs from St. Paul's exaltation of God's "foolishness" over human "wisdom" in the first three chapters of 1 Corinthians, through Tertullian's *Credo quia absurdum,* to Kierkegaard and his modern successors. Dostoevsky himself may have considered Don Quixote akin to a holy fool. While modeling Myshkin partly after the knight, he begins in his third plan for *The Idiot* to imagine the prince as "a regular *yurodivyi*" (*Notebooks,* 69. Cf. 6th plan, 122). And in the novel's final version Rogozhin addresses him by that same epithet (1:1, 37). According to one scholar who has studied the fool and the wanderer (*strannik*) as archetypes in Russian literature, "there is hardly any of Dostoevsky's leading characters who would not be *iurodivyi-strannik* in potential or an actual one in disguise."[65] This is not to deny, however, that certain important differences emerge between Don Quixote and the holy fools when his character is examined against Fedotov's four principles of *salia.*

First, despite Don Quixote's constant humiliation, he, unlike the *saloi* or *iurodivye,* rarely represses his vainglory; on the contrary, he imagines himself

64. E.g., Fernando Rielo, *Teoría del Quijote: Su mística hispánica* (Madrid: Porrúa Turanzas, 1982), 17.

65. Ewa M. Thompson, "The Archetype of the Fool in Russian Literature," *Canadian Slavonic Papers* 15 (1973):245-73; here 263.

to be the most valorous knight of his age (e.g., *Quixote*, 2:16). This distinction between him and the holy fools stems from their differing ideas of what constitutes the greatest human sin. For the holy fools, as for Dostoevsky, that sin is pride and vainglory itself. In contrast, Don Quixote suggests to a group of mock-shepherds that the worst sin is ingratitude (*desagradecimiento*), or dissatisfaction with the gift of God's world (2:58) (Soltys, "Don Quijote en la obra de Dostoyevski," 34–35).

Second, like the holy fools Don Quixote imagines himself to be serving the world on a special mission. But unlike them he seeks to accomplish that mission not by the power of the Spirit, but by action.

Third, unlike the holy fools Don Quixote is not a city-dweller, and his sojourn in the one city he visits (Barcelona) is relatively brief. However, like them he at times allows himself to be seen seminaked by other persons (e.g., 1:25 and 35), and on occasion insists on sleeping in fields and woods without a roof overhead, much to Sancho's annoyance (e.g., 2:19).

Fourth, Don Quixote's "madness" differs from that of the *saloi:* whereas the knight's is real, the holy fools' is not. With the exception of a few modern exegetes like Serrano-Plaja who argue that Don Quixote is more a skilled actor than a bona fide lunatic, readers rarely question the reality of the knight's insanity. In contrast, the holy fools' madness was purportedly a sham they enacted intentionally to provoke derision and vilification from the world, and in turn to "laugh" at the world themselves. Such behavior is not found in Western Christianity; the closest parallel crops up in the carnival or "laughter" culture analyzed by Bakhtin, such as the "carnivalized Catholicism" of St. Francis, who spoke of himself and his disciples as "God's jugglers" (*ioculatores Domini*) engaging in "spiritual joy" (*laetitia spiritualis*).[66] Though Bakhtin views the *Quixote* as a preeminent landmark in carnivalistic literature, the knight is not comparable to the holy fools in the same way that St. Francis is; unlike Francis, he is not joyful, and unlike the *saloi,* he does not feign his foolishness. Don Quixote indignantly resists any insinuation that he is a fool, as when he responds to the rebuke of the grave ecclesiastic at the duke's dinner table (2:32). Despite these differences, however, Dostoevsky must have viewed Don Quixote and the holy fools as kindred spirits as the life of any *iurodivyi,* like that of the knight, exemplifies the radical disjunction of "two orders": that

66. *Rabelais,* 57. Cf. Syrkin, "Behavior of the 'Fool for Christ's Sake,' " 158–60, 160 n.33.

of the real and that of the ideal, or, in the case of the holy fools, "that of the world and that of God" (Fedotov, *Russian Religious Mind,* 3:21-22).

In addition to Don Quixote's faith, compassion, suffering, humiliation, and foolishness, at least one other of his traits must have struck Dostoevsky as religiously important: his childlike behavior, suggestive of Christian innocence and simplicity. In frolicking about the countryside and "playing" knight, Don Quixote "behaves like a child, but he is not a child" (Serrano-Plaja, *"Magic" Realism,* 28). Myshkin too is portrayed as a childlike adult although "we cannot say that he is playing . . . like Don Quixote" (31). Consequential for Dostoevsky is the spiritual significance of children: "In Dostoevsky's work are children not, in fact, a kind of constant to show the superior world? And those who come closest to them—Alyosha Karamazov or Myshkin—do they not seem to be like those who are nearest the kingdom of God?" (34). Besides Christ's warning that "Except ye be converted and become as little children, ye shall not enter into the kingdom of heaven" (Matt. 18:3), two other traditions must have encouraged Dostoevsky to exalt the child: Russian kenoticism and Western Romanticism. The kenotic ideal follows through on Christ's advice that the adult should "humble himself as this little child" (Matt. 18:4). At the same time, continuing a tendency that began with Bacon, Traherne, and Vaughn in England, and Rousseau in France, some of the most prominent writers of the Romantic Age in Europe and America equated the child with the Edenic Adam and elevated the child's "freshness of sensation" as a norm for adult experience, especially poetic experience (see Abrams, *Natural Supernaturalism,* 379-83, 411-15).

Having considered six traits in Don Quixote that correspond to Dostoevsky's notion of true religion, we can appreciate why he viewed the knight as the most beautiful character in Christian literature, and a figure comparable to Christ. Yet the question remains, How did Dostoevsky arrive at his stated conviction that Christ was the "only one positively beautiful person"? Though his public writings would later stress his propagandistic belief that the unique calling of Russian Orthodoxy and the Russian people was to preserve the "purity" of Christ's "Divine image" (e.g., "Perplexed Air," 1873, *Diary,* 63), his 1868 letter to Sofia is concerned with Christ not as divine, but rather as a "person" who lived "on earth."

While Dostoevsky was influenced by the Romantic idealization of the knight through his reading of Schiller, Byron, Heine, and Turgenev, his exposure to the emphasis on Christ as human came through his reading of the "historical" lives of Jesus by Strauss and Renan. It was possibly during the period of his activity as a revolutionary in the Petrashevsky group (1846–49) that Dostoevsky first encountered the work by Strauss, to whom he alludes as a hater of Christ several times in *The Diary of a Writer.*[67] Renan's work appeared in Paris on 23 June 1863, shortly before Dostoevsky's second visit there, and is mentioned twice in his notebooks for *The Idiot.*[68] So he was clearly under the sway of Renan's humanized conception of Christ while he worked on that novel. Even more telling is the *Diary*'s one allusion to Renan. After remarking that Belinsky was obliged as a socialist "to destroy the teaching of Christ, to call it fallacious and ignorant philanthropy," Dostoevsky notes that the great critic was not even fazed by

> the beatific image of God-man, its moral inaccessibility, its wonderful and miraculous beauty. . . . Bielinsky [*sic*] did not stop even before this insurmountable obstacle, as did Renan, who proclaimed in his *Vie de Jésus* —a book permeated with incredulity—that Christ nevertheless is the ideal of human beauty, an inaccessible type which cannot be repeated even in the future. (7)

Dostoevsky seems to have viewed Renan's work as a confirmation of his own religious credo, which he had disclosed almost a decade before in the letter to Fonvisin quoted earlier. In stating his preference for Christ over truth, he had claimed that while being an inveterate "child of unfaith and skepticism," he knew of "nothing lovelier, deeper, . . . and more perfect than the Saviour" (*Letters,* 70–71). He was now struck to find that Renan, despite the "incredulity" permeating *Vie de Jésus,* calls Christ "the ideal of human beauty" (nota bene: "human"). As a testimony to the lasting impression that description made on Dostoevsky, his own humanized conception of Christ as the only "positively beautiful person" on earth becomes analogous to his idealized image of Don Quixote as the most beautiful character in Christian literature. Let us now turn to consider *The Idiot,* in whose hero Christ and Don Quixote are combined.

67. "Old People," 1873, *Diary,* 8; "One of the Contemporaneous Falsehoods," 1873, *Diary,* 150, 151. See also Drouilly, *Pensée politique et religieuse,* 100.
68. *Notebooks,* 5th plan, 105; notes on pts. 3 and 4, 240.

4

Don Quixote's Religious Transformation in The Idiot

It was not with the intention of depicting a positively beautiful person that Dostoevsky began *The Idiot*, which of all his novels came the hardest for him, largely because of the wretched circumstances of his life at the time (see Wasiolek, Introduction to Dostoevsky, *Notebooks*, 1–9). That aim did not emerge until after he had been through some six plans, and as late as a month prior to his submission of the novel's first part to the publisher. In a letter dated 31 December 1867/12 January 1868 to his friend Apollon Maikov, he disclosed his cherished "idea" of portraying "a wholly beautiful man [*izobrazit' vpolne prekrasnogo cheloveka*]." In adding "This idea formerly has appeared in artistic form" (quoted by Miller, *Dostoevsky and "The Idiot,"* 73), he presumably had in mind Christ, Don Quixote, Pickwick, and Valjean, whom he cited as paradigms in the letter he wrote the next day to Sofia about his idea.

As a "beautiful" person Myshkin is conceived in terms comparable to Goethe's *Wilhelm Meister* and Hegel's *Phenomenology of the Spirit*.[1] There is

1. See Anthony J. Cascardi, *The Bounds of Reason: Cervantes, Dostoevsky, Flaubert* (New York: Columbia University Press, 1986), 130.

also a striking correspondence between Dostoevsky's statements to Maikov and Sofia about the supreme difficulty of trying to portray such a figure, and Emerson's remarks on the considerable demands exacted by his own attempt to sketch "representative men." Just as Dostoevsky was encouraged by Renan's *Vie de Jésus* to view Christ as the one perfect man, so Emerson recalled after reading the same book:

> When I wrote *Representative Men*, I felt that Jesus was the "Representative Man" whom I ought to sketch; but the task required great gifts, — steadiest insight and perfect temper; else, the consciousness of want of sympathy in the audience would make one petulant or sore, in spite of himself.[2]

While he shared Emerson's awareness of people's "want of sympathy," Dostoevsky was not insensitive to traces of goodness in those around him; indeed, of the "robber-murderers" in prison with him, he once testified in a letter to Mikhail that "there were among them deep, strong, and beautiful natures, and it often gave me great joy to find gold under a rough exterior" (from Omsk, 22 February 1854, *Letters*, 65). But from his early youth on, Dostoevsky had viewed the world as an environment hostile to human virtue. At age sixteen he had written to Mikhail: "I feel that our world has become one immense Negative, and that everything noble, beautiful, and divine, has turned itself into satire" (from Saint Petersburg, 9 August 1838, *Letters*, 3).

This insight is consistent with Kierkegaard's speculation in the late 1840s that Christ, his disciples, and any true Christian would become comical "counterparts" of Don Quixote, were they to appear in the modern secular world.[3] The religious existence of a true Christian living in the secular age would seem no less anachronistic than did Don Quixote's chivalric existence in his own unchivalric age. This correspondence must have seemed obvious to Dostoevsky, given his fixation on the problems of atheism, nihilism, and other contemporary ideologies contradictory to Christianity. After all, had not the atheist Belinsky once speculated in an outburst aimed at Dostoevsky that

2. *The Journals of Ralph Waldo Emerson*, 10 vols., ed. E. W. Emerson and W. E. Forbes (Boston: Houghton Mifflin, 1909–14), 9:579.

3. *Søren Kierkegaard's Journals and Papers*, 7 vols., trans. and ed. Howard V. Hong and Edna H. Hong (Bloomington: University of Indiana Press, 1967–78), 1:132–33. Cf. 2:274; 282–83.

Christ would be "effaced" were he to return amidst the science and politics of the modern world? (Dostoevsky, "Old People," *Diary,* 7).

Written a decade prior to "The Legend of the Grand Inquisitor," wherein a returned Christ is condemned in sixteenth-century Seville, *The Idiot* presages that tale's theme of the savior's anachronicity. Prince Myshkin, as Joseph Frank puts it, "lives in the eschatological tension that was (and is) the soul of the primitive Christian ethic, whose doctrine of totally selfless *agape* was conceived in the same perspective of the imminent end of time."[4] At the same time, he inhabits Dostoevsky's age, not the age of primitive Christianity. As the *Quixote*'s "Russian version," Myshkin's story reveals for Simon O. Lesser "the inadequacy of mere goodness in the world of today" ("Saint and Sinner," 211), much as Don Quixote's story shows the folly of chivalry in the postmedieval world. For this reason Myshkin stands as the preeminent religious transformation of Cervantes's hero in the nineteenth century.

Analysis of the Text

For Stieglitz, one of the debaters at the priory in André Malraux's *Les Noyers de l'Altenburg* (1945), the *Quixote, The Idiot,* and *Robinson Crusoe* are the only books that "hold their own against prison life," and as such they comprise "one and the same" book, containing "the three isolated heroes of the world-novel."[5] Aside from the social isolation of Don Quixote and Myshkin, and their other similarities mentioned earlier, one comparison of the *Quixote* and *The Idiot* has shown that both texts contain elements derived from their authors' lives (for example, the knight's idealism, the prince's epilepsy); that both employ the device of paired alter egos (Don Quixote/idealism versus Sancho Panza/pragmatism, Myshkin/good versus Rogozhin/evil); that both present microcosms of society, representing a polyphony of voices from different socioeconomic classes; that *The Idiot* contains sections structurally analogous to the interpolated tales of the *Quixote* (such as the digressions on the Yepanchin family, Nastasya's love affairs, and the problems of the Ivolgins);

4. "A Reading of *The Idiot,*" *Southern Review* 5 (1969): 303–31; here 308.
5. *The Walnut Trees of Altenburg,* trans. A. W. Fielding (London: Lehmann, 1952), 90. Cf. André Malraux, *Anti-Memoirs,* trans. Terence Kilmartin (New York: Holt, Rinehart, and Winston, 1968), 25–26.

that both depict suffering as a form of life; that both employ a psychoanalytic principle in their use of dreams and the subconscious (as in Don Quixote's descent into Montesinos's cave and Ippolit's self-revelations); that the concept of time in both is circular, as one episode or moment seems to mirror the one(s) preceding it; that Myshkin undergoes a change of character analogous to the "sanchification" of Don Quixote; that Kolya, in accepting Myshkin's philosophy, plays a role analogous to Sancho's; that Don Quixote and Myshkin both seek the divine and the sublime; that Myshkin, like Don Quixote, is platonic in his love of women and comports himself inadequately with them; that both characters are Christ-like.[6]

Myshkin's Christic aspect is as essential to his character as his quixotic aspect. The extensive entries of 10 April 1868 in Dostoevsky's notebook for part 2 of *The Idiot* allude to the evolving hero three times as "Prince Christ" (*Kniaz' Khristos*) (198, 201, 205). Thus Myshkin strikes some scholars as a "symbol of Christ"; that is, not as Christ himself, but as someone with "a special similarity to Christ."[7] A "general parallel" has been observed between Myshkin's "tragic fate" and Christ's Passion (Frank, "Reading of *The Idiot,*" 304), and the prince may seem "a failure as Christ was a failure, helpless to check the hurt that we do to each other, but ready . . . by his own faith to give to all an image of the best of themselves."[8]

Accepting Myshkin as "almost a parody" (Holquist, "Gaps in Christology," 132) of Christ and Don Quixote, our analysis of *The Idiot* will focus on his association with both figures, and trace their mergence in his development through four roles in the course of the novel: the roles of (1) a "heavenly stranger" in the temporal world; (2) a "poor knight" in the mode of Pushkin's hero; (3) an embodiment of the sacred "binding idea" of "love thy neighbour as thyself"; and (4) an "idiot redux" (my phrase), or a man reduced—literally "led back"—to idiocy by the catastrophe of existence in the profane world.

1:1–16: The Heavenly Stranger

From its opening chapter *The Idiot* parallels the *Quixote* in certain ways while inverting it in others. In both novels the themes of mental illness and journey-

---

6. Soltys, "Don Quijote en la obra de Dostoyevski," chap. 7 ("La comparación entre *Don Quijote y El idiota*"), 108–47.

7. Guardini, "Symbol of Christ," 359. Cf. Nigg, *Christliche Narr,* 400.

8. Edward Wasiolek, *Dostoevsky: The Major Fiction* (Cambridge: MIT Press, 1964), 109.

ing are introduced early on. But whereas the *Quixote* introduces a middle-aged hidalgo who promptly *lapses into* madness in the security of his reading-room, *The Idiot* introduces a young epileptic, Prince Leo Nikolayevich Myshkin, who recently *recovered from* "idiocy" in the security of a Swiss sanitarium where he underwent treatment for the last four years. And whereas Cervantes's story begins with Don Quixote's sallying forth astride his horse as a knight, Dostoevsky's story begins with a journey's end—Myshkin's arrival by train in the Russian city of Saint Petersburg.

As Don Quixote is joined early on by a partner with an opposite personality and physique, so Myshkin first appears in the company of an antithetical character in his third-class compartment. The stereotypically devilish face of Semyon Parfyonovich Rogozhin (dark curly hair, fiery eyes, malicious smile, deathly pallor, etc.) and Myshkin's conventionally saintly or Christ-like visage (fair hair, hollow cheeks, piercing but gentle eyes, little white beard, etc.) suggest the dialectic of good versus evil that will characterize their relationship, and provide a moral counterpart to the metaphysical antitheses of idealism versus realism, soul versus body, spirit versus material that the Romantics found in the Don Quixote–Sancho Panza friendship.

Like the anachronistically armored Don Quixote, Myshkin is attired in a way that seems utterly out of place in his cold surroundings. While Rogozhin is "warmly dressed in a large lamb's-wool-lined black overcoat" (27), Myshkin is "obviously quite unprepared," wearing as a cloak "the sort of thing travellers often wear during the winter months in a distant foreign country, . . . without . . . having to bargain for such long stretches of country" (28).

> A meagre bundle of old, faded silk material, which apparently con-
> tained all his belongings, dangled from his hands. He wore thick-soled
> shoes and gaiters—all of it quite un-Russian. His dark-haired fellow-
> passenger in the lamb's-wool-lined coat scrutinized it all, . . . and, at
> last, asked with that callous grin with which people sometimes so
> casually and unceremoniously express their pleasure at the misfor-
> tunes of their fellow-men:
>   "Chilly?" (28)

Here, Myshkin's kinship to Don Quixote as a strange figure is strengthened by the emphasis on his alien ("un-Russian") appearance, and Rogozhin's

Schadenfreude ("Chilly?") calls to mind the delight which so many characters in the *Quixote* take in the mad knight's sufferings. Symbolically, Rogozhin is already wearing his victim's skin on his back; if the notorious distinction between devouring "wolves" and helpless "sheep" in Dostoevsky's fiction holds true,[9] the young man's lamb's-wool-lined coat signifies his affiliation with the predatory lupine type, which finds antecedents in Cervantes's "fair huntress" and her ducal husband, as well as in Fielding's "parson-hunting" squire. Though the prince's given name, Leo, hardly implies a lamblike vulnerability, it does recall the lion image used by medieval allegorists as a symbol for Christ,[10] and his patronymic stems from the Russian *myshka*, "little mouse," a creature known for its helplessness before predators.

During his conversation on the train with Rogozhin and the busybody civil servant Lebedev, who butts in, Myshkin begins to betray a naïveté akin to Don Quixote's. When asked some "questions" by Rogozhin, he shows "not the slightest suspicion of how scornful, irrelevant, and frivolous some of them were" (28). In response to a derogatory remark by Lebedev against doctors, he admits: "Naturally, I'm not in a position to argue with you, because there are so many things I don't know" (29). And when he betrays no embarrassment for his impecuniousness and paucity of belongings, and confesses that he has no carnal knowledge of women (like the chaste knight and the virginal Christ), Rogozhin labels him a "holy fool" (37). (Ironically, Rogozhin's given name, Parfyon, stems from the Greek *parthénios,* "the virginal," which already intimates his paradoxical fraternity with the prince.)

Like Don Quixote as he sallies into the world of Spain, Myshkin seems a total stranger as he reenters the Russian world. From the start he appears lost, alienated, and helpless, admitting to one person: "I haven't been in Russia for over four years and I really can hardly say that I ever left it, for when I did leave it I was scarcely in my right mind. I knew nothing then, and I know even less now. I'm in need of good, kind people" (1:3, 48–49). Like Don Quixote he has no wife or immediate family. As the orphaned, sole surviving male member of the Myshkin lineage, he is an anachronism. Lebedev, upon learning the prince's patronymic, points out: "It's an historic name, sir. . . . I'm afraid no Myshkins are to be found anywhere nowadays" (1:1, 31). The Myshkin family

9. Nikolai K. Mikhailovsky, *Dostoevsky: A Cruel Talent,* trans. Spencer V. Cadmus, Jr. (Ann Arbor: Ardis, 1978).

10. This symbol's *locus classicus* is chap. 1 of the *Physiologus* (Greek version, c. 2d century; Latin version, c. 4th century).

is referred to as "very ancient" (1:2, 39), and the prince, in announcing himself to General Yepanchin's valet, informs him that "Mrs. Yepanchin is a Princess Myshkin, the last of them, and except for her and myself there are no more Myshkins left" (42). His skill in the medieval art of calligraphy, which he demonstrates to General Yepanchin and Ganya Ivolgin, only adds to his anachronous aura.

Most decisively "quixotic," according to Segundo Serrano Poncela, is "the inadequacy [*la inadequación*] between reality and the prince's postures toward it." The noteworthy difference is that Myshkin, unlike the knight, "has a clear awareness of the limits of his folly; knows to laugh at himself when reality is so harsh that it succeeds in wounding him, and through the occurrence of such a defensive doubling [*repliegue*], he disarms the teaser—something that never occurs in Don Quixote." Thus the prince's conversation with the Yepanchins' astonished footman and the latter's resulting stupor seems "typically quixotic" ("Don Quijote en Dostoievski," 19). Anticipating the similar reactions of General Yepanchin (1:3) and Ganya Ivolgin (1:7), the valet at first reacts coldly to this strange visitor, but is gradually warmed or—to borrow Serrano-Plaja's term—"myshkinized" (*"Magic" Realism,* 41; cf. 48) by the prince's disarming humility, innocence, simplicity, and honesty.

While resembling Don Quixote in his anachronicity and "myshkinization" of others, Myshkin is like Christ in his compassion toward sufferers, his seemingly clairvoyant insight, and his association with a couple of minor Christic motifs. One of these is his intimacy with children. In reminiscing to Mrs. Yepanchin and her three daughters about his four years in a Swiss village, he recalls (1:6): "There were always children there, and I spent all my time with the children, only with the children" (89), who "could not get on without me, and were always flocking round me" (90). Paraphrasing Jesus he explains: "It is through children that the soul is cured" (90). Another Christic motif occurs when Myshkin turns the other cheek after being slapped in the face by Ganya (1:10); in this instance he displays the typically Russian *smirenie,* "an entire attitude of non-resistance to evil or supposed evil, or self-humiliation" in which "the battling spirit of Don Quixote has its antithesis."[11]

Myshkin's *smirenie* is directly related to the most crucial of all his Christic traits: his extraordinary compassion toward human suffering. This compassion first reveals itself when he recalls his trauma of having witnessed the guillotin-

---

11. Wolfgango L. Giusti, "Sul 'donchischiottismo' di alcuni personaggi del Dostohevskij," *Cultura* 10 (1931): 171-79; here 175; quoted by Serrano-Plaja, *"Magic" Realism,* 64-65.

ing of a criminal at Lyons (1:2). The horror of that experience led Myshkin to view capital punishment as "an immeasurably greater evil than the crime [of murder] itself" since the sentenced murderer, unlike his victim, must suffer the "terrible agony" of knowing that his own impending execution at a precise time is absolutely "certain" (46). The prince adds, presumably with Gethsemane in mind: "It was of agony like this and of such horror that Christ spoke" (46).

Myshkin's compassion also joins him with Don Quixote (cf. Serrano-Plaja, *"Magic" Realism,* 69–80). The prince's apparent notion that pity, compassion, and love should outweigh the law of justice accords with the merciful declaration the knight makes to the guards upon liberating the galley slaves (1:22), and with his speech defending that action to his squire and the priest (1:30). However, whereas Don Quixote's compassion is fundamental to his repeated self-definition as a knight and presumably arises no less out of his desire to fulfill that role than out of any inherent altruism, Myshkin's compassion stems strictly from his own innate goodness; he is not seeking to fulfill any particular role. There is also a difference in the ways the compassion of the two characters relates to their understanding of people. The knight is responsive to such external symptoms of the afflictions of others as the sound of a farm-boy's cries or the sight of the galley slaves' chains, but proves incapable of discerning their private thoughts, feelings, and intentions. In contrast, Myshkin's compassion is heightened by his ability to intuit the inner lives of almost everyone he meets, sometimes by simply scrutinizing the person's face. Like Christ and numerous Russian saints known for their clairvoyancy,[12] he is particularly acute at discerning people's hidden sufferings, as when he sees through Ganya's amiable facade upon first meeting him: "I expect when he is alone he doesn't look like that at all and, quite possibly, he never laughs," the prince cannot help reflecting (1:2, 47). The prince later intuits the extraordinary suffering of Nastasya, whom he has never met, by examining her visage in a photograph (1:3). When asked by Ganya whether he thinks Rogozhin will marry Nastasya, he prophesies with uncanny accurateness: "He might marry her to-morrow and, perhaps, murder her a week later" (59). Still later we are told that Myshkin "could see through things . . . and was capable of giving an excellent account of them" (1:7, 110). Eventually Ganya himself remarks the prince's uncanny insight: "You notice things other people never notice" (1:11, 141).

12. E.g., John 2:24–25: "[Jesus] knew all men, And needed not that any should testify of man: for he knew what was in man." The alleged clairvoyancy of some Russian saints is remarked by Fedotov, *Russian Religious Mind,* e.g., 2:289–90.

We learn more about the history behind Myshkin's hypersensitivity to human suffering from his initial interview with Mrs. Yepanchin and her daughters, to whom he relates several pertinent memories from his years abroad (1:5-6): his suffering of a painful series of epileptic attacks while en route from Russia to Switzerland; his feeling of profound sympathy one evening at the sound of a donkey braying in the Basel marketplace; his meetings with a suicidal prisoner and a victim of a mock-execution; and his involvement in the tragic story of Marie, a girl from the Swiss village where he lived. Seduced and then abandoned by a traveling French businessman, the fatherless girl lost her mother, was ostracized by the villagers and publicly mocked by the pastor in church, and eventually died of consumption. At least two aspects of these memories strengthen the connection between Myshkin and Christ. The first is the special fondness he felt for the "long-suffering" donkey, the animal on which Jesus allegedly rode upon entering Jerusalem in fulfillment of the prophecy of Zechariah 9:9. The second is Myshkin's compassion toward Marie (cf. Mary Magdalene). As the only person in the village who pitied her and never considered her "guilty," he displayed the sort of pity that Jesus showed toward the adulterous woman (John 8:2-11).

Myshkin's quixotic and Christic dimensions are complemented by his relationships with two ostensibly antithetical women: a Dulcinea-figure in the person of Aglaya Yepanchin, and a Mary Magdalene–figure, Nastasya Filippovna Barashkov. Aglaya, the youngest of the Yepanchin daughters, is "The most beautiful girl in the family" (1:4, 62), whose "future, as [her sisters] had most sincerely decided among themselves, was not to be an ordinary one, but an embodiment of the ideal of heaven on earth" (62). Conversely, the beautiful Nastasya was orphaned as a child and subsequently seduced by a philandering rich man, Mr. Totsky, who "kept" her four years in a little house in a remote village ironically called Eden. Nastasya's "fall," which parallels Marie's, sets her actual past in a contrast with the prediction of Aglaya's "ideal" future, and implicitly conjoins Nastasya with the dissolute Rogozhin, whose life is described as "A hell on earth" (1:1, 36). Furthermore, the prediction that "Aglaya's future husband was to be a model of perfection and a paragon of all virtues" (1:4, 62) finds depraved inversions in the "suitors" Nastasya now has in Petersburg, where Totsky has "installed" her: Rogozhin and Ganya are vying with money to purchase her hand in marriage, while General Yepanchin secretly bargains to make her his mistress.

Aglaya and Nastasya do share one important quality with each other, as well as with the Dulcinea of Don Quixote's fantasy: their striking beauty. Myshkin's initial response to the photograph of Nastasya—"She's wonderfully beautiful" (1:3, 54)—is echoed almost verbatim by his remark to Aglaya: "You're extraordinarily beautiful" (1:7, 99). Yet he notices a key difference between the two women in their beauty. When Mrs. Yepanchin insists that he "read" Aglaya's face, Myshkin can only bring himself to say that she is "almost as beautiful as Nastasya Filippovna, except that her face is quite different" (100). Nastasya's beauty differs from Aglaya's in that it betrays "so much suffering" (103), and this "strange beauty" has aroused a "feeling of compassion" (102) in the prince. By secretly kissing her portrait moments earlier, he linked his compassion toward her with that which he had felt toward the unfortunate Marie, whom he once kissed (1:6). Unlike other people, the prince sees in Nastasya—as he saw in Marie—not "guilt," but suffering. While General Ivolgin's epithet for Nastasya, "shameless whore" (1:12, 147), reflects her ill-repute, the prince will whisper to her at her birthday party: "Everything about you is perfection" (1:13, 161). This statement reminds us of Don Quixote's addressing prostitutes as "damsels" (*Quixote,* 1:2), and a coarse farm-girl as his Dulcinea (2:10). Myshkin's quixotism becomes even more pronounced when, to the amazement of Nastasya and her guests, he announces his wish to marry her (1:15). After Nastasya responds sarcastically, "What are you going to live on if you're really so much in love that you don't mind marrying Rogozhin's slut—you, a prince?" (184), Myshkin remains undaunted, as does Don Quixote when the prostitutes and, later, the farm-girl, mock him for his genteel manner toward them.

> "I shall be marrying an honest woman, and not Rogozhin's slut," said the prince.
>
> "Me an honest woman?"
>
> "You."
>
> "Oh well, you've got that out of—novels! That, my darling Prince, is the sort of thing they believed in the old days. Nowadays the world's grown wiser, and all that's nonsense! And how can you be thinking of marriage when you want a nurse to look after you yourself!"
>
> The prince got up and said in a trembling, timid voice, though at the same time with an air of profound conviction:
>
> "You're quite right, Nastasya Filippovna; I know nothing and I've seen nothing, but I—I think you'll be doing me an honour, and not I

you. I'm nothing, but you've suffered and emerged pure out of such a
hell, and that is a great deal. What, then, are you ashamed of?
(184-85)

Myshkin's quixotism comes to the fore in this exchange. His insistence that
"Rogozhin's slut" is "an honest woman" again recalls the knight's transformation
of prostitutes into "damsels." Nastasya's suggestion that he "got that out
of—novels," and her distinction between the "nonsense" which "they believed
in the old days" and the "wiser" attitude of the world "nowadays," hearken back
to the contradiction between Don Quixote's anachronistic fantasies and his
contemporary reality. Despite Myshkin's "trembling, timid voice," which is
hardly reminiscent of Don Quixote's customarily bold, assertive tone, the
prince's "air of profound conviction" and the chivalric terms in which he states
his readiness to defend Nastasya ("I'm ready to die for you," "I won't let anyone
say a bad word about you" [185]) recall the knight's dedication to Dulcinea.
Finally, the prince's outburst elicits "sniggering," "smiling," and "amazement"
among the guests, as well as General Yepanchin's question, "He isn't raving, is
he?" (185)—reactions practically identical with the way most people respond
to Don Quixote.

But if, as Murray Krieger suggests, "Myshkin's initial championing of
Nastasya is presented to us in the framework of Quixotism" (*Tragic Vision*,
216), an important qualification must be made: while Don Quixote's idealization of Dulcinea is based on an illusion, Myshkin's championing of Nastasya
stems from his notion that she "suffered and emerged pure out of such a hell."
The idea that suffering purifies the sufferer stems not from the *Quixote*, but is
congruent with the Russian Orthodox stress on *kenosis*, and related to the
Roman Catholic doctrine of purgatory, which found some, though not full,
acceptance in the Eastern Church over the centuries.

The images of Christ and Marie/Mary Magdalene that are manifest in
Myshkin and Nastasya may account for the *anagnorisis* the latter two shared
upon first meeting at Ganya's flat (1:9). Considered naturalistically as well as in
conjunction with their biblical counterparts, their feeling that they have "seen"
each other "somewhere" before might be explained as follows. Myshkin may
"recognize" Nastasya in the sense that her suffering of "fallenness" not only is
identical with that which he pitied in Marie, but recalls that which Christ
pitied in Mary Magdalene and the adulterous woman. At the same time

Nastasya may "recognize" Myshkin in the sense that she undoubtedly knows certain icons whose representations of Christ and the saints Myshkin's physiognomy (described in 1:1) resembles. Moreover, she may discern in Myshkin the sort of compassion exemplified by Christ toward "fallen" women. Healed by Jesus of "seven devils" (Luke 8:2), Mary followed him to Jerusalem and addressed him reverentially after his resurrection as Rabboni or "Master" (John 20:16). Likewise, Nastasya, saved by Myshkin from having to marry the wicked Ganya (1:14), announces to the guests at her party: "The prince means a lot to me, for he is the first man I've ever come across in my life in whom I can believe as a true and loyal friend. He believed in me at first sight, and I believed in him" (175). She later tells Myshkin: "You're the first human being I've seen!" (1:16, 195).

Myshkin's and Nastasya's "recognition" of each other may also be considered on philosophical and mythic levels of meaning. Philosophically, their mutual déjà vu implies for Guardini that they have already met in the realm of platonic "ideas," and that "within the actual historical meeting, something eternal has unveiled itself" ("Symbol of Christ," 369). Mythically, V. I. Ivanov construes the two characters as "beings who have come down from on high." The prince symbolizes the "Heavenly emissary" and "liberator" who must "deliver the world's soul from the bondage of an evil enchantment" and "free Andromeda from her chains, abduct Eurydice or Alcestis from Hades, waken the Sleeping Beauty," while Nastasya represents the "Eternal Female," or "that Beauty who comes down upon earth to save the world . . . , but then, like the Ashtaroth of the Gnostics, becomes imprisoned in matter and desecrated," and must await her deliverer.[13]

This interpretation would help explain why Myshkin and Nastasya see each other as embodying, beneath the imperfect, accidental roles of "idiot" and "fallen" woman, something perfect or essential. Myshkin perceives in Nastasya the perfection of an essential "beauty" that transcends the "fallenness" of her temporal condition. Nastasya perceives in Myshkin the perfection of an essential "human being" uncorrupted by the the world's wickedness, who is capable of feeling selfless love (*agape*) and compassion. Caught up in her accidental suffering and guilt, Nastasya may have forgotten her essential perfection, of which she must be reminded by the heavenly emissary, Myshkin. This is

13. Vyacheslav I. Ivanov, *Freedom and the Tragic Life: A Study of Dostoevsky,* trans. Norman Cameron (New York: Noonday, 1952), pt. 2, chap. 3 ("The Stranger"), 86–106; here 96–97.

implied when she recognizes him for the second time at Ganya's flat ("I do think I've seen his face somewhere"):

> "And aren't you ashamed of yourself?" cried the prince suddenly with deep, heartfelt reproach. "You're not the woman you pretend to be. Why, it isn't possible!"
>
> Nastasya Filippovna looked surprised. She smiled, but seemed to be concealing something behind her smile. She was a little embarrassed and, glancing at Ganya, went out of the room. But before she reached the entrance hall, she suddenly returned, went up to Mrs. Ivolgin, took her hand, and raised it to her lips.
>
> "He was right, I'm not really like that," she whispered rapidly and fervidly, flushing all over, and, turning round again, walked out (1:10, 138-39)

Oblivious of her own essential perfection, Nastasya used to have presentiments that someone like Myshkin would appear and free her from her suffering. As she prepares to depart with Rogozhin from her party after rejecting Myshkin's marriage proposal because she did not want to "ruin" him, Nastasya tells the prince:

> "I dreamed of you long ago, when I still lived in the country with [Totsky]. . . . I used to think and dream, think and dream, and always I was imagining someone like you, kind and honest and good and as silly as you, so silly that he would suddenly come and say, "It's not your fault, Nastasya Filippovna, and I adore you!" (1:16, 192)

From the prince's disclosure moments earlier it seems that he has intuited her yearning for him all along: "When I saw your portrait this morning, I seemed to have recognized a face I knew well. I felt at once as though you had called me" (189).

Regardless of whether Myshkin was brought to Petersburg in answer to a "mysterious call," as he suggests (1:5, 81), or through "God's intention," as Mrs. Yepanchin believes (1:7, 105), it is clear that he, like Christ as Word-made-flesh (John 1:14), and like Don Quixote as hidalgo-turned-knight, appears as a stranger amidst human society. Remembering his departure from Switzerland he states:

> "As I sat in the train, I thought: 'Now I'm going among people; I may not know anything, but a new life has begun for me.' I made up my mind to do my duty honestly and resolutely. I may find it painful and dull to be among people. . . . Perhaps even here they will regard me as a child—it can't be helped! For some reason everyone regards me as an idiot, too." (1:6, 97)

What sort of world is it where so good a man may be considered "an idiot"? For Dostoevsky, as Berdiaev points out, the city is "the scene of the human tragedy," and Petersburg is "a spectral vision begotten by erring and apostate men" (*Dostoievsky,* 40). Some of the most "apostate" vices are exhibited by the guests at Nastasya's party, most notably the hypocrisy and dishonesty of the participants in the "parlour game" proposed by Ferdyshchenko (1:14); the money-worship displayed by the guests when Nastasya tosses a bundle containing a hundred thousand rubles into the fireplace (1:16); and the lecherous coveting of Nastasya by Ganya and Rogozhin, around which the entire episode revolves. General Yepanchin, a secret sinner himself, assesses the whole proceedings most aptly: "This is Sodom—Sodom!" (190). From an earlier complaint by Ganya's younger brother, Kolya, we may assume that the rampant immorality at Nastasya's party reflects (in Dostoevsky's view) the degeneracy not only of Saint Petersburg, but also the whole nation: "In our age everyone is a sordid adventurer! And that is particularly true of Russia" (1:12, 154).

On entering this corrupt world, the prince has produced an effect that seems both Christic and quixotic. Like the Christ of John's Gospel he has caused a "scandal" (*skándalon*), which in its New Testament sense (literally, a stumbling-block or offense), connotes that elementary phenomenon which occurs whenever people's "sensation of a strange and almost incomprehensible phenomenon," such as purity, nobility, strength, or holiness, is "transformed" into irritation, revulsion, and hate (Guardini, "Symbol of Christ," 371). This was exemplified when Ganya slapped him and he responded only by staring at his assailant "with strange, reproachful eyes," and "a strange and completely incongruous smile" (1:10, 138). At the same time, "In Myshkin is repeated the story of Don Quixote: his light falls upon unyielding, sluggish, resistant matter, but proves powerless to reshape it, so that he becomes no more than a figure of comedy" (Ivanov, *Freedom and the Tragic Life,* 98). This was most evident when, wearing "his dirty boots, his wide-brimmed hat, his cloak, [and] his look of profound embarrassment" (1:13, 157), he arrived at Nastasya's party, and "her guests at once prepared to welcome the unbidden visitor with mirth and laughter" (158).

Through the rest of the novel, it will become apparent that the prince's "scandal" and his "comedy" outweigh and counteract any positive effect that he may produce in others, and are symptomatic of a tragic phenomenon: his existing in a world where, as a true Christian and essential "human being," he is fundamentally out of place, and hence quixotic.

2:1–12: The Poor Knight

As Nastasya's recognition of Myshkin in part 1 was an implicit *anagnorisis* of his Christic nature, so there occurs in part 2 an explicit *anagnorisis* of his quixotism. It is Aglaya who recognizes Myshkin's likeness to Don Quixote. After reading a letter from the prince, she places it in a volume of *Don Quixote de la Mancha* and mysteriously bursts out laughing (2:1). Later, in the company of her family, the prince, and others, she explains the link between Pushkin's "A Poor Knight" and Don Quixote (2:6), and then recites the ballad aloud, slyly changing the letters inscribed on the hero's shield, A. M. D. (*Ave Mater Dei*), to A. N. B. (*Ave Nastasya Barashkov*) (2:7).

Aglaya's exegesis of "A Poor Knight" illuminates its connection to Don Quixote. As she explains to her mother, the "poor knight" should be deeply respected because he is "capable of having an ideal," and "having believed in it, he devoted his whole life to it. . . . The poem doesn't specify exactly what the ideal of the 'poor knight' was, but it is evident that it was some bright image . . . of pure beauty" (2:6, 265–66). By insisting that the motto on his shield reads A. N. B. instead of A. M. D., despite Kolya's attempt to correct her, Aglaya reaffirms her allusion to Myshkin (= "poor knight") and Nastasya (= "image of pure beauty" = Virgin Mary), and then combines Don Quixote, the "poor knight," and, implicitly, Myshkin, in a single image:

> "[I]t is clear that the poor knight no longer cared who the lady was or what his lady did. . . . That's where his merit lies, for even if she

became a thief afterwards, he would still have to believe in her and break a lance for her pure beauty. . . . Such feelings in themselves leave a profound and, from one point of view, highly praiseworthy impression behind, not to mention Don Quixote. The 'poor knight' is also a Don Quixote, only serious and not comic." (266)

Though Aglaya (like Dostoevsky) does not know it, her conception of those two characters and Myshkin as a trinity sets them in the same class as Kierkegaard's "knight of faith."[14] As exemplified in *Fear and Trembling* by Abraham's willingness to sacrifice his son out of absolute faith, the Kierke-gaardian knight makes a leap of faith requiring a teleological suspension of the ethical. Likewise, Pushkin's knight devotes himself so wholeheartedly to his lady that in Aglaya's view, he would believe in her even if she were a thief — as Myshkin "believes" in Nastasya despite her "fallenness."

Paradoxically, while Aglaya's interpretation of the poem implies an *anagnorisis* of Myshkin as a "serious" Don Quixote, the prince's posture toward reality does not seem on the surface so quixotic now as it did in part 1. He appears to have undergone a transformation analogous to the "sanchification" of the knight (Soltys, "Don Quijote en la obra de Dostoyevski," 118). This does not mean he has shed his quixotic aspect entirely. The "most unbusinesslike manner" (2:1, 201) in which he handles the fortune which he unexpectedly inherits might remind us of Don Quixote's indifference toward money. But the prince seems to accommodate himself to the reality around him in a way he did not before. In recounting the "moments of intense life" and "great hopes" that he experienced in Moscow during his recent sojourn there (between pts. 1 and 2), he recalls to Mrs. Yepanchin his "feeling of joy that I was not a stranger, not a foreigner, *there*. I was suddenly very pleased to be back in my own country" (2:12, 332). This newly felt pleasure may account for his comical attempt to dress in accordance with the latest Muscovite fashion.

If anyone, who had known him on his first arrival in Petersburg six months before, had seen him now, he would have concluded that, if anything, he had changed for the better in appearance. But that was

14. I am by no means the first to compare Myshkin to Kierkegaard's knight of faith. See Frank, "Reading of *The Idiot,*" 329. Cf. Cascardi, *Bounds of Reason,* 94–95. On the frequent comparison of Don Quixote and the knight of faith, see E. Ziolkowski, "Don Quixote and Kierkegaard's Understanding."

not so. It was only his clothes that were completely different: they were all new, made in Moscow by a good tailor, but even they were not quite right: they were much too fashionable . . . , and, moreover, they were worn by a man who quite obviously took no interest in them, so that anyone who wanted a good laugh would perhaps have found something to smile at if he happened to look intently at the prince. (2:2, 208)

This passage alerts us to a contradiction underlying Myshkin's "changed" appearance. Just as his switch from wearing unfashionable clothes (in pt. 1) to wearing hyperfashionable ones makes him no less ridiculous-looking than before, so, consistent with his ruminations about "*double* thoughts" (2:11, 325), his new pleasure at being in Russia is undermined by a deep sense of discomfort and misgiving. His state of mind is reminiscent of the melancholy and doubts betrayed by the knight toward the end of the *Quixote.*

The prince's discomfort results from external as well as internal causes. Externally he is plagued not only by Aglaya's mockery through her recitation of the Pushkin poem already discussed, but also by Rogozhin's attempt to murder him (2:5), and the attempt by a band of "young nihilists" to discredit his integrity by publicly slandering his character and past (2:8). Internally he is discomfited by his returning illness, which begins in the form of a headache during his visit to Rogozhin's house (2:3), and which culminates in his seizure at the moment Rogozhin attacks him with a knife later that day. Myshkin's illness accounts for his "extraordinary craving for solitude" (2:5, 241) and the series of bizarre, agitated thoughts and feelings that plague him as he wanders about Saint Petersburg in the hours between the visit and the attack. Having had a presentiment of that attack during the visit, he feels compelled by a "morbid" impulse to "look round uneasily, as if expecting to see someone" (242). His paranoia seems to exacerbate his quixotic compulsion to question both his perception of reality and the reality itself, as when he ponders "whether he really had stood just now before that shop window, perhaps five minutes before, or whether he had imagined it all, or got it all mixed up. Did that shop and the things in its window really exist?" (242). Myshkin thus develops a "morbidly suspicious state of mind" in which he blames himself for "two extremes: for his extraordinarily 'senseless and tiresome' trustfulness and at the same time for his 'contemptible and gloomy' suspiciousness" (2:11, 317). In his agony,

> he was suddenly overcome by an uncontrollable desire to leave every-
> thing here and go back to where he had come from, to some far-away
> solitary place, and to go away at once without even saying good-bye to
> anyone. He had a feeling that if he stayed here even a few days longer,
> he would irrevocably be drawn into this world, and that this world
> would become his world henceforward. But he did not debate the
> question with himself even for as long as ten minutes; he decided at
> once that to run away was 'impossible,' that it would be almost
> cowardice, that he was faced with such problems that now he had no
> right . . . not to do all he could to solve them. (322–23)

Like Don Quixote's stated discomfort in the Age of Iron, Myshkin's desire to leave Russia and return to "where he had come from" out of a fear of being "drawn into this world" signifies his reluctance as an essential human being to immerse himself in the realm of the accidental. While Myshkin may be viewed as "a soul that has plunged from that 'place beyond the skies' (*epouránios topos*) described by Plato, where, with the gods, men unborn contemplate the forms of eternal beauty" (Ivanov, *Freedom and the Tragic Life,* 90), his recollection (*anamnesis*) of those forms is of no practical purpose. Indeed, his fate demonstrates a "failure of *kairos* to affect *chronos*" (Holquist, "Gaps in Christology," 144), which takes a toll on his spirituality. Despite his "Christlike decision to mix with the affairs of the world" (Krieger, *Tragic Vision,* 213), he proves incapable of resolving his conflict of faith and doubt.

The development of this theme is not accompanied by any diminishment of the prince's Christian virtues: his *agape,* charity, compassion, etc. Myshkin confides to Rogozhin: "I loved [Nastasya] not because I was in love with her, but because I pitied her" (2:3, 226). For the prince, compassion is "the only law of all human existence" (2:5, 248). Because he embodies this "law," he is acclaimed as a morally superior person by several characters, including the nihilist Keller, who extols his "simplicity and innocence" (2:11, 324); Lebedev, who remarks that the prince "will judge in a human way" (326); and another nihilist, Antip Burdovsky, who writes to the prince, after the latter forgives him for slandering him: "I'm entirely convinced . . . that you are perhaps better than other men" (2:12, 335). In addition, Mrs. Yepanchin reaffirms her earlier view of Myshkin as a heavenly emissary, telling him: "I've waited for you as for Providence," believing that "God himself has sent you to me as a friend and brother" (333).

The theme of faith and doubt comes to light during Myshkin's visit to Rogozhin's house, when he becomes depressed by the sight of a reproduction of Hans Holbein the Younger's gruesomely realistic *Christ in the Tomb* (1521) hanging over a doorway (2:4). On mentioning that he saw the picture abroad and cannot forget it, he is at first ignored by Rogozhin. But after a moment, the following exchange takes place:

> "Tell me, Prince, I've long wanted to ask you, do you believe in God?" Rogozhin suddenly broke into speech after walking a few steps.
>
> "How strangely you speak and—look!" the prince observed involuntarily.
>
> "I like looking at that picture," Rogozhin muttered after a short pause, as though he had forgotten his question.
>
> "At that picture!" the prince exclaimed, struck by a sudden thought. "At that picture! Why, some people may lose their faith by looking at that picture!"
>
> "Aye, that also may be lost," Rogozhin assented unexpectedly. (236)

Why should Rogozhin feel compelled to ask Myshkin of all people whether he believes in God? (When asked this by Myshkin, Rogozhin skirts the question: "Oh, for no reason. It just occurred to me. I meant to ask you before." [236]) The prince's remark that the Holbein picture could cause people to "lose their faith"—a remark that repeats what Dostoevsky himself uttered, as recorded by his wife Anna Grigorievna, when he saw that picture in the Öffentliche Kunstsammlung in Basel[15]—opens the possibility that his own faith was shaken by the sight of it. And the fact is, he never answers Rogozhin's question. Instead he tells him of "four encounters" he recently had, each of which pertains to the problem of faith. Based on these experiences, the "conclusion" that the prince finally relates to Rogozhin is really no answer at all:

---

15. Quoted by the editor in Dostoevsky's *Notebooks for "The Idiot"*, 106n.6.

> "[T]he essence of religious feeling has nothing to do with any reasoning, or any crimes and misdemeanours or atheism; it is something entirely different and it will always be so; it is something our atheists will always overlook, and they will never talk about *that*. But . . . you will notice it more clearly in a Russian heart. (238)

If Myshkin's "point" is "to show religious faith and moral conscience existing as an irreducible datum in the Russian people *below* the level of reason, or even of any sort of conventional social morality" (Frank, "Reading of *The Idiot;*" 317), this does not address Rogozhin's inquiry as to whether he believes in God. Myshkin's telling of the encounters might seem similar to Christ's use of parables; indeed, Mrs. Yepanchin earlier scolded him, as the Pharisees scolded Christ, for "talking in riddles" (1:5, 81). Yet an important distinction must be drawn. Christ's parables are supposed to make heaven's secrets distinguishable to whoever "heareth the word, and understandeth it" (Matt. 13:23). Conversely, Myshkin's four tales in effect create a Bakhtinian polyphony of several autonomous voices; that is, the voices of the four persons he met (an atheist, a murderer, a soldier-thief, and a peasant mother), each of which expresses a different attitude toward God, and behind all of which Myshkin's own attitude remains obscured. Guardini contends that Rogozhin's question is moot, since Myshkin, like Christ, "lives in the presence of God" and hence "can obviously not 'believe,' for in his very existence, he does not leave him" ("Symbol of Christ," 377). Nonetheless, we may suspect that the prince does have faith, but that his faith is insecure. This is further suggested by the fact that he and his faithless friend become "brothers" through their symbolic exchange of crosses before his departure from the latter's house. Indeed, according to the perceptive Kolya, Myshkin is "an extraordinary sceptic" who has begun "to disbelieve everything" (2:11, 328).

As chivalry is dead in the Spain into which Don Quixote sallies as a knight, so nihilism and atheism are rampant in the Russia which Myshkin has entered as a kind of Man-God. In Rogozhin's words, "lots of people don't believe nowadays" (2:4, 236). Myshkin's exposure to the problem of unbelief in Russia comes in a variety of ways: through the first of his "four encounters"; through his friendship with Rogozhin, who is fighting "to regain his lost faith by force" (2:5, 248); and through his relationship with the young nihilists, whom Mrs. Yepanchin attacks as "heathens" (2:9, 301). Still, overshadowing the prince's

encounter with unbelief in other Russians is his horror at Holbein's starkly
realistic depiction of the lifeless body of Christ after its removal from the cross,
an image that inspires no more hope for resurrection or afterlife than does the
final stanza of the Pushkin poem whose hero Aglaya linked to Myshkin:
"Returning to his distant castle, / There he lived and sighed, / Ever silent, sad,
and cheerless, / Of reason bereft, he died" (quoted in *Idiot,* 2:7, 269).

Among the things that remain to be seen in the novel's second half are the
catastrophic events that leave Myshkin himself "Of reason bereft" and necessi-
tate his return to his own "distant castle": the Swiss sanitarium.

3:1–10: The Binding Idea

In his rumination on "practical men" and "civil servants" at the opening of part
3 the narrator observes: "Lack of originality has from time immemorial been
regarded as the chief characteristic and the best recommendation of a sensible,
business-like, and practical man," with the result that "Inventors and men of
genius have almost always been regarded as fools at the beginning (and very
often at the end) of their careers" (339). This observation is not without
relevance to Myshkin's quixotism. While the prince lacks practicality, he does,
like "inventors and men of genius," and like Don Quixote (labeled "in*genio*so"
in his novel's title), appear "original." Hence he, like them, is regarded as a
"fool."

However, Myshkin is distinguishable from the inventor, the genius, and
Don Quixote in his relation to the particular idea that makes him "original."
The originality of each of the others can ultimately be defined by the ideas that
underlie whatever they do or produce that is "original": for example, the idea
behind the inventor's invention or the genius's creation or discovery; or the
"más extraño pensamiento" behind Don Quixote's career as a knight. In
contrast, Myshkin's originality like that of a saint is traceable not to his
conception of a particular idea, but to his *embodiment* of one: "love thy
neighbour as thyself," which implies charity, compassion, and mercy.

Though never stated thus, the idea of "love thy neighbour" in parts 1 and 2
was reflected in the prince's compassion toward Marie and Nastasya, and in his
forgiveness of Ganya for slapping him, and of the young nihilists for slandering
him. The same idea now finds its most striking expression, albeit in negative
terms, when Myshkin meets Rogozhin (3:3) for the first time since the latter's

attempt to kill him. Myshkin forgives Rogozhin, begs him not to let any past "hatred" stand between them, and is met by the reply: "You don't know what hatred is!" (376).

The problem with "love thy neighbour as thyself" as this idea is embodied in Myshkin is its hopeless impracticality. Only among an angelic population could so lofty a rule be truly viable; among a cruel humanity it stands as an infinitely attractive idea, but one whose fulfillment in praxis seems all but impossible. When some saint or "heavenly emissary" who exemplifies it appears in the world, he or she becomes a kind of walking hierophany and may seem (and *be!*) quixotically out of place. Such is the case with Myshkin, and this predicament seals his unhappy fate. As Don Quixote's mad illusions bring his chivalric fantasy into conflict with reality, so "the inner logic of [Myshkin's] character requires that the absolute of Christian love should conflict irreconcilably with the inescapable demands of human life" (Frank, "Reading of *The Idiot,*" 316). This truth compels Prince Sh., the fiancé of one of Aglaya's sisters, to warn Myshkin that "it is not easy to achieve heaven on earth, and you do seem to count on it a little: heaven is a difficult matter" (3:1, 353). A later statement by Nastasya is more to the point: "Can one love everyone, all men, all one's neighbours? I have often asked myself that question. Of course not, and, indeed, it would be unnatural" (3:10, 463).

It is not insignificant that these two allusions to the impossibility of fulfilling the ethic of Christian love on earth occur respectively in the first and last chapters of part 3. In the narrative between them Myshkin is identified for the first time by other characters as an exemplar of something explicitly "Christian" and "essential." Concurrently, his quixotic discordance with the world is accentuated by the strain in his relationship with Aglaya, and by his increasing sense of alienation from society.

In embodying the idea of "love thy neighbour," whose fulfillment would ideally bind the individual with all other humans, Myshkin also implicitly embodies another idea whose fulfillment would ideally bind the human with God. As enunciated by Christ (Matt. 22:37–39; Mark 12:29–31), "love thy neighbour" is subordinate to the preceding idea of "love the Lord thy God with all thy heart, and with all thy soul, and with all thy mind." Given that the fulfillment of "love the Lord thy God" and "love thy neighbour" (with the Greek verb being in both cases *agapésein*) would bind the individual human with God and all mankind, the subordination of the latter idea to the former implies that in order for all humans to be bound together through *agape* all mankind must be bound to God through that same force.

A society of humans bound together by virtue of its culture's being uniformly grounded in the divine—suggesting Tillich's notion of a "theonomous" culture—is surely what Lebedev has in mind when he angers the other guests at Myshkin's birthday party by drunkenly theorizing aloud that the current age lacks a "binding idea" like that which "bound and guided men's hearts and fructified the waters of life" in medieval Europe (3:4, 391). This theory bears upon Myshkin's embodiment of "love thy neighbour"; his existence as such is naturally oriented toward binding humans together. He tried to articulate this notion earlier when he told General Yepanchin: "it's just because people are lazy that they are apt to divide themselves into different groups just by looking at one another and can't find any common interests" (1:3, 50). The prince will later repeat Lebedev's thesis when he distinguishes between the "one idea" by which people during the reign of Peter the Great were "animated," and the ideological diffusion—the hallmark of what Tillich termed a "heteronomous" age—of "modern man":

> "In those days people seem to have been animated by one idea, but now they are much more nervous, more developed, more sensitive— they seem to be animated by two or three ideas at a time—modern man is more diffuse and, I assure you, it is this that prevents him from being such a complete human being as they were in those days." (4:5, 528)

As an embodiment of the single idea of "love thy neighbour" Myshkin exists in contradiction to the ideologically "diffuse" modern age: a heteronomous, polyphonic age with atheistic and nihilistic tendencies; an age when youthful murderers "don't want even to admit that they are criminals, and think that they had a right to do what they did" (3:1, 351).

The first several chapters of part 3 highlight Myshkin's tragic quixotism. To begin with, the narrator's observation that among the prince's "peculiar characteristics" are his "naïveté" and "good faith, unsuspicious of derision or ridicule" (3:1, 349) could easily be applied to Don Quixote. However, here as elsewhere, a certain ambiguity betrays the narrator's unreliability. Throughout the novel's first half the prince exemplified a "naïveté" comparable to that of

Don Quixote in social exchanges. But consistent with his own insight into people's thoughts and feelings, and in contrast to the knight's blindness toward such matters, the prince proved almost always to be aware of when he was being mocked. The description of Myshkin as "unsuspicious of derision or ridicule" is contradicted when he tells Mrs. Yepanchin, Radomsky, and several others: "There are certain ideas, certain great ideas, which I mustn't start talking about, because I'm quite sure to make you all laugh" (3:2, 354). Moments later he states his awareness "that after twenty years of illness there must be some trace of it left, so that people can't help laughing at me" (355).

The "strange incident" to which this outburst gives rise reveals the quixotic discordance between Myshkin and the degenerate society around him. After bursting out at the prince, "Why are you saying this to *them?*" Aglaya exclaims:

> "There's no one here who is worth such words! . . . No one, no one here is worth your little finger, nor your mind, nor your heart! You're more honest than any of them, better, kinder, cleverer than any of them! There are people here who are not worthy to bend down to pick up the handkerchief you've dropped. Why then are you humbling yourself . . . ? Why are you all twisted up inside? Why have you no pride? (355)

While Myshkin's humility and lack of "pride" distinguish him from Don Quixote, Aglaya's image of a man of superior "mind" and "heart" among unworthy people matches the exalted, Romantic portrait of the knight in the poem she recited earlier. However, just as the same characters in the *Quixote* who admire the knight for his sensible reflections on subjects other than chivalry cannot help laughing at his mad antics during his "fits," so Aglaya cannot help feeling ambivalent toward the prince. Moments after expressing her reverence for him she blurts out that she could never "marry a ridiculous man like you" (355). When he timidly assures her that he never intended to marry her, she bursts out laughing in his face. (Aglaya, the "ideal" woman, here takes after the "enchanted Dulcinea" who ridiculed the mad knight as he knelt earnestly before her [*Quixote,* 2:10].) Aglaya later makes explicit her ambivalence to him: "If, when I read you about the 'poor knight' that day, I wished to—to express my admiration for you at the same time, I also wished to express my disgust with you for your behaviour" (3:8, 442).

Myshkin's quixotism again manifests itself when he protects Nastasya from an assault in the Pavlovsk pleasure-gardens (3:2). Following the same pattern as his earlier intervention against Ganya on Varya's behalf, where he wound up getting slapped by Ganya (1:10), this "incident" results in his being flung back by the attacker and falling on a chair. While it is a far cry from saving a damsel from a dragon's jaws, Myshkin's rescue of a "woman in distress" accords with Don Quixote's chivalric fantasy. The prince displays that quality which is the sine qua non of any true hero or knight: courage. Asked by Aglaya whether he is a "coward," he replies: "N-no, I don't think I am, really. A coward is a man who's afraid and runs away, but a man who is afraid and doesn't run away is not a coward" (3:3, 367). Keller, another witness of the prince's intervention, later reflects: "It's fellows like him who're never afraid" (374).

Despite his courage, what Myshkin shows himself to be in the park incident is not a militaristic *héros* or *caballero* in the classical Homeric and chivalric senses, but someone as compassionate as Jesus (who showed ultimate courage in submitting himself to the cross). His rescue of Nastasya is done out of "the feeling of infinite pity he felt for her"; from the time he first beheld her photograph months before, "the feeling of compassion and even of torment for this woman never left his heart and it had not left it now" (362). Because his intervention is reminiscent of Christ's rescue of the adulterous woman, we should not be surprised later to find the phrase by which Christ dissuaded her condemners from stoning her echoed by the prince; in reference to Nastasya he tells Aglaya: "Oh, do not hold her up to scorn, do not cast a stone [*ne brosaite kamnia*]!" (3:8, 443).

Though Myshkin's Christian nature has been manifest all along, it is not until his birthday party in the middle chapters of part 3 that any character applies that label to him. Ironically, the tubercular nihilist Ippolit is the one who does so. After quoting to the crowd Myshkin's alleged claim that "the world will be saved by beauty," he exclaims:

> "You're a zealous Christian, aren't you? Kolya says you call yourself a Christian."
> The prince looked attentively at him and made no answer. (3:5, 394)

Ippolit's question is like Rogozhin's earlier inquiry about the prince's belief in God. In both cases Myshkin's questioner embodies the negation of the question being asked: as it took a man who had lost his faith to ask whether Myshkin believed in God, so it now takes an anti-Christian nihilist to ask whether the prince calls himself a Christian. Both questions are posed in a Bakhtinian "threshold" situation: Rogozhin stood on the threshold (symbolized by the doorway over which the Holbein picture hung) of trying to murder Myshkin; Ippolit now stands on the threshold (symbolized by the veranda door through which he will run) of attempting suicide. In both cases the prince is in effect being tried; his refusal to answer the questions of whether he believes in God or is a Christian is analogous to Christ's refusal to answer when asked by Caiaphas and Pilate whether he called himself "King of the Jews" and "Son of God."

Reminiscent of Kierkegaard's famous contention that the term "Christian" becomes meaningless in modern Christendom since everyone therein is thought of as a "Christian," while no one *is* truly a Christian, Myshkin's refusal to call himself one implies that the true Christian is not someone who labels himself as such, but someone who embodies what is essentially Christian. While labels appeal to the mind and intellect, religion and faith are for Myshkin matters of emotion and the heart; this was the lesson of his "four encounters," and is consistent with Mrs. Yepanchin's assertion that "the heart is the great thing; the rest is nothing" (1:7, 104). Nonetheless, Ippolit applies the term "Christian" to Myshkin several times in his lengthy "Necessary Explanation," which he reads aloud to all the guests. While he mocks Myshkin's "Christian meekness" (3:6, 407) and "Christian arguments" (3:7, 423), Ippolit is seemingly unaware that he and the prince responded in almost identical ways to Holbein's depiction of the dead Christ. Ippolit too saw the reproduction in Rogozhin's house, and he now describes it in all its gruesome detail (3:6). Recalling Myshkin's speculation that the mere sight of that picture could cause some people to "lose their faith," we are struck by the questions Ippolit now asks:

> "[I]f such a corpse (and it must have been just like that) was seen by all His disciples, by His future chief apostles, by the women who followed Him and stood by the cross, by all who believed in Him and worshipped Him, then how could they possibly have believed, as they looked at the corpse, that that martyr would rise again?" (419)

Furthermore:

"And if, on the eve of the crucifixion, the Master could have seen what He would look like when taken from the cross, would he have mounted the cross and died as he did? This question, too, you can't help asking yourself as you look at the picture." (419-20)

Our earlier suspicion that Myshkin's response to this picture suggested the insecurity of his faith is now supported by the fact that Ippolit, a nihilist, responds so similarly to it.

Before he runs out and unsuccessfully tries to shoot himself, Ippolit addresses Myshkin: "Let me bid farewell to a human being" (429). This recalls what Nastasya said to the prince upon departing with Rogozhin from her own party: "You're the first human being I've seen!" The parallel indicates that Ippolit and Nastasya share in recognizing Myshkin as a "human being," and also suggests a link between the two scenes. The parties of Nastasya and Myshkin mark the dates of the two characters' entry into the temporal world, commemorating symbolically their transition from a state of essential "perfection" (which is what Myshkin called Nastasya at her party) into a context where the one would "fall" and the other would become quixotic. Myshkin's "essential" aspect, which distinguishes him from others and accounts for his quixotism, is remarked by Aglaya during their conversation at the green seat in the park:

"I think you're the most honest and truthful man I know—more honest and truthful than anyone, and if people say about you that your mind—I mean, that you sometimes suffer from mental illness, it's unfair. . . . For although you really are ill mentally . . . , yet the most essential part of your mind is much better than in any of them. Indeed, it's something they never dreamed of. For there are two sorts of mind—one that is essential and one that isn't." (3:8, 438)

Aglaya's analysis of Myshkin's "mind" makes explicit what was implicit in Nastasya's perception of him as a "human being"; that is, that he, or his mind, represents something "essential."

Myshkin's discomfort in the world becomes more acute as his feeling of alienation from society causes him to regress toward his original status as utter "stranger." In his longing for solitude and escape, he withdraws into his ruminations and begins to question the distinction between dream and reality. This theme, akin to the conflict of illusion and reality in the *Quixote,* initially manifests itself in the first scene in the gardens, prior to the incident with Nastasya there. Standing awkwardly with Aglaya, Radomsky, and several of the latter's friends, Myshkin momentarily withdraws from the reality around him:

> The prince did not even notice that the other men were talking and paying compliments to Aglaya, and occasionally he almost seemed to forget that he was sitting beside her. At times he felt that he would have liked to go away somewhere, to disappear entirely, and he would not have minded going away to some gloomy and deserted spot to be alone with his thoughts if only no one knew where he was. . . . At moments he dreamed of the mountains, and one familiar spot . . . he always liked to remember and had been fond of visiting when he was there, from where he could look down on the village, on the faintly gleaming streak of the waterfall below, the white clouds, and the ruins of the ancient castle. Oh, how he wished he could be there now and think of one thing only—oh, all his life of that one thing only—it would have kept him occupied for a thousand years! And let them— let them all forget him entirely here. Oh, . . . and it would have been even better if they had not known him at all and if all this had been just a dream. But was it not all the same whether it was real or a dream? Sometimes he would suddenly begin to look attentively at Aglaya without taking his eyes off her for five minutes at a time, but there was a very strange look in them: he seemed to be looking at her as though she were a mile away or as though it were her portrait and not herself he was looking at. (3:2, 359)

By Aglaya's own distinction, the mental state depicted here might be summed up as the longing of an "essential" mind to extract itself ("to disappear entirely") from the accidental world of human society in which it feels utterly out of place. Only in solitude at that special "spot" in the Swiss mountains would the prince be able to immerse himself in his "essential" ruminations about that ineffable "one thing." From his "essential" perspective, the question of whether "all this"—that is, the world of human society—is "real" or "a dream" becomes pressing, because to him "all this" must appear nonessential. At the same time, from the vantage of those who feel at home in "all this," the idea that anyone might question whether they are "real" would seem absurd. Hence, after Aglaya interrupts the prince's brooding and asks him why he is looking "as though you were about to stretch out your hand and touch my face to feel if it was real" (359), she and the others laugh at him.

Myshkin's feeling of discordance, and his longing to escape, intensify to such a degree that by the time he returns to the park for his rendezvous with Aglaya he sees himself as "an outcast." As he awaits her at the designated green seat, he drops off into a melancholy reverie about the first year of his cure in Switzerland:

> One bright, sunny day he went for a walk in the mountains and walked a long time, tormented by a thought that . . . seemed to be eluding him. Before him was the brilliant sky, below—the lake, and around, the bright horizon, stretching away into infinity. He looked a long time in agony. He remembered now how he had stretched out his arms towards that bright and limitless expanse of blue and had wept. What tormented him was that he was a complete stranger to all this. What banquet was it, what grand everlasting festival, to which he had long felt drawn, always—ever since he was a child, and which he could never join? . . . Everything has its path, and everything knows its path; . . . only he knows nothing, understands nothing, neither men nor sounds, a stranger to everything and an outcast. (3:7, 433-34)

It is no mere coincidence that Myshkin has this daydream as he is awaiting Aglaya. She, whose name is the Greek term for splendor, beauty, or festive resplendence (*aglaía*), symbolizes that "grand everlasting festival" of the earth in relation to which he feels like "a complete stranger" and "outcast." She thus is the natural rival of Nastasya, the unearthly female of whom the prince was surely thinking when he told Ippolit earlier "that the world will be saved by beauty," and to whom that soteriological role is ascribed by the etymology of her name: *anástasis,* "resurrection." (It should be remembered that Mary Magdalene, Nastasya's biblical forbear, is the first person to whom Christ appears after his resurrection in the Gospels of Mark and John.)

However, just as Myshkin and Rogozhin, for all the antitheses they represent (good/evil, victim/attacker, etc.), became spiritual "brothers" through their exchange of crosses, so the female rivals, for all the antitheses *they* represent (innocence/suffering, idealness/fallenness, etc.), are paradoxically conjoined through their relationships with the prince. Suggested in part 1 through Myshkin's comparison of their beauty, the connection between the two women is again implied when, as he awaits Aglaya at the green seat, he lapses into a dream about a remorseful, horror-stricken woman (Nastasya), only to be awakened by Aglaya's "gay, fresh laugh" (3:7, 434). His compassion for the wretched woman of his dream—"nothing in the world would make him admit that she was a criminal" (434)—recalls Christ's refusal to condemn the adulterous woman, and Aglaya's interpretation of the "poor knight" as one who would still "believe in" his lady "even if she became a thief." Aglaya even hints at these associations in her attempt to persuade the prince to marry Nastasya, despite his insistence that he will not. "Then sacrifice yourself!" she tells him, conceiving of him as a martyr like Christ or the "poor knight." "It's the sort of thing that becomes you so well!" (3:8, 445).

At this point certain striking affinities between Myshkin and Nastasya begin to emerge. Both of them, like Don Quixote, suffer from an illness of some sort; the knight's madness finds counterparts in the prince's epilepsy and Nastasya's insanity. Upon learning that Nastasya has sent Aglaya letters trying to convince her to marry him, the prince, who has already expressed to General Yepanchin and Rogozhin his opinion that Nastasya is "mad" (3:3, 369) and "not—in her right mind" (378), asserts: "It's madness, it's proof of her madness" (3:8, 445). Just as Myshkin, who has entered the temporal world as "heavenly emissary," undergoes a constant existential strain reflected in his "idiocy," so Nastasya, the "eternal female" living in the temporal world as a "fallen" woman, undergoes a strain that results in her madness. By the end of part 3, she and Myshkin consider themselves out of place in this world, and share a readiness to return to that platonic "place beyond the skies" from which they originally descended. This metaphysical interpretation is warranted by the prince's secret longing to go off alone to his "place" in the Swiss mountains, and by Nastasya's prophetic avowals in two of her letters to Aglaya: "I shall be dead soon," and "I have renounced the world" and "have almost ceased to exist" (3:10, 464).

The gradual withdrawal of Myshkin and Nastasya from the "reality" of this world is reflected in the predominance of the dream theme, which presents the prince as dreamer, and Nastasya as subject of his dreams. The final chapter of part 3 begins with him having another "bad dream" about her, and when he reads her letters, they too strike him "like a bad dream" (461), leaving him suspicious that something "fantastic" has become "reality," and that he has "read it all before, a long, long time ago" (462). This déjà vu, like the *anagnorisis* that he and Nastasya had of each other in part 1, contributes to the impression that they "met" somewhere before, or discern in each other the images of their prototypes, Christ and Mary Magdalene.

That Nastasya associates Christ with Myshkin is evinced in one of her letters by her description of the image she has formed of Christ, not "according to the Gospel stories," but according to her own imagination:

> "I would depict Him alone. . . . I would have only a little child with Him—the child would be playing beside Him; . . . Christ has been listening to him, but now He is pondering, His hand still resting . . . on the child's fair little head. He is looking into the distance, at the horizon; a great thought, as great as the universe, dwells in His eyes; His face is sad. . . . The sun is setting. . . . That is my picture!" (463-64)

Consciously or unconsciously, Nastasya has clearly modeled her image of Christ after Myshkin. Figuring in that image are such hallmarks of Myshkin's character as the preference for solitude, the innocent, childlike nature, and the intimacy with children. In fact, Nastasya's depiction of Christ "alone" with a child, gazing "into the distance," and "pondering" some ineffable "great thought," closely resembles two of the prince's memories of wandering in the Swiss mountains (recalled in 1:5 and 3:7). Her image of the living Christ is highly Romantic, as opposed to Rogozhin's reproduction of Holbein's emphatically unidealistic image of the dead Christ. At the same time, her specification that Christ is "alone" and "sad" bears a striking resemblance to Pushkin's description of the "poor knight"—with whom Myshkin was associated earlier—as "sad and pale and lonely" in the third line of his poem.

It is as displaced symbols of Christ and Mary Magdalene that Myshkin and Nastasya appear in the final scene of part 3: their surrealistic midnight encounter on the road beside the park. The fact that the prince's "thoughts [were] in a tangle, and everything round him seemed to be like a dream" (466) again reflects his discordance with reality, just as Nastasya's manifestation as an "apparition" (466) figuratively reaffirms that she literally has "almost ceased to exist." This encounter seems a sardonic variation of the meeting of the resurrected Christ with Mary Magdalene:

[Nastasya] went down on her knees before him, there in the street, like one demented; he recoiled in horror, while she tried to catch his hand to kiss it and, just as recently in his dream, tears glittered on her long eyelashes.

"Get up, get up!" he said in a horrified whisper. "Get up at once!"

"Are you happy? Happy?" she asked. "Say only one word to me—are you happy now?" (466)

In presenting a Christ-like character who is reluctant to play Christ's role of "Master," and a Mary Magdalene who seems anything but healed of her "seven devils" (Myshkin cries a moment later: "She's mad!" [467]), this encounter also seems a strange inversion of Don Quixote's meeting with the "enchanted Dulcinea": whereas the mad knight kneels reverently before a coarse farm-girl who mocks him, the idiot prince faces a mad woman who kneels worshipfully before *him*. Nonetheless, with the Knight of the Sad Countenance, with Pushkin's "poor knight," and with Nastasya's "sad" Christ, Myshkin now shares one more trait: profound grief. In the chapter's closing passage Rogozhin, who appears the moment Nastasya disappears, asks Myshkin:

"By the way, old man, . . . why didn't you answer her question? Are you happy or not?"

"No, no, no!" cried the prince with unutterable sorrow.

"I never thought you'd say 'yes'!" Rogozhin laughed maliciously, and he went away without looking round. (467)

4:1–12: Idiot Redux

Unlike the Gospels, which close with the savior's resurrection, and the *Quixote,* which concludes with the madman's recovery, reconciliation, and peaceful death, *The Idiot* ends catastrophically with Nastasya's murder by Rogozhin, Rogozhin's loss of sanity, Myshkin's reversion to "idiocy," and Aglaya's spiritual death, which is signified (in Dostoevsky's view) by her marriage to a Polish count and her conversion to Roman Catholicism. The novel's tragic outcome is prepared for by a pair of themes that developed throughout the first three parts and culminate in this last part: the failure of Myshkin's Christian love to effect a deep, positive change in Rogozhin or any other character, with the exception of Kolya, for more than fleeting moments; and the prince's failure to resolve the tension between his ethereal compassion for Nastasya and his more human love for Aglaya.

Part 4 traces the final stages in Myshkin's return to complete alienation from society, and his reversion to being a fully private person, which the Greek term *idiótes* denotes. Mrs. Yepanchin, ever wavering between reverence and disdain for him, opines that he is "a sickly idiot . . . who doesn't know the way of the world and has no place in it" (4:5, 513). Even the narrator calls him "a strange sort of person" (523). His insomnia on the night before he is to attend a large party at the Yepanchins' betrays how uncomfortable he feels in society (4:6). On the following evening his ignorance of "the way of the world" is evidenced by his naïve impression of the crowd of guests at the party:

> The charm of elegant manners, simplicity, and apparent candour was almost magical. It could never have occurred to him that all that candour and nobility, wit and lofty personal dignity was perhaps only a magnificent artistic veneer. In spite of their impressive exterior, the majority of the guests were, indeed, rather empty-headed people who, in their smugness, did not realize themselves that much of their excellence was just a veneer. . . . The prince, fascinated by the charm of his first impression, did not as much as suspect that. (539)

The prince's intensifying quixotism is reflected by several undeniable parallels between his attendance at the Yepanchins' party and Don Quixote's attendance at the party arranged by the wife of Don Antonio Moreno (*Quixote*, 2:62). Both parties occur late in their respective narratives: Don Quixote's attendance at Don Antonio's immediately precedes his final defeat and return home, just as Myshkin's attendance at the Yepanchins' will be followed shortly by his relapse into idiocy and his return to Switzerland. At both parties the out-of-place hero becomes the center of attention and appears ridiculous. Don Quixote dances to exhaustion with two flirtatious ladies while remaining unaware that the party was specially planned by his hostess to amuse the guests with his strange delusions. Myshkin, similarly captivated by the glitter of "society" at the Yepanchins' party, which he takes "for the real thing, for pure gold without alloy" (542), disgraces himself by bursting out in a venomous tirade against Catholicism and then accidentally smashing an expensive Chinese vase, at which the entire room of guests explodes in laughter. Finally, the exhausted Don Quixote ends up collapsing on the dance floor and has to be carried to bed by Don Antonio's servants, just as Myshkin faints and falls to the carpet.

Myshkin's attendance at this party is reminiscent of Don Quixote in other respects as well. That he, like the knight, represents something anachronistic is implied when another guest tells him: "You seem to be very religious, which is so rare with our young men nowadays" (4:7, 547). And just as Don Quixote lapses into "fits" only when the subject of chivalry is broached, so it is only that other guest's mention of Catholicism that triggers Myshkin's outburst, which is "so out of keeping with his habitual and, indeed, timid restraint" (551). Also, while Myshkin's anti-Catholicism would seem blasphemous to the Spanish knight, the prince's argument for the "renaissance" and "resurrection" of mankind "by the Russian God and Christ" (551) strangely anticipates Unamuno's argument for the spiritual rejuvenation of Spain and Western civilization through reverence for Don Quixote as the "Spanish Christ." In Myshkin there is a hint of the same sort of struggle of faith and doubt that Unamuno finds in Don Quixote. During his harangue, the prince confesses: "I'm sometimes despicable, because I lose my faith" (557). This confirms our earlier suspicion that Myshkin's faith is unstable. His later "melancholy" and "depression" (4:8, 560) and "melancholy looks" (4:10, 593) are analogous to the depression that plagues Don Quixote toward the end of his career as a knight.

As provocative as the parallels between Don Quixote and Myshkin at the two parties might be, perhaps the most important analogy lies in what those parties show about the societies they represent. The depiction of most of the wealthier characters in the *Quixote* is commonly thought to be intended as a satire of the indolence and degeneracy of the Spanish aristocracy. Likewise, to attack the Russian aristocracy is clearly part of Dostoevsky's aim throughout *The Idiot,* and this attack culminates in the episode of the Yepanchins' party. Because Myshkin becomes "enchanted" (4:7, 553) by false appearances at the party, he fails to perceive that, behind its hypocritical facade of etiquette and polite manners, "society" is characterized by precisely all those negative traits he proclaims it not to possess: "pettiness," "exclusiveness," "backwardness," "inadequate education," "absurd habits," and "outward manners, nothing but antiquated form" containing "nothing *real*" (4:7, 555–56). His simple, childlike nature, which receives special emphasis in part 4,[16] leads him to commit a perceptual error comparable to Don Quixote's mistaking illusion for reality, but with a twist: whereas Don Quixote habitually mistakes fantasy for reality, Myshkin's error lies in his failure to realize—in keeping with one of Dostoevsky's favorite paradoxes—that the "real" can often seem more fantastic than "fantasy" itself. As he was told by General Ivolgin, who as a compulsive liar and fabricator of tales is eminently qualified to speak on this matter, "Truth, sir, very often seems impossible" (4:4, 503). Thus, while sorcerers and enchantment are merely figments of Don Quixote's imagination, Myshkin really does become "enchanted" by the social atmosphere of the party, and his enchantment leads him to conclude erroneously that the negative notions that he has been led (by Lebedev) to hold about society are "an inconceivable, impossible, and even absurd dream" (4:6, 543). However, on the next day an instance of something seemingly "fantastic" becoming reality presents itself as Myshkin, with Rogozhin, witnesses the highly improbable meeting between Aglaya and Nastasya at the latter's house:

> The prince, who the day before would not have believed it possible to see it even in a dream, now stood, looked and listened as though he had foreseen it long ago. The most fantastic dream became suddenly transformed into the most vivid and sharply defined reality. (4:8, 571)

The ensuing episode harbingers the novel's catastrophic end. After Aglaya, betraying her jealousy of Nastasya's special relationship with the prince, insults her by denigrating her character and life-style, two things happen that assure the tragic fates of the four characters present. Challenged by Nastasya to "choose" between her and Aglaya, Myshkin irreparably offends the latter by momentarily siding with the former, and thereby assures his ostracism from the Yepanchin family, and Aglaya's spiritual death. At the same time, Nastasya, in proudly challenging Myshkin to make that "decision," and then, in disdainfully ordering Rogozhin to depart, assures her own murder by Rogozhin and the subsequent mental breakdowns of both him and the prince.

16. Myshkin says: "What children we are, Kolya! . . . And—how lovely it is that we still are children!" (*Idiot*, 4:5, 517). Aglaya praises the prince's "beautiful and kind-hearted simplicity" (522), and Kolya calls him "a perfect child" (528). At the Yepanchins' party Myshkin tells everyone: "I know I'm just a child" (4:7, 556). And Aglaya tells Nastasya: "Never in my life have I met a man like him for noble simplicity of mind and for boundless trustfulness" (4:8, 572).

In triggering the plot's denouement, the meeting at Nastasya's house is the only occasion on which the four main protagonists meet in isolation. Viewed symbolically, they form a constellation of antitheses that may be summed up as follows. On the cosmological and moral levels they encompass heaven and the good (Myshkin); hell and evil (Rogozhin); earth and the beauty and perfection of innocence (Aglaya); purgatory and the beauty and purification of suffering (Nastasya). On the archetypal level Myshkin symbolizes Christ and incarnates love and compassion. He appears in the world tragically as the "poor knight" and comically as Don Quixote. Rogozhin symbolizes Satan and incarnates passion and hate. Posing as the "brother" of the Christ-like prince through their exchange of crosses, he mimics the role of Don Quixote's companion-foil Sancho Panza. Aglaya symbolizes Dulcinea in her "idealness," which conceals the reality of Aldonza Lorenzo. Nastasya symbolizes Mary Magdalene in her "fallenness," but within her lies the ideal of *Mater Dei,* the Virgin Mary, as suggested by the exchanged initials in Aglaya's recitation of the Pushkin poem.

These four symbolic characters relate to each other in symbolically different ways. Aglaya, as mocker, has made Myshkin qua Don Quixote and Nastasya qua "fallen" woman the butts of her disdain. Nastasya, as reverer, has made Myshkin and Aglaya the objects of her reverence as embodiments of "innocence" and "perfection." Rogozhin, as "wolf," preys on Myshkin and Nastasya as "sheep," murdering Nastasya with the same knife he earlier used in his attempt to murder the prince. And in the heavenly light shed upon them by the prince qua man-God, or "lion mouse" (*leo myshka*), and consistent with the etymologies of their given names (*aglaía, anástasia, parthénios*), Aglaya represents the Earth's "festive resplendence," while Nastasya and Rogozhin take on meanings that belie their purgatorial and hellish existence: "resurrection" and "the virginal."

Myshkin's compassion for Nastasya, who, "as he once said to Aglaya, 'pierced his heart for ever'" (4:8, 576), ultimately outweighs his more earthly love for Aglaya. This becomes apparent after Aglaya taunts Nastasya into a mad tirade.

> He could bear it no longer, and he turned imploringly and reproachfully to Aglaya, pointing to Nastasya Filippovna: "How could you? She's so—unhappy!"
> But that was all he had time to say, struck dumb by Aglaya's terrible look. There was so much suffering in that look and, at the

same time, so much hatred, too, that he threw up his hands in despair, uttered a cry, and rushed after her. But it was too late. She could not endure even the brief moment of his hesitation, covered her face with her hands, cried, "Oh, my God!" and ran out of the room. (576)

This climactic scene poses one of the most difficult problems of the novel: is Myshkin "right" to say what he says to Aglaya? Does not her "suffering," no less than Nastasya's, merit the prince's compassion? In the opinion expressed by Radomsky, the spokesman for society's ethical norm, Myshkin unquestionably did wrong:

"And—and did you not deceive that divine girl by telling her that you loved her?"

"Yes, yes, you're right," said the prince in great anguish. "Oh, I do feel that I'm to blame!"

"But is that enough?" cried Radomsky indignantly. " . . . You are to blame, and yet you persist! And where was your heart then, your 'Christian' heart? You saw her face at that moment, didn't you? Was *she* suffering less than *your other* woman . . . ?" (4:9, 585)

Indeed, Aglaya *was* suffering less than Nastasya, or suffering for a very different reason, and it was this difference that led Myshkin to side with Nastasya for that fateful moment. Prior to the Yepanchins' party, he discerned Aglaya's "state of great anxiety, great uncertainty, and . . . great mental suffering ('from jealousy,' the prince whispered to himself)" (4:6, 537). But from a true Christian and religious perspective, which in a Kierkegaardian sense transcends the strictly ethical and nominally "Christian" norm to which Radomsky appeals, Aglaya's jealous suffering pales in comparison with Nastasya's "fallen" suffering. If, as Myshkin once told Ippolit, "He who can suffer more is worthy of suffering more" (4:5, 526), then she who suffers more must be worthy of greater compassion. This principle, which impels the prince instinctively to side with Nastasya against Aglaya, cannot be explained or understood in terms of normal earthly love. As Radomsky puts it, "Aglaya loved like a woman, like a human being, and not like—a disembodied spirit!" (4:9, 587).

Myshkin's subsequent ostracism from the Yepanchins and their whole social network makes him an "outsider," like Don Quixote. It therefore seems appropriate that Radomsky, the only friend of the Yepanchins who will still visit the prince, "analyzes" him and his relationship with Nastasya in a way that highlights his quixotic attributes: "clearly and sensibly," and with "extraordinary psychological insight" (583). Like Aglaya's exegesis of "A Poor Knight," Radomsky's analysis of the prince calls Don Quixote constantly to mind. Alerted by the resemblance between Radomsky's opening phrase, "what begins with a lie must end with a lie," and the title of Dostoevsky's 1877 article on the *Quixote,* "A Lie is Saved by a Lie," we cannot but notice how many of the words and phrases that Radomsky uses to describe Myshkin would apply to Don Quixote: "intelligent," "strange," "not like other people," characterized by "inherent inexperience," "extraordinary simplicity," "phenomenal lack of a sense of proportion," "extraordinary honesty," and "sincere convictions" (583–84). Like Don Quixote, who sallies forth in quest of unknown adventures, having read too many chivalry books, Myshkin was—in Radomsky's words— "anxious to go back to Russia as to an unknown country," having "read too many books about Russia." Like Don Quixote, Myshkin is "a knight-errant, a virgin," "bewitched" by a woman's beauty (though, of course, Nastasya is real, unlike Dulcinea). Like Don Quixote, who is mentally ill, Myshkin suffers from a sickness: "epilepsy." And like Don Quixote, who encounters illusory persons and things on the road, Myshkin, on his first day in the "fantastic town" (Saint Petersburg), made "unexpected acquaintances" and found a "most unexpected reality."

That it is Radomsky who links Myshkin to Don Quixote in this allusive manner is telling. As a close friend of Aglaya's who was present at her recitation of the Pushkin poem, he presumably understands her association of the "poor knight" and the prince with Don Quixote. In the role he now plays, Radomsky takes after Don Diego de Miranda and Sansón Carrasco. As Don Diego is an exemplary Spanish gentleman who embodies the Renaissance ideal of *discreción,* so Radomsky is for Joseph Frank "the perfect model of a sympathetic and well-bred Russian gentleman, whose delicacy and courtesy is beyond reproach" ("Reading of *The Idiot,*" 311). Don Diego and Radomsky stand for the social-moral norms against which Don Quixote's chivalric enthusiasm and what Radomsky will call Myshkin's "intellectual enthusiasm" might be judged.[17] At the same time, in telling Myshkin "I'll show you yourself as in

17. There is, as we remarked earlier, disagreement among *Quixote* critics over whether

a looking-glass [*kak v zerkale*]" (584), Radomsky links himself allusively to Sansón; the bachelor's successive titles, "Knight of the Mirrors" (*Quixote,* 2:12–15) and "Knight of the White Moon" (2:64–65), likewise invoke images of reflection that suggest his aim of forcing Don Quixote to confront his true identity (as an object reflected in a mirror, or sunlight upon the moon), and to give up his illusory self-conception as a knight.

Another analogy between Myshkin and Don Quixote is affirmed by Radomsky's conclusion that the prince's basic "feeling" in defending the "fallen" Nastasya was "intellectual enthusiasm" (*golovnoi vostorg,* literally, "cerebral delight" or "rapture"):

> Radomsky went on excitedly. "It's quite clear that, carried away by your enthusiasm, as it were, you pounced on the chance of publicly proclaiming your generous idea that . . . you did not consider a woman dishonoured who had fallen from virtue not through any fault of her own. . . . But, my dear Prince, that's not the point. The point is whether your feeling was true, whether it was a genuine feeling, a natural feeling, or whether it was nothing but intellectual enthusiasm. What do you think? The woman taken in adultery—the same kind of woman—was forgiven, but she was not told that she had done well and that she was deserving of honour and respect, was she? Didn't your commonsense tell you three months later what the true position was?" (584–85)

Certain key allusions in this passage elucidate further Myshkin's mixture of quixotic and Christic qualities. His "enthusiasm" is something that he and other quixotic characters share with Don Quixote.[18] And Radomsky, in likening Nastasya to "the woman taken in adultery," suggests that the prince's kindness toward her has fulfilled the paradigm of Christ's compassion to an extreme that exceeds "commonsense." Common sense is the criterion on which Radomsky, like Don Diego and Sansón, judges. What he does not

Cervantes admired or scorned Don Diego. Similarly, critics of *The Idiot* disagree over how Dostoevsky might have viewed Radomsky. In Krieger's view, Radomsky has Dostoevsky's "approval," and "is there to help us judge Myshkin" (*Tragic Vision,* 225). But Wasiolek contends: "Radomsky—on whose words Krieger's whole thesis rests—is not the moral norm of the novel against which Myshkin is to be judged. Radomsky has one of those glib, rational, pragmatic, balance-sheet minds that Dostoevsky held in loathing" (Introduction to Dostoevsky, *Notebooks,* 16).

18. See Serrano-Plaja, *"Magic" Realism,* chap. 2 ("Enthusiast Virtue"), 28–95.

realize is that Christian compassion, like true faith and love, contradicts and transcends common sense, and that someone who embodies those virtues may appear like an enthusiast, or a "poor idiot," which is what Radomsky calls the prince as soon as they part (588).

Myshkin, the heavenly emissary, in siding with Nastasya, the eternal female, allied himself with a being who was no more "of this world" than he. Therefore, as scholars and critics of this novel have failed to note, its final chapters subtly present Nastasya too as a Quixote. As Don Quixote read too many chivalry books, so Nastasya is reputed by Radomsky and Aglaya to have "read too much poetry" (4:8, 573). As Don Quixote went mad, so Nastasya suffers from a "disordered mind and sick soul" (571); is told by Aglaya that her "self-love amounts to—to madness" (571); and is compared by the narrator to a "mad woman" (575), a description supported by Myshkin's remark to Radomsky: "Yes—she is mad!" (4:9, 586). Nastasya's kinship to the knight is implicitly confirmed after her death when Myshkin finds in her room a copy of *Madame Bovary* (1857), whose adulterous heroine is commonly regarded as a female Quixote.[19]

Not meant for this world, Nastasya dies in the end, as did Don Quixote and Emma Bovary. But the quixotic prince, left in this world as an "idiot" at his novel's close, must still await that final fate before he may rejoin Nastasya in their "place beyond the skies." Let us turn now to consider the resurrection and "fourth sally" of the Manchegan knight in twentieth-century literature, and his religious transformation in Monsignor Quixote.

---

19. E.g., Helmut Hatzfeld, "*Don Quijote* und *Madame Bovary,*" *Jahrbuch für Philologie* 3 (1927):54-70, 116-31; Vittorio Lugli, "Flaubert e il *Don Chisciotte,*" *Cultura* 15 (1927):401-7; Maurice Bardon, "Don Quichotte et le roman réaliste français: Stendhal, Balzac, Flaubert," *Revue de Littérature Comparée* 16 (1936):63-81; Cascardi, *Bounds of Reason,* esp. 159-99, 263-70. See also Levin, *Gates of Horn,* 248-51, "Quixotic Principle," 240; Adams, *Strains of Discord,* 85-90.

Part Three

Father Quixote: Twentieth-Century Quixotic Priest

> *"Don't worry, friend Sancho," said the barber, "for we will entreat your master, and advise him, even urging it upon him as a case of conscience, to become an emperor and not an archbishop, because it will be easier for him."* (*Quixote,* Ormsby translation, 1:26, 193)

> *All this Sancho listened to and fixed well in his memory. He thanked them heartily for their decision to advise his master to become an emperor instead of an archbishop, for he felt sure that, when it came to bestowing rewards on their squires, emperors could do more than archbishops-errant.* (1:27, 196)

Soon after *Monsignor Quixote* appeared, critics conveyed two views of its theme and relation to Cervantes's classic. One reviewer suggests that despite some obvious "parallels" in plot between the two novels, "Most of the adventures are clearly Greene's invention and are meant to serve his own thematic purposes, which are connected in only the loosest fashion to those of Cervantes." The same reviewer regards *Monsignor Quixote* as "a whimsical meditation on faith and doubt and the varieties of human folly."[1] Another critic observes that Greene "actually transposes elements of Cervantes's novel directly into the modern world, retaining the La Mancha setting and alluding to some of the original incidents." However, he identifies Greene's "basic theme" with the message of "The Grand Inquisitor" that "anyone who goes about the world behaving as Christ and his true followers did is liable to seem mad and

---

1. Robert Towers, "An Amiable Graham Greene," in *New York Times Book Review,* 19 September 1982, 32.

dangerous to most people, but especially so to the princes and bureaucrats of the Catholic Church."[2]

While describing aptly the double theme of *Monsignor Quixote,* these two critics overlook that theme's Kierkegaardian and Unamunian dimensions. If Greene's novel is a "meditation on faith and doubt," his linking of that problem with the quixotic hero is attributable to the impression made on him by Unamuno's view of the knight as the prototypical vitalist whose faith is established on uncertainty. And if *Monsignor Quixote* is thematically consonant with "The Grand Inquisitor," it is because Christ appears no less "mad and dangerous" to the Catholic Inquisitor of sixteenth-century Seville than the Kierkegaardian knight of faith with whom Unamuno equated Don Quixote would seem to many modern church officials. Two decades before Dostoevsky created Prince Myshkin, and three decades before "The Grand Inquisitor" appeared in *The Brothers Karamazov,* Kierkegaard predicted that when "secular sensibleness" permeates the whole world, "the only remaining conception of what it is to be Christian will be the portrayal of Christ, the disciples, and others as comic figures. They will be counterparts of Don Quixote, a man who had a firm notion that the world is evil" (*Journals,* 1:132–33).

Monsignor Quixote represents a culmination of certain religious tendencies in *Quixote* criticism that began with Kierkegaard and Dostoevsky, crystallized in Unamuno,[3] and persist today. In 1982, when Greene's novel was published, there also appeared a study by Fernando Rielo entitled *Teoría del Quijote: su mística hispánica* (Theory of the Quixote: Its Spanish Mysticism). Described in the book's prologue as a mystic poet, critic, and philosopher, Rielo equates Don Quixote and Christ as "Cristo de La Mancha" and "Quijote Nazareno" (*Teoría,* xix), and detects in the *Quixote* certain mystical patterns (e.g., what he views as the *noche oscura* symbolized in the adventure of Montesinos's cave) that seem to link the knight to the great Spanish mystics, St. John of the Cross and St. Teresa. *Teoría del Quijote* thus provides a remarkable theoretical complement to the titular hero of *Monsignor Quixote,* a Catholic priest who believes himself to be descended from Cervantes's knight, and whose favorite reading includes works by those two mystics. And just as Rielo cites Unamuno and follows him in comparing Don Quixote and St. Ignatius, so Unamuno's

---

2. John Spurling, *Graham Greene* (London: Methuen, 1983), 52.

3. On the relation of Greene's novel to the *Quixote* and some of Unamuno's writings, see Patrick Henry, "Cervantes, Unamuno, and Graham Greene's *Monsignor Quixote,*" *Comparative Literature Studies* 23 (1986):12–23.

comparison is alluded to several times in Greene's novel, and Father Quixote pays tribute to the great philosopher by visiting the university town where he taught and died.

Monsignor Quixote and *Teoría del Quijote* reflect what might be called the religious trend in twentieth-century criticism of Cervantes's novel, a trend yet to be defined or traced. To establish the critical background for the sanctification of the knight in Greene's novel, which I will analyze later, a working definition and an overview of works in this trend from Unamuno to Rielo are in order.

5

The Religious Trend in Twentieth-Century Quixote *Criticism*

The religious current in twentieth-century *Quixote* criticism defines itself by two main tendencies: the perception of Don Quixote as an exemplar of Christian faith, or a knight of faith; and the comparison of him to certain saintly figures, and above all, Christ. In this trend the "soft" tendency of viewing Don Quixote sympathetically, and the Romantic tradition of idealizing him, achieve their most extreme expression: sympathy for the knight becomes religious reverence, and idealization tends toward deification.

Shunned by most professional Cervantists, the religious trend evolved almost exclusively outside their circles, finding its roots in Kierkegaard, Turgenev, and Dostoevsky, and attracting a late-nineteenth-century contributor in George E. Morrison, who in the preface to his play (1895) about Don Quixote, called him "the Christ of fiction."[1] The trend flourished during the *Quixote*'s tercentenary (1905) and the next year in works by Unamuno, Rubén Darío,

---

1. *Alonzo Quixano, Otherwise Don Quixote* (London: Elkin Matthews [1895]).

and José Enrique Rodó, and then spread throughout Europe and the Americas. Of those three Hispanic writers only one was born and lived in Spain, and none was a *cervantista* or scholarly specialist in Spanish literature: Unamuno, a Basque Spaniard, was a professor of Greek at the University of Salamanca, a philosophical essayist, a novelist, and poet; the Nicaraguan Darío was a poet and critic; Rodó, from Uruguay, was an essayist and politician. Because Unamuno's writings on the *Quixote* became touchstones for later contributors to the religious trend, his interpretation will furnish the starting point for our examination.

The comparison of Don Quixote and Christ invites one prefatory generalization. We have seen that those two figures were viewed in the nineteenth century as poets by the aesthetically conscious Romantics, and that this tendency led to Dostoevsky's comparison of them as "beautiful" characters. In our century, fraught as it has been with wars and injustices, comparisons of the same two figures have tended more to present them as liberators and champions of justice. Finding its biblical source in Paul's letter to the Galatians (3:28 and 5:1), the modern concept of Jesus as liberator is traceable from Dostoevsky and Tolstoy, through Abraham Lincoln and Julia Ward Howe, to Mahatma Gandhi and Martin Luther King, Jr.[2] The preoccupation with human freedom is also reflected in a number of Jesus' transfigurations in twentieth-century fiction, particularly those cast as Christian Socialists or communists.[3] At the same time, Romantic exegetes have always admired the knight for liberating the galley slaves. Such admiration is especially pronounced among twentieth-century critics who have seen him as a symbol of justice and liberation in the immediate contexts of the Spanish-American War, the revolutions of Mexico and Russia, World War I, the Spanish Civil War, and World War II. The resulting analogy between Don Quixote and Christ as liberators finds its earliest anticipator in that most dashing leader of the Spanish American wars of independence, Simón Bolívar. Known as *El Liberador,* Bolívar proclaimed on his deathbed: "The three greatest fools of History have been Jesus Christ, Don Quixote, . . . and me!"[4]

---

2. See Pelikan, *Jesus Through the Centuries,* chap. 17 ("The Liberator"), 206–19.

3. See T. Ziolkowski, *Fictional Transfigurations,* chap. 3 ("The Christian Socialist Jesus"), 55–97; chap. 6 ("Comrade Jesus"), 182–224.

4. Quoted by Unamuno, "Don Quixote-Bolívar," in *Our Lord Don Quixote,* 383–400; here 386.

Unamuno

A hallmark of the *generacíon del 98,* that brilliant group of Spanish men of letters led by Miguel de Unamuno around the turn of the century, was the prominence that the *Quixote* assumed in their thinking and writing as a work expressive of their activist yearnings. After the disaster of Spain's war with the United States, the *noventayochistas* were unified in their aim of effecting a spiritual regeneration of their nation. In working toward that end, they sought inspiration in great figures of the past, most notably the Spanish mystics and Don Quixote. Their interpretations of the *Quixote,* especially those of Unamuno, "Azorín" (José Martínez Ruiz), and later Ortega, are reflections on the spiritual meaning of Spain's cultural history. In sublimating the knight's virtues while repudiating the pejorative connotations of such terms as *quijote, quijotadas,* and their derivatives, these men transformed him into a paradigm of dignity and a symbol of revitalization.[5]

For Unamuno, Don Quixote became the archetypal Spaniard: the ideal hero and creative spirit. It is well known that the philosopher changed his view of the knight several times. In his notorious essay of 1898, "¡Muera don Quijote!," he calls for the "death" of Don Quixote, meaning mad, quixotic adventures, and the "life" of Alonso Quixano, meaning sound, steady work. But in the first of his philosophical novels, *Love and Pedagogy* (1902), he exalts quixotic madness—calling it "herostratism" after the Ephesian Herostratus, who burned down the Temple of Artemis to immortalize himself—over quixotic sanity. He reiterates this position in his essay "Glosses on 'Don Quixote'" (1902-3), and in his philosophical-theological commentary, *The Life of Don Quixote and Sancho* (1905). The intensely religious view set forth by that book finds its hermeneutic justification in an essay Unamuno published that same year, "On the Reading and Interpretation of 'Don Quixote.'"

In this largely polemical essay, Unamuno complains that the *Quixote's* "poetry," its "truly universal element," is overlooked because "we tend to become enmeshed in its literature, in its temporal and particular elements."[6] He attacks contemporary Spanish critics and Cervantists for paying excessive

5. Paul Descouzis, *Cervantes y la generación del 98: la cuarta salida de don Quijote* (Madrid: Iberoamericanos, 1970), 19. See also Close, *Romantic Approach,* chap. 5 ("Unamuno, 'Azorin,' Ortega"), 134-85.

6. "On the Reading and Interpretation of 'Don Quixote,'" in *Our Lord Don Quixote,* 445-63; here 453.

attention to (what he regards as) insignificant details in the text, and for speculating about Cervantes's authorial intent. Such critics have displayed "philosophical" and "poetic incapacity" (448) in their failure to penetrate the text's "inner meaning" (449). In attacking these "pedants and spiritual sluggards" as "the school of the Cervantist Masora" (448), Unamuno contends that Cervantes's authorial intent is irrelevant for "what the rest of us see in the book":

> Ever since *Don Quixote* appeared in print . . . , the book has no longer belonged to Cervantes, but to all who read and feel it. Cervantes extracted Don Quixote from the soul of his people and from the soul of all humanity, and in his immortal book he returned him to his people and all humanity. Since then, Don Quixote and Sancho have continued to live in the souls of the readers of Cervantes' book and even in the souls of those who have never read it. (449–50)

Once the hero has achieved this semantic autonomy, the author and his intentions become dispensable, and the text achieves a sacred status. Reiterating a point from "Glosses on 'Don Quixote,'" Unamuno recommends the *Quixote* as "the national Bible of the patriotic religion of Spain" (452), to be read allegorically in the same way as Holy Scripture. This entails separating Cervantes from the text, and substituting "Quixotism" for "Cervantism" (459). Cervantes was "enormously inferior to his work" (455); in writing it, he merely served as "the minister and representative of humanity," and "the instrument by which sixteenth-century Spain gave birth to Don Quixote" (456).

Unamuno's essay establishes the theoretical basis for his exegetical procedure in *The Life of Don Quixote and Sancho.* This he makes clear in his forewords to the second and third Spanish editions (1914, 1928), the former of which describes his chapter-by-chapter commentary as "free and personal," one that does "not pretend to discover the meaning Cervantes aimed to impart to his work, but only the meaning which I myself give it" (4). Unamuno communes with the *Quixote* in the light of his own highly vitalist philosophy and existential religion, addressing the knight as "my lord" (*mi señor*), and identifying with the latter's quest for immortality. Though "hard" critics and *cervantistas* have shunned his commentary, considering it hermeneutically invalid,[7] it stands as a *locus classicus* for *Quixote* criticism's religious trend, whose two main aspects are the interpretation of Don Quixote as a knight of faith (*caballero de fe*) and the comparison of him to Christ.

The first aspect reflects the influence of Kierkegaard on Unamuno's religious and theological thinking. As elsewhere in Unamuno's writings, this influence is evident in *The Life of Don Quixote and Sancho.* Kierkegaard's concept of truth as subjectivity manifests itself in Unamuno's suggestion that nothing is more certain than that which is grasped through immediate experience, and hence, that Don Quixote's illusions are the perfect image of reality.[8] The experience of Kierkegaardian *Angst,* which Unamuno terms *congoja,* is implied in the latter's view of the knight as a man led by his longing for immortality to a devastating sense of his own mortality. Both these elements, the notion of truth as subjectivity and the experience of *Angst,* are essential to Kierkegaard's concept of the knight of faith in *Fear and Trembling;* accordingly, it is as such a type that Don Quixote is perceived by Unamuno.

Don Quixote exemplifies four distinct kinds of faith for Unamuno, though the philosopher makes no attempt to systematize them: faith in God, faith in oneself, faith in one's illusions, and the faith one inspires in other people. Unamuno finds the first type expressed in the knight's initial sally: "Don Quixote's obedience to the designs of God is one of the qualities we should most observe and admire in his life. His obedience was perfect, blind." Although Don Quixote's vainglorious "search for eternal name and fame, the desire to have his history written in time to come," gives his generous undertaking a "sinful basis," that sinfulness makes the knight "deeply and intimately human," since heroes and holy persons always set out in quest of temporal and eternal glory.[9]

Don Quixote's "perfect faith" in God, which Unamuno finds epitomized in the adventure of the lions (2:17, 190), is directly linked to his faith in himself. This second type of faith is revealed in the adventure of Andrés, where the knight reprimands the boy's abusive master and then assures the boy that he no

---

7. E.g., C. P. Otero, "Unamuno and Cervantes," in *Unamuno: Creator and Creation,* ed. José Rubia Barcia and M. A. Zeitlin (Berkeley: University of California Press, 1967), 171–87.

8. See Jesus-Antonio Collado, *Kierkegaard y Unamuno: la existencia religiosa* (Madrid: Gredos, 1962), 273. Cf. Jorge Uscatescu, "Unamuno y Kierkegaard o la interiodad secreta," *Arbor* 103, nos. 403–4 (1979):25–40.

9. *The Life of Don Quixote and Sancho,* 1:2, *Our Lord Don Quixote,* 34. The colon separates the part and chapter numbers, which correspond to the pertinent part and chapter of Cervantes's *Quixote.*

longer has anything to fear. Italicizing the pertinent quotation from the *Quixote,* Unamuno urges:

> Notice that sentence *"he will not beat you again, for I have only to lay my command on him, and he will respect it,"* which characterizes the Knight's profound faith in himself, a faith in which he exalted himself, for since he did not yet have deeds to show, he thought of himself as the son of the deeds he planned to undertake. (1:4, 43)

The connection between the first two kinds of faith is later evidenced when the knight assures Princess Micomicona (Dorotea) that—in Unamuno's words— "with the help of God and of his own arm she would soon see herself re-established in her kingdom" (1:29, 120).

> Here we must admire how Don Quixote merged his faith in God and his faith in himself into one. . . . The fact is that there is no faith in oneself to equal that of a servant of God . . . ; nor a faith like that of a man who, like Don Quixote, though he be lured on by fame, seeks above all the kingdom of God and his justice. (121)

Unamuno remarks Don Quixote's faith in himself once more when the knight, confined in the cage, still expresses his belief that his name will live forever (1:47).

Concomitant with Don Quixote's faith in God and in himself, and equally admired by Unamuno, is the knight's faith in his illusions. This third type of faith is illuminated by Don Quixote's dinner at the inn after his first sally. Unamuno reminds us that the madman, on hearing a reed whistle blown by a hog-gelder,

> was confirmed in the belief that *he was in some famous castle, where he was being regaled with music, that the codfish he was eating was trout, the black bread white, the whores ladies, and the innkeeper warden of the castle. . . .*
>
> With good reason has it been said that nothing is impossible to the believer, and that there is nothing like faith to season and soften the hardest and bitterest bread. (1:2, 37)

Unamuno later equates Don Quixote's faith in his illusion of Dulcinea with faith in the existence of a spiritual realm. The encounter with the Toledan merchants (1:4), whom the knight orders to praise Dulcinea's beauty, strikes Unamuno as "one of the most quixotic of Don Quixote's adventures; that is, one that most lifts up the hearts of those redeemed by his madness." In this adventure, as Unamuno recounts it, the knight prepares "to conquer the spiritual kingdom of faith. He wanted to make those men, whose moneyed hearts could only see the material kingdom of riches, confess that there is a spiritual kingdom, and thus to redeem them in spite of themselves." Unamuno is especially impressed by Don Quixote's demand that the merchants, without seeing Dulcinea, swear that she is the world's most beautiful lady: "Admirable Knight of Faith! And how profound his sense of faith! He was a true product of his country, which also set out, a sword in the right hand and in the left hand a crucifix, to force remote peoples to confess a creed they did not know" (45).

While Unamuno will allow that Don Quixote "created" Dulcinea "in pure faith" (2:64, 276), the madman's willful belief in his illusion that the barber's basin is a helmet illustrates the philosopher's subjectivistic, voluntaristic concept of truth; that is, that truth equals one's belief in an object as that object is imposed by one's will. As one of the central theses of Kierkegaard's *Concluding Unscientific Postscript* (1846) is that truth is subjectivity, Unamuno praises Don Quixote for insisting that what looks to Sancho like a basin looks to him, the knight, like a helmet, and that to a third person it might look like something else: "That is the pure truth: the world is what it seems to each of us, and wisdom consists in making it into the image of our will, as we rave without reason, filled with faith in the absurd" (1:24, 112). Later, reflecting on the debate between Don Quixote and a crowd of mockers over whether the basin is a helmet or a basin, Unamuno asserts: "The more one believes in a thing, the truer it is believed, and it is not intelligence, but will, which imposes this truth" (1:45, 142).

The fourth type of faith is that which Don Quixote inspires in others. Unamuno is hardly nonplussed by the mockers' pretense of sharing Don Quixote's belief that the basin is a helmet; for Unamuno they are no different from the human masses ("sheep") who, following their prophets ("Knights of Faith"), take up arms to defend a religious "proposition" (143). Being "quixotized despite themselves, engaged in a struggle and fighting . . . to defend the Knight's faith, even without believing it," the mockers illustrate that "it is the martyrs who make the faith rather than faith which makes the martyrs" (144).

Since no one becomes as intensely "quixotized" as Sancho Panza, the chapter in which the knight first solicits his services as a squire inspires Unamuno to reflect on the contagiousness of Don Quixote's faith in the absurd. For Unamuno, Sancho's belief in Don Quixote's promise of an island shows that "a sane man following a madman gives greater evidence of quixotism than does a madman pursuing his follies. Faith is contagious, and Don Quixote's is so robust and fiery that it redounds upon those who love him" (1:7, 56). Henceforth Sancho's quixotization and his acquirement of his master's faith will be a recurrent theme. How "contagious" Don Quixote's faith is becomes apparent as early as the altercation with the Yangüesans, where the squire's act of joining his master in a charge against those heartless men implies for Unamuno that "Sancho's faith in Don Quixote is even greater, if that is possible, than that of his master in himself" (1:15, 86; cf. "Glosses," *Our Lord Don Quixote,* 359). Unamuno identifies other examples of Sancho's quixotization and faith (1:18; 1:23; 1:25; 1:45), so that by the episode of the "enchanted Dulcinea," he can describe the squire's life as "a slow process of handing himself over to the power of quixotic and quixotizing faith," which is "a true and lively faith, a faith nourished by doubts" (2:10, 174). In the end, having developed this theme further (2:33; 2:47-55), Unamuno can assure the spirit of the deceased knight that Sancho remains "to replace you, a Sancho full of faith. For your faith, Knight, is now stored up in Sancho" (2:74, 313).

Unamuno's view of Don Quixote as a knight of faith furnishes the paradigm for one of the two definitive tendencies of the religious trend in subsequent *Quixote* criticism. The other tendency, the comparison of Don Quixote to Christ, also finds paradigmatic expression in Unamuno's commentary. Though he compares Don Quixote to other heroes and holy figures such as the Cid, Pizarro, St. Teresa, and most notably St. Ignatius,[10] the analogy with Christ has the most far-reaching ramifications, and is one of the features that Unamuno's interpretation of the knight shares with Dostoevsky's.[11]

However, Unamuno's interpretation differs from the Russian author's on a crucial point: his idea of the knight as actually "existing" in a special sense.

10. See Ignacio Elizalde, "Ignacio de Loyola y Miguel de Unamuno," *Arbor* (Madrid) 106, no. 413 (1980):29–41.

11. See Marrero, *El Cristo de Unamuno,* chap. 2 ("Don Quijote y Cristo, o el Quijotismo de Unamuno y el de Dostoyevski"), 155–204.

Unamuno provides the theoretical justification for this idea in "On the Reading and Interpretation of 'Don Quixote,'" where he refers to the thesis expounded by the German theologian and philosopher of religion Albert Kalthoff in *Das Christusproblem* (1902) regarding the question of Jesus' historical existence. Kalthoff construes Christ as having been no more than a symbol of the Christian Church, itself born of the Jewish communities as the result of a socioeconomic movement. Christ is therefore not the "historical" Jesus of liberal Protestant historians, but rather—as Unamuno sums up Kalthoff's view—"the ethical and religious entity who has come down to us, living, growing, and adapting himself to the diverse needs of the times within the collective consciousness of Christendom" (450). Unamuno mentions Kalthoff's doctrine not in order to agree with or refute it, but only to clarify his own approach to the *Quixote:*

> Certainly it will occur to no one, unless it be to me, seriously to maintain that Don Quixote really and truly existed and did all the things that Cervantes tells us about, in the way that almost all Christians maintain and believe that Christ existed and did all the things the Gospels tell us about. Nevertheless, it can and should be maintained that Don Quixote existed and still exists with a life and existence perhaps more intense and effective than if he had lived and existed in the ordinary manner. (450–51)

Having heralded Don Quixote the "Castilian Christ" in his essay "The Knight of the Sad Countenance" (1896), Unamuno draws at least seven analogies between the knight and the savior. First, quoting Jesus' claim that "Whosoever loses his soul shall gain it," Unamuno asserts: "Alonso Quixano lost his wits and judgment to find them in Don Quixote: a glorified judgment" (1:1, 30). Second, "Like Christ Jesus, of whom Don Quixote was ever a faithful disciple, he was ready for whatever adventures the roads brought him" (1:2, 33). Third, when Don Quixote commanded the Toledan merchants to acknowledge the supremeness of Dulcinea's beauty, they "asked Don Quixote, as the Jews did Christ, for some signs so that they might believe" (1:14, 84). Fourth, when the knight becomes "forever the butt and laughingstock of barbers, curates, graduates, dukes, and idlers of every breed," it signifies his "passion by mockery"; just as Christ was mocked by those who cried "Behold the man!," so Don Quixote is mocked by those who say "Behold the madman!" (1:29, 122). Fifth, commenting on the ecclesiastic's rebuke of Don Quixote at the duke's castle, Unamuno feels certain that were Christ ever to return to earth, "that grave ecclesiastic, or his successor, would be among the Pharisees, and they would take him for a madman or a dangerous agitator and would seek to give him an equally ignominious death" (2:31, 209–10). Sixth, Jesus "went up to only one city, to Jerusalem alone, and Don Quixote went up only to Barcelona, the Jerusalem of our Knight" (2:46, 235). Seventh, when the knight expresses dismay and spiritual anguish on beholding a group of saints' images and contrasts their holy lives with his own chivalric existence, "[t]here is nothing surprising in his reaction, when one considers that Christ, borne down by grief in the olive grove, asked his Father if he could spare the lees in the chalice of bitterness" (2:58, 256). To top things off, according to Unamuno, the whores at the inn whom Don Quixote mistakes for maidens assume the role of Mary Magdalene (1:2, 36); Sancho, in his carnality, becomes the knight's Simon Peter (1:10, 65); and Dulcinea, deified by Don Quixote, is for him what the Virgin Mary is for the Spanish people (2:67, 291).

The perception of Don Quixote as a knight of faith and as Christ-like is presupposed in Unamuno's polemical essay "The Sepulcher of Don Quixote," which appeared in the Madrid journal *La España Moderna* in 1906 and was later published as the preface to the second and subsequent Spanish editions of *The Life of Don Quixote and Sancho.* The essay calls for a "holy crusade of going to rescue the Sepulcher of Don Quixote from the hands of the university graduates, curates, barbers, dukes, and canons who occupy it," that is, from "the champions of Reason" who "stand guard over it so that the Knight may not rise from the dead."[12] Pursuing the anticipated analogy between the sepulchers of Christ and Don Quixote, Unamuno draws one distinction: whereas the alleged location of Christ's tomb was known by the "fervent crusaders" of old, the location of Don Quixote's will *not* be known by "our crusaders," but "must be sought in the battle to save it" (12). Repeating his suggestion from "On the Reading and Interpretation of 'Don Quixote,'" Unamuno speaks of "Quixotism" in cultic terms as "a new religion" whose "founder" and "prophet" was Don Quixote. This religion requires "the courage of standing up to ridicule" (12). To qualify, the crusader must possess two other virtues embodied by the knight: "faith" (19) and "Holy Solitude" (22).

12. "The Sepulcher of Don Quixote," in *Our Lord Don Quixote,* 9–22; here 11, 12.

Unamuno's religious view of Don Quixote develops further in *The Tragic Sense of Life in Men and Nations* (1913), his philosophical sequel to his commentary. The book's theme is the conflict of religion and science, faith and reason, belief and unbelief, that has plagued Western consciousness since the Renaissance. For Unamuno, this conflict is epitomized in Don Quixote and Sancho. Citing from Mark 9:24 the famous words of the epileptic's father, "Lord, I believe; help thou mine unbelief," Unamuno claims to have shown in his commentary that this sort of "human faith" is the same as that which Sancho and his master hold in the latter's "extravagances": "Our Lord Don Quixote is the prototype of the vitalist whose faith is founded on uncertainty, and Sancho is the prototype of the rationalist who doubts his own reason."[13]

The final chapter of *The Tragic Sense,* entitled "Don Quixote in the Contemporary European Tragicomedy," attempts to distill from the lesson of "Quixotism" a directive for confronting the enmity between faith and reason. According to Unamuno, reason tends to make a mockery of faith, and to "despise" it, and for this reason one must have recourse to Don Quixote "to learn how to face ridicule and overcome it" (328). As a "sublime fool and madman," Don Quixote "made himself ridiculous," and thereby "achieved immortality" (331–32). He became the Spanish Christ because he, like Jesus, suffered the "passion" of mockery. On the one hand, "The tragedy of Christ, the divine tragedy, is the tragedy of the Cross" (341), though the cultured skeptic Pilate "sought to make it into a comedy by making mock of it, and thought up the farce of the king with the reed scepter and crown of thorns, and he cried out 'Behold the man!' " (341–42). On the other hand,

> the human tragedy, the intra-human tragedy, is the tragedy of Don Quixote, whose face was daubed with soap that he might make sport for the servants of the Duke and Duchess, while the masters . . . might cry out "Behold the madman!" And the comic tragedy, the irrational tragedy, is the passion following on mockery and ridicule. (342)

Unamuno's perception of Don Quixote's "passion" as a "comic tragedy" accords with Kierkegaard's view of the knight. In considering what it would imply for one "to act the part of Quixote, to imagine oneself ridiculed and mocked," Unamuno invokes from *Concluding Unscientific Postscript* the

13. *The Tragic Sense of Life in Men and Nations,* trans. Anthony Kerrigan (Princeton: Princeton University Press, 1972), 133.

observation that—in Unamuno's words—"the regenerate (*Opvakte* in Danish) desire that the wicked world should mock them, the better to assure themselves of their own regeneracy as they see themselves mocked" (355). In that same work Kierkegaard's pseudonym Johannes Climacus characterizes Don Quixote as "the prototype for a subjective madman" and associates him with the "comic," the "tragic," and "tragic-comic romanticism," defining the comical as "the painless contradiction" with a "way out," and the tragic as "the suffering contradiction" with *no* "way out."[14] Correspondingly, Unamuno relates his own notion of Don Quixote as "a man conscious of his own tragic comical quality" (351) to Horace Walpole's subjectivist dictum that life is a tragedy for those who "feel" and a comedy for those who "think" (342).

As a result of his innovative notion of Don Quixote as a character who "exists" outside his text, Unamuno differs from Kierkegaard in his attitude toward the *Quixote's* ending. In two journal entries that Unamuno probably did not know, Kierkegaard objects to three points about that ending: that Don Quixote died; that he died a rational man; and that his story had any ending at all (*Journals*, 1:357; 2:206). Though Unamuno shares Kierkegaard's longing for the knight's life to be "an endless fantasy," he is not bothered by the fact that the novel ends, or that it ends the way it does. By conceiving of two Don Quixotes, one who regained his sanity and died in the novel, and another, "the real one, the one who remained on earth and lives among us, inspiring us with his spirit" (351), Unamuno can imagine the knight as a truly immortal character. These two Don Quixotes have thus had separate though equally saintly and salvific fates. Upon dying, the former

> went down into Hell, . . . and there he freed all the condemned, as he had freed the galley slaves, and he closed the gates of Hell, and took down the inscription Dante saw there, "Abandon all hope!," and replaced it with one reading "Long Live Hope!" And then, escorted by the souls he had freed, . . . he went to Heaven. And God laughed paternally at him, and this divine laughter filled his soul with eternal felicity. (351)

All the while, "the other Don Quixote remained here, among us, fighting with desperation" or "from despair," which makes him literally a *desesperado*

14. *Concluding Unscientific Postscript,* trans. David F. Swenson (Princeton: Princeton University Press, 1941), 35, 175, 459–63.

like Pizarro and St. Ignatius (351). It is Unamuno's hope that the unworldly "doctrines" of this "reborn Don Quixote" will not triumph in this world, for "if the world wished to make Don Quixote king, he would retreat to the woods . . . , just as Christ withdrew to the mount when, after the miracle of the loaves and fishes, they sought to proclaim Him king" (357).

The conclusion of *The Tragic Sense* is religious and activist, appealing to Don Quixote as a symbolic catalyst to Christian renewal within the spiritually sterile modern world. Alluding to the prophetic role of John the Baptist, Unamuno proclaims that "Don Quixote's new mission in the world today" is "to clamor in the wilderness" (357), so that "the solitary voice which falls like a seed upon the desert will bear fruit in the form of a gigantic cedar singing, with its infinity of tongues, an eternal hosanna to the Master of life and of death" (358). The knight's foe in this mission is the "graduate Carrasco of pan-European regenerationism," or those "scientists" who "create wealth, create nationality, create art, create science, create ethics, above all create—or rather transpose—*Kultur,* and thus kill off both life and death" (358).

The cultic tendency in Unamuno's attitude toward Don Quixote climaxes in several later writings. His essay "Don Quixote's Beatitude" (1922) depicts the knight as posthumously entering the other world and being embraced and blessed by Jesus Christ himself (*Our Lord Don Quixote,* 426–28). Another essay, "Saint Don Quixote of La Mancha" (1923), calls for the canonization of the knight and the establishment of a "Quixotic Church" (*Our Lord Don Quixote,* 429–33). An untitled sonnet of his, composed in 1924 and published in his collection of sonnets, *De Fuerteventura a París* (1925), is addressed to the knight, and opens with a reverent allusion to

> Tu evangelio, mi señor Don Quijote,
> al pecho de tu pueblo, cual venablo
> lancé.[15]

> (Your Gospel, my lord Don Quixote,
> into the heart of your people, as a javelin
> thrust.)

Finally, in a book published in 1930, six years before his death, Unamuno claims to have

15. *Obras completas,* ed. Manual Garcia Blanco, 9 vols. (Madrid: Escelicer, 1966–71), 6:683.

taken what is most intimate from the soul of our people, its eternal essence, its divine over-reason for being [*sobrerrazón de ser*], the game of its quixotic Christianity [*cristiandad quijotesca*] to the awareness and understanding of the peoples of the Latin, Anglo-Saxon, Germanic, Slavic languages . . . , to human civilization![16]

Unamuno's immodest reference to the universal impact of his concept of Spain's "quixotic Christianity" finds no fuller substantiation than in the contributions by subsequent authors to the religious trend in *Quixote* criticism, almost all of whom show signs of his sway.

Darío and Rodó

In addition to Unamuno's writings, two classic sources for the religious trend are Darío's poem "Letanía de Nuestro Señor Don Quijote" (Litany for our lord Don Quijote), composed in 1905, the same year Unamuno's commentary appeared; and Rodó's brief essay "El Cristo a la jineta" (The Christ in short stirrups), published the next year. Like Unamuno, Darío presents the knight as a saintly symbol of faith, and Rodó compares him to Christ.

Darío led the so-called Modernist movement among Hispanic American poets, and is credited with having brought *modernismo* to Spain, where his work was admired by all members of the Generation of '98, albeit begrudgingly by Unamuno. His "Letanía de Nuestro Señor Don Quijote," consisting of twelve stanzas addressed to the knight, opens by hailing him as "Rey de los hidalgos, señor de los tristes" ("King of the hidalgos, lord of the sad"), and

> Noble peregrino de los peregrinos,
> que santificaste todos los caminos
> con el paso augusto de tu heroicidad.[17]

16. *Dos discursos y dos artículos* (Madrid: Historia nueva, 1930), 31; quoted by Marrero, *Cristo de Unamuno*, 178.

17. All quotations of this poem are from Rubén Darío, *Obras poéticas completas*, rev. ed. (Madrid: Aguilar, 1945), 755-57.

(Noble pilgrim of pilgrims,
Who sanctifieth all roads
By the majestic gait of your heroism.)

After commiserating with the knight for having to endure such trivializing rituals of a tercentenary celebration as "elogios, memorias, discursos" ("eulogies, memories, speeches"), the poet launches into the "litany" proper, which expresses an attitude toward him no less cultic than Unamuno's. Like Unamuno, who addressed similar prayers to the knight (e.g., *Life of Don Quixote,* 2:64; *Our Lord Don Quixote,* 277). Darío calls him "lord," and in effect canonizes him by beseeching him to fulfill saintly functions: "Ruega por nosotros" ("Pray for us"), "por nos intercede" ("intercede for us"), "suplica por nos" ("supplicate for us"), "libranos" ("liberate us"). Don Quixote thus becomes a kind of patron saint and liberator of those who are

> ... hambrientos de vida,
> con el alma a tientas, con la fe perdida,
> llenos de congojas y faltos de sol.

> (... hungry for life,
> with soul probing, with faith lost,
> full of agonies and deprived of sun.)

The "tristezas" ("sorrows") and "dolores" ("pains") from which Don Quixote is to free these souls include "los superhombres de Nietzsche" ("the supermen of Nietzsche"), "cantos áfonos" ("aphonous songs"), "recetas que firma un doctor" ("prescriptions that a doctor signs"), "las epidemias de horribles blasfemias" ("epidemics from horrible blasphemies"), and "las Academias" ("academies"). The most important prayer is the closing one: "liberate us!" Alluding to the poet's bondage in the decadent, faithless modern world, this entreaty presupposes the knight's image as liberator. That same role, as we will see, allows for the seventh of twenty analogies drawn by Rodó between Don Quixote and Christ.

Four years younger than Darío, Rodó is known for his fusion of Modernism and spiritualism. Like Darío's "Letanía," Rodó's "El Cristo a la jineta" addresses Don Quixote directly, albeit in the form of an essay rather than a poem. The essay's title is perhaps a play on Sancho Panza's glowing description of the man in green as a saint in short stirrups: "santo a la jineta" (Porrúa edition, 2:16, 382). Revering the knight as a "Warlike Christ" (*Cristo guerro*), a Christ "militant" and "armed,"[18] Rodó draws a score of analogies between him and Christ. These can be summarized as follows:

	Christ	*Don Quixote*
(1)	was alleged to be of the blood of David;	claimed to be descended from a king;
(2)	was born in a humble village which his birth raised from obscurity;	was of a humble village, which through his name lives in the world's memory;
(3)	was called the "Galilean" after his region's name;	was called "Knight of La Mancha" after his region's name;
(4)	was consecrated by John the Baptist;	was dubbed by a castle warden (actually an innkeeper);
(5)	passed forty days and forty nights in seclusion in the desert;	passed an extended period alone in the Sierra Morena;
(6)	purified harlots at his side through his charity;	transfigured Maritornes and wenches of the town through his gentility;
(7)	blessed those who suffer persecution for justice;	suffered for justice by freeing the galley slaves;
(8)	attracted his following with his promise of the heavenly kingdom;	attracted his sole companion (Sancho, who represents the masses) with his promise of an island;
(9)	healed the sick;	helped the aggravated and the needy;
(10)	implored the spirits of the damned;	sought to remedy enchantments;
(11)	was refused recognition as Messiah by common sense;	was refused recognition as knight-errant by common sense;

18. "El Cristo a la jineta," from *El mirador de Próspero*, in José Enrique Rodó, *Obras completas,* ed. Emir Rodríguez Monegal (Madrid: Aguilar, 1957), 521–22; here 521.

(12)	was mocked for his messianism;	was mocked for his knighthood;
(13)	was opposed by his mother and brothers, with whom he renounced his ties;	was opposed by his niece and housekeeper, and confined by them to his home;
(14)	aroused the indignation of the priests when celebrated as the Christ by the crowd at Jerusalem;	aroused the indignation of the grave ecclesiastic when celebrated as a knight-errant at the duke's home;
(15)	suffered persecution, mockery, and ignominy at Jerusalem;	suffered persecution, mockery, and ignominy at the duke's home;
(16)	was denied by Peter;	was denied by Sancho (who told the duchess the knight was mad);
(17)	was derided by the label "This is the King of the Jews" on his cross;	was derided by the label "This is Don Quixote of La Mancha" sewn on his jacket's back in Barcelona;
(18)	was handed over by Judas;	was handed over by Sansón Carrasco;
(19)	possessed two natures—the human, which died, and the divine, which resurrected and rose to heaven.	possessed two natures—the human in Alonso Quixano, who died and left his estate for others, and the divine in Don Quixote, who resurrected in order to complete his adventures.
(20)	Christ's Gospel was written by a tax-collector, St. Matthew.	Don Quixote's Gospel was written by a (former) tax-collector, Cervantes.

Through this synoptic reading of the *Quixote* and the Gospels, the Don Quixote–Christ comparison crystallizes more fully than anywhere previously. Moreover, just as Darío's "Letanía" addressed Don Quixote as an intercessory saint for those who have lost faith, and just as Unamuno will contend in *The Tragic Sense* that the knight remains with us spiritually as a *desesperado* fighting on behalf of faith, so Rodó suggests in closing that Don Quixote "resurrected" after dying, and that "you [Don Quixote] still walk through the world, and still undo wrongs, and rectify injustices, and wage war with enchanters, and aid the weak, the needy and the meek" (522).

Unamuno, Darío, and Rodó were by no means the last to regard Don Quixote in this way.

Ortega and Madariaga

Less than a decade after the publications of Unamuno's commentary, Darío's poem, and Rodó's essay, and a year after Unamuno's *The Tragic Sense* appeared, José Ortega y Gasset published his *Meditations on Quixote* (1914). Twelve years later, after appearing serially from June 1923 to February 1925 in the Buenos Aires journal *La Nación,* Salvador de Madariaga's "psychological essay," *Guía del lector del "Quijote"* made its debut as a book (1926), known in English as *Don Quixote: An Introductory Essay in Psychology* (1934). Unamuno's *The Life of Don Quixote,* Ortega's *Meditations,* and Madariaga's *Essay,* together with Ramiro de Maeztu's *Don Quijote, Don Juan y la Celestina* (1926), seem to represent the four sides of a "rectangle" of modern Spanish thought: the four authors had in common that they all were members of the Generation of '98, that all were reacting against erudition, and that all were *quijotistas,* not *cervantistas.* But their books differ insofar as Unamuno's is religious; Ortega's, cultural-philosophical; Madariaga's, psychological; Maeztu's, activistic and political.[19]

The approaches of Ortega and Madariaga to the *Quixote* differ markedly from that of Unamuno, from each other's, and from the one taken around the same time in Miguel Cortacero y Velasco's now obscure *Cervantes y el evangelio* (1915), which interprets the *Quixote* symbolically as a deliberate "plagiarism" (*un plagio*) of certain major episodes and aspects of the Bible, especially the Gospels.[20] Though this is not the place to broach the philosophical complexities of Ortega's work and the psychological nuances of Madariaga's, one of their books perpetuates Unamuno's view of Don Quixote as knight of faith, and the other, his association of the knight with Christ.

That association occurs in Ortega's *Meditations,* which is manifestly inspired by Unamuno's commentary on the *Quixote,* but which expounds a philosophy

19. See Alberto Porqueras-Mayo, "El *Quijote* en un rectángulo del pensamiento moderno español," *Revista Hispánica Moderna* 28 (1962): 26–35.
20. *Cervantes y el evangelio; o, el simbolismo del Quijote* (Madrid: Fuentenebro, 1915), 3.

of rational vitalism in reaction to the latter's irrational vitalism (Close, *Romantic Approach*, 170). Drawing a sharp distinction between *Don Quixote* the book, and Don Quixote the character, Ortega emphasizes that his aim is "to investigate the Quixotism of the book," as opposed to that of "character" (*Meditations*, 50). Though he complains that "the errors to which the isolated consideration of Don Quixote [as a character] has led are really grotesque," Ortega affirms the analogy between Don Quixote and the redemptive Christ, describing the knight as "the sad parody of a more divine and serene Christ: he is a Gothic Christ; torn by modern anguish, a ridiculous Christ of our own neighbourhood." Ortega continues:

> Whenever a few Spaniards who have been sensitized by the idealized poverty of their past, the sordidness of their present, and the bitter hostility of their future gather together, Don Quixote descends among them and the burning ardor of his crazed countenance harmonizes those discordant hearts, strings them together like a spiritual thread, nationalizes them, putting a common racial sorrow above their personal bitterness. "For where two or three are gathered together in my name," said Jesus, "there am I in the midst of them." (51)

While Ortega's perception is consistent with Unamuno's view of Don Quixote as the Spanish Christ, Madariaga draws on Unamuno's image of the knight of faith. In presenting Don Quixote as a man who willfully holds faith in his illusions and heroically struggles against his doubts, Madariaga traces the decline of that faith and the ultimate victory of those doubts in the course of the novel. He also derives from Unamuno's commentary much of his insight into the process whereby the squire's "spirit" is seduced and drawn up by his master's fantasies. This theme will become a major premise in a number of later contributions to the religious trend, including *Monsignor Quixote.*

Suarès, Kafka, and Frank

In the twelve years between the appearance of Ortega's *Meditations* and the publication of Madariaga's *Essay* as a book, both in Madrid, three works by non-Spanish writers contributed to the religious trend in *Quixote* criticism: André Suarès's *Cervantes,* of which the first French edition was published in Paris in 1916 (a Spanish translation appeared that same year in Madrid under the title *Don Quijote en Francia*); Franz Kafka's parable "Abraham," composed in a letter of June 1921; and Waldo Frank's "The Will of Don Quixote," which constitutes the ninth chapter of his book *Virgin Spain* (1926). Suarès was a French critic, philosophical essayist, and literary portraitist; Kafka, a Czechoslavak-born German novelist and short-story writer; Frank, an American novelist, journalist, and writer of cultural and literary criticism.

In the year of the Battle of Verdun, Suarès published his *Cervantes* to commemorate the three-hundredth anniversary of the author's death (1616). The book opens: "There comes the saint of justice, Don Quixote, the noblest and simplest of men."[21] This *santo de la justicia* "thinks like a child," and is "a prodigy of good will and the ensign of all hope" (31–32). Like Unamuno, Suarès exalts the knight's frenzied and insane aspects. At a time when all Europe is at war and chaos reigns, the knight embodies "the frenzy for justice" (*el delirio de la justicia*), representing the cause "of the poor, of the oppressed and of the suffering. But he does not plead; with sword held high, he assails triumphant evil, like an archangel" (55). Calling Don Quixote "the knight-errant of holy equity, which is perfect charity" (57), Suarès speaks of "the madness for liberty which animates Don Quixote," who "breaks all chains, and pardons even scoundrels if he finds them oppressed. The most noble being is the freest one and the one most enamored of liberty" (59).

Like Darío, Suarès presents Don Quixote as a saintly liberator and symbol of freedom, especially in his seventh chapter, entitled "Libre." But whereas Darío's entreaty, "liberate us!" followed his poem's listing of general woes in the pre-war Western culture, Suarès has in mind France's affinity with Don Quixote as an opponent of the immediate evil incarnate in the military subjugation of Belgium and Serbia by the German and Austro-Hungarian militaries:

> Don Quixote conducts our battle.
> He is the one who flings himself against the windmills of science and barbarism, in order to liberate tortured Belgium and Serbia who is being dragged by her hair, two noble sisters in torment. He defies all

21. *Don Quijote en Francia,* Span. trans. Ricardo Baeza (Madrid: Minerva, 1916), 31.

the giants. France loves him and does not doubt him. They hold the same gods and the same horror at wickedness. (58)

As liberator and opponent of evil, Don Quixote seems Christ-like to Suarès, as he did to Unamuno, Rodó, and Ortega. The knight's eyes represent "the nails of the Cross in the face of a buffoon" (*los clavos de la Cruz en un rostro de polichinela*) (34). He appears as "the Cross on horseback [*la cruz a caballo*], divine and mocked" (34), "the grotesque shadow of God in man" (*la sombra grotesca de Dios en el hombre*) (57–58), and is, like Christ, "the man of sorrow who causes laughter" (58). At times, he "thinks like Socrates, a Christian Socrates [*Socrates cristiano*]. For Socrates, it is sufficient for men to think what is good. For Don Quixote, it is sufficient for men to try to do what is good" (147).

Kafka's "Abraham," whose religious allusions are Hebrew rather than Greek or Christian, transforms the gerontic patriarch of its title into a character combining the figures of Don Quixote and a misfit schoolboy. After imagining Abraham as a ready and eager waiter who was unable to take a break from his duties to sacrifice Isaac, Kafka continues:

But take another Abraham. One who wanted to perform the sacrifice altogether in the right way and had a correct sense in general of the whole affair, but could not believe he was the one meant, he, an ugly old man, and the dirty youngster that was his child. True faith is not lacking in him, he has this faith; he would make the sacrifice in the right spirit if only he could believe he was the one meant. He is afraid that after starting out as Abraham with his son he would change on the way into Don Quixote. The world would have been enraged at Abraham could it have beheld him at the time, but this one is afraid that that world would laugh itself to death at the sight of him. However, it is not the ridiculousness as such that he is afraid of—though he is, of course, afraid of that too and, above all, of his joining in the laughter—but in the main he is afraid that this ridiculousness will make him even older and uglier, his son even dirtier, even more unworthy of being really called. An Abraham who should come unsummoned! It is as if, at the end of the year, when the best student was solemnly about to receive a prize, the worst student rose in the expectant stillness and came forward from his dirty desk in the last row because he had made a mistake of hearing, and the whole class burst out laughing. And perhaps he had made no mistake at all, his name really was called, it having been the teacher's intention to make the rewarding of the best student at the same time a punishment for the worst one.[22]

Kafka was not the first to represent Abraham as quixotic. The comparison is implicit in Fielding's characterization and naming of his quixotic parson, Abraham Adams, as well as in Kierkegaard's *Fear and Trembling,* which depicts Abraham as the paradigmatic knight of faith, a putative transfiguration of Don Quixote (see Welsh, *Reflections,* 189-92). The same comparison becomes explicit in *The Life of Don Quixote and Sancho,* reflecting Kierkegaard's impact on the author; Unamuno presents the knight as living in a direct, personal, unmediated, relationship with God, like "that hero of faith, Abraham, on Mount Moriah" (1:5, 50), and describes the adventure of the lion as a divine test through which God tried "the faith and obedience of Don Quixote, as He had tried the faith of Abraham in directing him to . . . sacrifice his son" (2:17, 190). It is known that Kafka read *Fear and Trembling* around October 1917, some three and a half years before he wrote "Abraham," and that, under Kierkegaard's influence, he considered Don Quixote a knight of faith. However, Kafka's perception of Cervantes's knight may have been even more colored by his reading of Salomon Maimon's *Lebensgeschichte* (1792), in which Jossel of Klezk, a Chassidic fanatic noted among Polish Jews for his extravagant asceticism and cabalistic experiments, is said to have behaved like Don Quixote.[23]

"Abraham," whose portrayal of a quixotic man of faith informs Kafka's two posthumous novels, *The Castle* and *The Trial* (see Welsh, *Reflections,* 192-96), can be read as a parody of *Fear and Trembling.* The parable's crux is the victimization of the man of faith by a divine joke: "An Abraham who should come unsummoned!" Don Quixote appears as a foolish Abraham when, summoned only by his own mad fantasy, he sallies forth as a knight, convinced that God has commissioned him to do so. While Kierkegaard was preoccupied

22. From a letter, June 1921, to Robert Klopstock, in Kafka's *Briefe 1902-1924,* ed. Max Brod (New York: Schocken Books, 1958), 332-34; included in Franz Kafka, *Parables and Paradoxes,* trans. Clement Greenberger (1946; New York: Schocken Books, 1958), 43-45.

23. See Salomon Maimon, *An Autobiography,* trans. J. Clarke Murray (London: Gardner, 1888), 134-35. See also Ritchie Robertson, "Kafka und Don Quixote," *Neophilologus* 69 (1985):17-24.

with Abraham's quixotic leap of faith and suspension of the ethical, and while Unamuno revered the knight for maintaining his faith in an absurdity despite his doubts, neither author considered the two figures as victims of a divine joke. Kafka's parable does precisely that: it presents God as a jokester by implicitly likening him to the schoolmaster who calls the worst student (read Abraham or Don Quixote) to the head of the class to have him suffer the "punishment" (*Bestrafung*) of his classmates' laughter.

While Kafka's parable takes the view of Don Quixote as knight of faith to a parodic extreme by exploiting the implications of a foolish, "unsummoned" Abraham, Waldo Frank's "The Will of Don Quixote" continues the identification of the knight with Christ. As a renowned Hispanophile well-read in Unamuno, Frank was perhaps the first American to draw this link, and one of the most important transmitters of the religious trend in the United States.

Like Unamuno, Frank regards the *Quixote* as a revelatory book, calling it "a divine farce, a sort of comic Mystery."[24] But in contrast to Unamuno, he does not separate the novel from its author; on the contrary, like Suarès, who sees Don Quixote as "the Great Cervantes himself in the armor of a knight-errant" (*Don Quijote en Francia*, 35), Frank asserts: "Before all else, *Don Quixote* is in form the life of Cervantes" (222). Where Frank differs from *both* Unamuno and Suarès is in his refusal to glorify the knight's madness; for Frank, Don Quixote is "a man possessed: not a madman" (208). Nonetheless, this notion leads Frank to compare Don Quixote to Christ, as did Unamuno and Suarès. What Don Quixote has in common with Jesus, the Hebrew prophets, Vardhamana, Jakob Boehme, Plotinus, or "any poet" as opposed to a mere madman, is that he is "possessed of an Ideal" (208). In traversing "a world neo-platonically real" (209), or a "medievally real" world that is "a hypertrophy of such births as Chivalry, Romance and Sainthood," Don Quixote possesses a "character of wholeness, or deliberate disregard for fact" (210). While his "transfiguring of the world to his own will is a medieval act," his motivating "will" is "the enacting of Justice" (210). This typically "Hebrew" will for justice as the means for unifying the world "links" him with the Jewish prophets (211), and the "ideal" toward which his "immaculate conception of Justice" aims is nothing other than "freedom and liberty" (212).

Introduced by Kafka and explored further by Frank, the connection between Don Quixote and Hebrew religion adds to the religious trend an element that

24. "The Will of Don Quixote," in *Virgin Spain: Scenes from the Spiritual Drama of a Great People* (New York: Boni, 1926), 191–226; here 195.

will reach full fruition several decades later in Dominique Aubier's attempt to link the *Quixote* to the *Zohar* and other classic Jewish texts.[25] At the same time, Frank's association of the knight with liberty and freedom elaborates on a point already emphasized by Darío and Suarès. Like them, Frank pays special attention to the galley-slave adventure, comparing Don Quixote to Christ as liberator:

> The freeing of the legally judged robbers, the letting of the lions out of cages, is farce: and yet it illumes [*sic*] a justice above laws whose vision is Christlike and whose enactment brings upon the knight a Christlike fate. In laughing at Don Quixote, we crucify him. Mockery and buffets create the knight of the Sorrowful Figure: our own roars of glee at his well-earned mishaps hail the ridiculous Christ. (212–13)

Here an ironic transition has taken place in the relationship between the Christ-like knight and his readers. Whereas a kind of personal, I–Thou relationship was assumed in Darío's prayer ("liberate us!"), Frank asserts that by our laughing at Don Quixote, we become his crucifiers. The forum of the knight's Passion thus shifts from within the narrative to the reader's response: while Unamuno and Rodó viewed the duke's household and the people of Barcelona as mockers in the Passion, "we" the readers now assume that role. But this does not mean that we lack reverence for Don Quixote; Frank allows that by the story's end, "we—the more humbly in that we have mocked and roared—avow our veneration" (217).

For Frank, Don Quixote symbolizes the vain search for "the salvation of wholeness" that has preoccupied the Western world and accounted for our "spiritual chaos" since Columbus sailed. Out of this search have arisen "the national concept of the State," "the Marxian Internation [*sic*]," "faith in science as Revelation," Rousseau's push for "the return to the unity of man's primordial needs," Nietzsche's "superman," and the Darwinian

> hope that God might be inserted as the principle of flux in the biologic process. All these prophecies and dogmatic actions strove alike to enlist mankind once more in a full unity of life and impulse.

25. *Don Quichotte, prophète d'Israël* (Paris: Laffont, 1966).

All who believed in them, to the extent of their devotion, have been Quixotes. (223)

Though the chivalric "magics" by which Don Quixote attempted "to make the world One" seem "shoddy and unreal," they are no more so than the various concepts and ideologies by which, since Dante, we have tried unsuccessfully "to build a universal House" (223). This insight leads Frank to juxtapose Don Quixote and Faust as "the great antistrophes of the Commedia of Dante" insofar as they are "bodies of Europe's dissolution—forms of our modern formlessness and of our need to be whole" (224). Don Quixote has a "deeper" meaning than Faust, since he "sought the grace of union not by absorbing the world into himself [as Faust did], but by transmuting himself into an impersonal symbol of the world" (225). The knight "failed" in his chivalric career, but "his book lives," and therefore his "cause," like that of "all the prophets and all the Christs," remains and "strikes us as truer than the realities which brought about his death" (225). Frank concludes:

> In the violence of his divorce from the world which he aspired to unite, in the ridiculousness of his discord from it, Don Quixote stands the last prophet of our historic Order [*sic*]. He bespeaks our need: a dynamic understanding which shall enlist ideal and reason, thought and act, knowledge and experience; which shall preserve the personal within the mystical will; which shall unite the world of fact . . . , with the world of dream. (225–26)

Cardona, Camp, and Kazantzakis

The religious trend in *Quixote* criticism continued to develop outside Spain during the late 1920s, and through the next decade, up to the outbreak of World War II. From this period, two contributions directly influenced by Unamuno are Rafael Cardona's reflective commentary *El sentido trágico del Quijote* (The tragic sense of the Quixote), published in San José, Costa Rica, in 1928; and a novel by the French writer, Jean Camp, *Sancho,* which appeared in Paris in 1933. Both authors adopt the view of the knight as a saintly, Christ-like figure from Unamuno, to whom they pay explicit homage by including prefatory quotations from *The Life of Don Quixote and Sancho.*

Cardona begins by asking: "Is there a tragic sense in the *Quixote?*"[26] Following Unamuno, Ortega, and "Azorín" in their quest for profound philosophical meanings in the novel, Cardona urges that "when we have laughed sufficiently" in reading it, "we feel the action of a kind of poison [*uno como veneno*] gradually invade . . . our soul; and as we penetrate the universal and interior meaning, we observe that each day there are fewer reasons for laughing at Don Quixote" (17). This idea goes a step beyond Frank's notion that we "crucify" the knight by our mockery. But that notion is recalled by Cardona's musing that Don Quixote, through his lapse into madness, "interred his human vanity and assumed the calvary of ridicule and of prophetic sorrow [*el calvario del ridículo y del dolor profético*]" (28).

Finding in the *Quixote* a "skeptical and amiable depth" like that in Erasmus's *Praise of Folly,* and a "Christian sentiment toward life that gives a real sense of all human vanity" (26), Cardona compares the knight to Hegel's "Individualized universalism, converted into a singular sentient being," in whom "all that is human, lacking in reason, comes to lose itself in the divine" (26). Don Quixote is superior to such figures as Hamlet, Faust, and Segismundo, for unlike them he is a complete man, one who embodies "the hero of charity, of unusual wandering, the paladin of liberty, the dreamer of justice, the religious practitioner, the graceful, profound, and inimitable orator" (32–33).

In keeping with Unamuno, Cardona deems Don Quixote's madness to be an essentially Christian trait and exalts it as "messianic dementia" (*demencia mesiánica*) (16) and "messianic fervor" (*fervor mesiánico*) (43). Interpreting the text allegorically, he construes the Manchegan's reading of chivalry books as symptomatic of "spiritual hunger" (*hambre espiritual*) (21–22), and equates the knight's relation to Dulcinea with the relation of Christians to the Virgin Mary (55). He also draws analogies between Don Quixote and Christ, as when he observes: "The peace of the earth is, in [Don Quixote's] opinion, as in Christ's, the moth which eats away, and the rust which corrupts; he has come to the world as a sword against giants—tyrants—and against beasts—nations" (32). Elsewhere he remarks: "Don Quixote, who has studied the Gospels and practices them, foresaw that no intelligible discourse is necessary for his squire, and that, meanwhile, the less he understands, the more he will be

26. *Sentido trágico del Quijote* (*acotaciones y quijoteos*) (San José, Costa Rica: Convivo, 1928), 15.

amazed; and as Jesus spoke to his disciples, he speaks through parables" (39). Still elsewhere, Cardona suggests rather gruesomely that such mockers of Don Quixote as the duke and the muleteers "devour him alive" (*se lo comieron vivo*), and "his yellowish flesh turns out to be so tasty to them that they decide to immortalize him in a kind of mystic communion that redeems them of Reason, as that other Jesus Christ redeems them of sin in the Catholic liturgy." In short, "We devour Don Quixote as we devoured Jesus Christ, as we will always devour prophets" (152).

Five years after Cardona's book appeared in Costa Rica, Camp's *Sancho* was published in France, where the religious trend had already manifested itself in Suarès's *Cervantes* and Paul Hazard's well-known analytical study (1931) of the *Quixote* and its author.[27] Anticipating Greene's *Monsignor Quixote* insofar as it adapts Unamuno's religious view of Cervantes's knight and squire to the form of a novel, *Sancho* is even headed by a quotation from Unamuno:

> Oh poor Sancho, how bravely you battle for your faith. . . . Your career was one of inner battle, between your coarse common sense, incited by cupidity, and your noble aspiration toward the ideal, lured by Dulcinea and your master! . . . You went on from enchantment to enchantment to reach the heights of redeeming faith.[28]

Inspired by this notion of Sancho's spiritual "struggle," Camp observes in his preface that while the squire is coarse, greedy, and ignorant, "his heart is the stable of Bethlehem, where the humble virtues of the poor graze: trust, sincerity, integrity and affection" (11).

The novel has two parts. Part 1, "The Squire," consists of six chapters that retell some of Sancho's most famous adventures with Don Quixote, who is presented as Christ-like. When he first invites Sancho to accompany him in quest of adventures, he addresses him with words straight from the Gospels:

27. Hazard's *"Don Quichotte" de Cervantes,* a synthesis of many previous works in *Quixote* criticism, includes references to such seminal contributors to the religious trend as Turgenev, Unamuno, and Suarès. In his chapter on "Religion," Hazard draws an Erasmian analogy between the Manchegan knight and Christ, both of whom in his view express a "Christian wisdom" (*sagesse chrétienne*) that appears mad and ridiculous from a worldly perspective (200–219; see 211–12).

28. A French translation of this passage appears on the unnumbered page following the title-page in Jean Camp, *Sancho* (Paris: Portiques, 1933). I have drawn this English rendering of Unamuno's statement from his *Life of Don Quixote,* 1:36, *Our Lord Don Quixote,* 136–37. Hereafter, unless otherwise indicated, all translations from *Sancho* are mine.

" 'Leave your children and your wife and follow me,' he commanded him like Christ" (26). Asked by the peasant whether their adventures will assure them daily food, the knight replies with an equally familiar expression from the same source: "Consider the lilies of the fields, Sancho: they neither toil nor spin" (26). Later, after Sancho tricks his master in the episode of the enchanted Dulcinea, an "internal voice" addresses the guilt-stricken squire as Christ's betrayer: "Hold out your hand, Judas, for the thirty pieces of silver" (47).

Camp's opening chapter contains a key quotation from Unamuno, "the old owl of Salamanca" (19). The quotation is drawn from Unamuno's commentary on the *Quixote's* last chapter, which addresses the spirit of the dead knight:

> "Sancho the Good, who went mad when you were cured of madness and on your deathbed, Sancho it is who will establish quixotism upon the earth forever. When, noble Knight, your faithful Sancho mounts Rocinante, dressed in your armor and bearing your lance, then you will be resuscitated in him, and your dream will come true." (*Sancho,* 19–20)[29]

The bearing of this passage on Camp's plot becomes apparent in part 2 ("The Epopee"), which relates the course of Sancho's life after his master's death. Sancho goes with Sansón Carrasco to Don Quixote's tomb and is commanded by the knight's spirit to conduct a crusade to the land of Muhammad and the infidels. Despite his wife's protestations and the skepticism of the local priest, he undertakes the mission with Sansón and the monk Serapio as his lieutenants, and undergoes a spiritual conversion away from his former, worldly self, donning "a new spirit" (89). After miraculously attracting a thousand followers from all over La Mancha "to raise the banner of Don Quixote" (95), the former squire leads them southward, invoking Dulcinea as their guardian. When some indignant clergymen protest against the presence of "trollops," "rogues," and "wenches" in this "human river," he replies by invoking the examples of Don Quixote and Christ:

> "My master spurned no one, and Christ before him. Do you know, my brothers, whether that is not a roundabout way that God uses for attracting the young to the crusade? The lilies of Lady Dulcinea will

29. As translated in Unamuno, *Life of Don Quixote,* 2:74, *Our Lord Don Quixote,* 314.

purify all impurity and those of Mary Magdalene were not so depraved
that they did not end by shedding their sins." (114)

Speaking thus in a Christ-like manner, this spiritually transformed Sancho is
revered as a holy man by his followers: "They had recognized Sancho as one of
their own. His words had conquered, convinced them, and, like the apostles of
the Gospel, they quite simply had followed the prophet" (116).

The account of the journey contains a number of allusions to Don Quixote
and Christ. After a storm kills many of the pilgrims, one of the survivors
informs Sancho that while it was going on he had a vision of Christ, St. John,
and Don Quixote, who "smiled in his grey goatee and signalled to Jesus" (126).
On the crusade's twentieth night, Sancho becomes sexually aroused by a dream
involving Dulcinea, succumbs to concupiscence and engages in a rather familiar act with a whore, only to be caught by his followers. In the face of their
reproach, he paraphrases what Christ said to those who condemned the
adulteress: "Let whoever has never sinned cast the first stone at me!" (174).
When he flogs himself before the other pilgrims to show his repentance, we are
reminded of the self-whipping that the knight required of him (in the *Quixote*)
to disenchant Dulcinea. Later, after recounting the pilgrims' calamitous crossing
of the sea at Gibraltar, the narrator asserts that although only "a handful"
survived, "that is sufficient for making a holy world out of this unknown land
which holds Dulcinea prisoner. Don Quixote was alone when he undertook his
exploits! The apostles were but a dozen and the whole world has retained their
voice of truth" (214).

In the end, Sancho is left weary, delirious, and abandoned by all on the North
African desert, where he experiences a series of hallucinations. The spirit of
Don Quixote astride Rocinante appears before him and praises him for having
led "all the poor and all the dreamers" (230). In their final exchange, Sancho
addresses the spirit as "Master," and the spirit in turn links himself to Christ:

> "You taught me, my Master, to smile at insults, to pardon blas-
> phemers."
> "I learned that from another who was greater than I." (231–32)

When the knight disappears, Sancho has a delusive vision of his wife, and then
of Barataria, the land which he once governed (in the *Quixote*). But as he

rejoices that he is about to be a king, he feels a Christ-like "crown of thorns" pushed down on his head, and drops dead, his corpse remaining to be eaten by a hyena.

Camp and Cardona were not alone as proponents of Unamuno's sanctification of Don Quixote outside Spain during the late 1920s and the 1930s. Another foreign adopter was the Greek writer and friend of Unamuno, Nikos Kazantzakis, who made three trips to Spain during that period: the first in August and September 1926; the second from October 1932 to March 1933; the third, in the autumn of 1936, the year of Unamuno's death and the outbreak of the Spanish Civil War.[30] The *Quixote*'s impact on Kazantzakis cannot be overestimated since Cervantes was his favorite author.[31]

Kazantzakis's contribution to the religious trend must be understood against the background of his personal devotion to Don Quixote as one of God's "saviors," a concept expounded in his *Spiritual Exercises,* known also as *The Saviors of God,* composed in Berlin between December 1922 and April 1923. For Kazantzakis, God is not omnipotent. Rather, "He clings to warm bodies; he has no other bulwark. He shouts for help," and "Within the province of our ephemeral flesh all of God is imperiled. He cannot be saved unless we save him with our own struggles; nor can we be saved unless he is saved."[32] Adopting from Nietzsche, Bergson, and William James their theories of heroic pessimism, antirationalism, and vitalism, Kazantzakis, much like Unamuno, considered the exertion of our vitality to be the highest virtue to which we can aspire, and the means by which we, as the material embodiment of God, are to "save" him from entrapment. Whereas Christians encourage the imitation of Christ, Kazantzakis espoused the imitation of Nietzsche's *Übermensch* and Bergson's *élan vital.* He found this vitalistic life-force manifest in all the "saviors of God," among whom he included, besides Don Quixote and Nietzsche, Moses,

30. See Pandelis Prevalakis, *Nikos Kazantzakis and his Odyssey: A Study of the Poet and the Poem,* trans. Philip Sherrard (New York: Simon and Schuster, 1961), 20, 148–51, 160. In the period 1933–34, as noted on 189 n.254, Kazantzakis published his own translations of some poems by Unamuno. He recounts his friendship and last visit (1936) with Unamuno in his collection of travel articles, *Spain,* trans. Amy Mims (New York: Simon and Schuster, 1963), pt. 2, 172–78. (Pt. 1 contains articles written in 1933 and originally published under the title *Spain;* the articles in pt. 2 were written in 1936 and published that year under the title *What I Saw for 40 Days in Spain.*) See also Carlos Miralles Sola, "Casantsakis y España," *Arbor* 66, no. 256 (1967): 92–104.

31. See Manuel Orgaz, "Don Quijote en Grecia," *Cuadernos Hispanoamericanos* 34 (1958): 368–70.

32. *The Saviors of God: Spiritual Exercises,* trans. Kimon Friar (New York: Simon and Schuster, 1960), 104–5.

Psycharis, the Buddha, Alexander the Great, Muhammad, Genghis Khan, Leonardo da Vinci, St. Teresa, El Greco, Shakespeare, and Lenin.[33]

Though by his own account Kazantzakis had devoted himself since childhood to all historical and mythic "conquerers, explorers, [and] Don Quixotes" who combined heroic and saintly qualities,[34] Don Quixote assumed for him an importance second only to that of Odysseus, with whom he identified as closely as did Unamuno with the knight. Kazantzakis's first novel, *Toda Raba* (1929), refers to Faust, Hamlet, and Don Quixote as "the three great guides of the human soul," each subordinate to "Don Ulysses."[35] This was written in the period between his first two visits to Spain. During the first half of 1932, about a year and a half before the second trip, he composed a dramatic scenario entitled *Don Quixote*. A year later he recorded some experiences from that trip in a book, *Spain* (1933), which contains numerous references to the knight.

Consistent with Unamuno's mystical identification of Don Quixote with the Spanish people, Kazantzakis regards the knight as Spain's "mystic fulfillment" and "profound synthesis," construing "the holy martyr Don Quixote" and his "mystic wife, Saint Teresa" as "the sacred couple of Spain," and Spain itself as "the Don Quixote of nations."[36] For Kazantzakis, as for Unamuno, Don Quixote represents the "cry against reason" (19), and is a salvific figure: "The world had emerged from God's hands, rife with injustice and shortcomings. And he, the Knight of the Ideal, was duty-bound to set it right. For Don Quixote's work begins where God's leaves off" (40). As in *Toda Raba*, this "eternally roving Knight of the Ideal" is aligned with Ulysses, Hamlet, and Faust as one of "the four ruling princes of human souls," but here he is elevated above the others: "For perhaps of all the princes, Don Quixote most faithfully mirrors the fate of man" (43).

Several paragraphs later Kazantzakis makes his most obvious contribution to the religious trend. Reflecting on the carving by Gregory Hernandez which represents the crucifixion procession, Kazantzakis divides all the participants, including Christ, into two "types," the Sanchos and the Don Quixotes. He begins with

33. Peter Bien, *Nikos Kazantzakis* (New York: Columbia University Press, 1972), 18–19.

34. Nikos Kazantzakis, *Report to Greco,* trans. Peter Bien (New York: Simon and Schuster, 1965), 190.

35. *Toda Raba,* trans. Amy Mims (New York: Simon and Schuster, 1964), 94.

36. *Spain,* 18. Cf. 40–41: "Spain too was governed by the saintly madness of Don Quixote."

the bandits and Roman soldiers; the Incense Bearers and the common people, jeering and ridiculing the naked Christ. . . . Here are all the Sancho types: people of the flesh, heavy eaters and drinkers with thick sagging lips and mocking eyes, some innocent, some wily. And along with them, all the Don Quixote types: the slender, palpitating, terrified apostles; the heroic, powerless women; and at the high peak of reality and imagination, the Grand Martyr—the Don Quixote of heaven, with His crown of thorns. (44-45)

In viewing Christ as heaven's Don Quixote, Kazantzakis adheres to what he imagines to be the normal Spanish view. After all, "To the Spaniard, is Jesus Christ perhaps but another aspect, the most pathetic, the most hidden and sacred, of Don Quixote?" (45).

In 1934 Kazantzakis wrote a canto of 160 lines entitled "Don Quixote" expressing his recent experience of Spain and his religious view of the knight. Echoing the assertion in *Spain* that "Don Quixote's work begins where God's leaves off," one of the early stanzas has the knight confirm this duty for himself as he sets out on his quest with his soul "shouting for freedom":

> "Be still, my soul," that ancient archon cried;
> "whatever God has left half finished here,
> I, as his warrior, shall complete it now!"[37]

The canto then depicts the struggle between Don Quixote's body and his heart as he seeks to fulfill his role as a savior of God, though that phrase is not used. After entering the "pitiless wasteland," which strikes him as "such a merciless and sterile country," the knight reflects: "I see I must have taken God's road indeed." When "Lady Freedom" approaches, he is beseeched by his "scraggly horse," which represents his body, to abandon the mission:

> "Alas, where are you going, master? Take pity

---

37. All quotations of this canto are from Kimon Friar's translation, which is included between pts. 1 and 2 of Kazantzakis, *Spain*, 149-55. "Don Quixote" is one of a series of cantos that Kazantzakis composed to his saviors of God (one canto to each) from November 1932 to July 1934.

on the poor flesh, for soon the sun will set.
Ah, let's return at once to that cool stable,
the earth, tilled with most fresh and most sweet clover."

Thus did the body speak, that sluggish seed
on the tall tree of God.

Despite this bodily opposition, Don Quixote heeds his heart, which reminds him of the "secret fragrance of our only love, / our nonexistent Lady, Dulcinea," and urges him:

["]Forward! Without a single hope, but even
as though the eyes will one day see all that
they long to see, fight on, O gallant knight!["]

Like Christ, who is nowhere mentioned, Don Quixote must endure mockery and martyrdom for his actions:

["]The icy stars above you will laugh long,
and men below will shout derision at all
you do, but you, with the seducing joy

of most ferocious freedom and death
will sweetly smile, O greatly martyred soul,
and leave drops of your rich blood everywhere.["]

Further, the heart assures him that he will be resurrected:

["]And you, in the divine lie fortified—
that resurrection still exists—shall paint
the eggs of springtime with your holy blood.["]

The heart closes its exhortation by informing him that he is "the youngest, favorite son of God," and God's "only worthy champion" (read "savior"), whose task it is to "snatch" God "from man's foul condition," and to "begin the

Second Creation." In the end Don Quixote, or "Captain Sole," becomes the lonely victim of the murderous "siren / of all deeds unattainable":

> Deeply within that untamed virgin's eyes
> our ancient archon gazed and there beheld

> loneliness, poverty and pain, and not
> a single man approached the loved one's breast.
> Captain Sole bit his lips till the blood ran.

> All life now, like a long complaining myth,
> wrapped itself round the swift reel of his mind
> until he started off from God's dark depths,

> and, floundering in the tight nets of his dream,
> entered into his Lady's kingdom thus.

Nowhere does the canto mention any human companion; Don Quixote's "loneliness" is epitomized by the epithet "Captain Sole," a reminder of Unamuno's praise for the knight's "holy solitude."[38] The use of that epithet here suggests the connection between Don Quixote and the character named Captain Sole whom Odysseus encounters in the twentieth book of Kazantzakis's epic "Modern Sequel" to *The Odyssey*, which he had begun writing in 1924, but which went through seven drafts before he completed it in 1938.[39]

Consistent with the religious trend in *Quixote* criticism, the knight's transformation in *The Odyssey* reflects his reputation as a saintly liberator prone to martyrdom. In book 20, Captain Sole (a type of Don Quixote) takes up his dusty armor once more and sallies forth on his bony old camel, Lightning (Rocinante's counterpart), to save humanity from slavery and injustice.

38. See "Sepulcher," *Our Lord Don Quixote*, 20-22. Cf. *Life of Don Quixote*, 2:44, *Our Lord Don Quixote*, 223-24; *Tragic Sense*, 352.

39. This connection is confirmed by Kazantzakis in a letter, 3 February 1930, written from Gottesgab: "In the final books [of my *Odyssey*] Odysseus meets the great leaders of souls — entirely changed of course: Buddha, Faust, Hamlet, Don Quixote, the Poet, Christ — and gives me the opportunity to put into contact and to contrast Odysseus' soul with all of them" (quoted by Prevelakis, *Kazantzakis and his Odyssey*, 181 n.131). See also Emmanuel Hatzantonis, "Captain Sole: Don Quijote's After-Image in Kazantzakis' *Odyssey,*" *Hispania* 46 (1963):283-86.

He is promptly caught by cannibals, whose slaves bind him to a stake and prepare the spits and fires for roasting. This scene involves some familiar motifs: the cannibals' "shouting and laughing" (line 165),[40] and their placing of "a crown of shavings on his proud and narrow skull" (line 168), resemble the mockery of Christ with the crown of thorns, while the cannibalistic scenario recalls Cardona's claim that we "devour Don Quixote as we devoured Jesus Christ." This prophet-eating motif recurs after the fortuitous arrival of Odysseus, who spies Captain Sole in his predicament and hurries to rescue him. The cannibals, fearing "the great ascetic" (line 185), set Captain Sole free, but the chieftain tells a fable illustrating that savage humanity will always devour its would-be saviors (lines 220–45). Nonetheless Captain Sole, once freed, dashes in a rage to free the slaves, shouting:

> "I am not disarmed! Justice is my protective shield!
> Earth issued from the hands of God imperfect, foul,
> and it's my duty to perfect it, I alone!
> So long as slavery, fear, injustice rack the world,
> I've sworn, my friend, never to let my sharp sword rest.
> Follow me, all ye faithful! Be bold, lads! Don't fear!
>
> (lines 290–95)

Odysseus admires Captain Sole, praising him as a "rebellious heart" (line 302) who is "fortified . . . with dreams" (line 303), and as "the earth's crimson wing, the only one she has" (line 314). But the Greek hero spurns the solitary dreamer for his impracticality and distance from reality. Wishing Captain Sole well, Odysseus continues on his journey.

Predmore

In 1939, the year World War II broke out, a short essay by Richard L. Predmore entitled "La apoteosis de don Quijote" (The apotheosis of Don Quixote) appeared in an Argentine journal.[41] Discussing Turgenev, Rodó, and

40. All quotations are from Nikos Kazantzakis, *The Odyssey: A Modern Sequel,* trans. Kimon Friar (New York: Simon and Schuster, 1958).
41. *Revista de Filología Hispánica* (Buenos Aires) 1 (1939): 262–64.

Unamuno, and citing Darío in a note, this American Cervantist points out their tendency to deify the knight and compare him to Christ. Predmore himself does not deify Don Quixote. And while he mentions Dostoevsky in passing, he makes no reference to other writers who compared the knight to Christ prior to 1939, such as Kierkegaard, Morrison, Ortega, Cortacero, Suarès, Frank, Cardona, Hazard, Camp, or Kazantzakis. Nonetheless, "La apoteosis de Don Quijote" is a landmark for the religious trend in *Quixote* criticism because it was the first critical work to call attention to the trend.

Contributors after World War II

After the war, the first work of *Quixote* criticism in Spanish to perpetuate the religious trend was Antonio Rodríguez's interpretive essay *El Quijote, mensaje oportuno* (1947, The Quixote, a timely message), which describes the knight as the "sublime precursor of the saints and heroes who, through their work and conduct, have raised the banner of the ideal to heights where the cracklings [*chisporroteos*] of calumny could not reach it." Don Quixote is for Rodríguez "the personification of the progressive, revolutionary, active ideal," and "the symbolic expression of all those who under different names— Prometheus, Christ, Spartacus—and in different epochs, have struggled for liberty, progress, and human happiness."[42]

As memories of the recent Spanish Civil War and World War undoubtedly sensitized Rodríguez to the likeness of Don Quixote and Christ as revolutionaries and liberators, so the acknowledgment of that likeness by the noted political historian Isidro Fabela is explainable by the fact that he himself was an honored veteran of the Mexican Revolution. In 1953 Fabela delivered before the Academia Mexicana Correspondiente de la Española a lecture "A mi Señor Don Quijote" (To my Lord Don Quixote), which later appeared as a book (1966). In it he declares that "we love and admire" the knight,

> because he suffers, because he is a master of sadness who teaches us to suffer for the realization of the ideal; because he possesses the attributes of the Nazarene who came to redeem us with his sacrifice on the

42. *El Quijote, mensaje oportuno. Apuntes para un ensayo de interpretación* (Mexico: Nación, S.C.P.E.R.S., 1947), 39.

cross. Only, Don Quixote is not gentle like Jesus Christ, but combative and bold; he lacks the gift of clear-sightedness and the equilibrium of the Divine Man, because he is enraptured [*enajenado*]; but as he is, in the midst of his madness, he is also a redeemer, a poet of mercy, a fighter for liberty, an apostle of justice, an imponderable defender of the woman who is made of what was the best that God held in His hands when He created her.[43]

This description of the knight as Christ-like but "combative and bold" recalls Rodó's portrayal of him almost fifty years earlier as "Christ in short stirrups," "warlike Christ," and "militant Christ."

Of course, not all post-war scholars compare Don Quixote and Christ simply as activist liberators and revolutionaries. In his three *meditaciones,* "Molinos de viento" (1954, Windmills), Francisco Maldonado de Guevara finds the sails of the windmill against which Don Quixote tilts symbolic of Jesus' cross.[44] Two other authors were struck by the knight's Christ-like aspect as it is revealed in his relationship to his squire. Álvaro Fernández Suárez observes in his *Los mitos del Quijote* (1953, The myths of the Quixote):

It is clear that Don Quixote, in supposing Sancho to be "stupid," "simple," or ... capable of believing [*capaz de creer*], was judging him in a similar way as Christ was able to judge the simple, the credulous, his disciples, and the fishermen of Galilee; that is to say, not considering this simplicity a state of inferiority of the spirit, but on the contrary, believing that intellectual simplicity will set free the most profound and substantial wisdom, that of the heart. In this way, it can be said without irreverence that in Don Quixote's choice of Sancho, as in Christ's choice, there was a certain ... saintly cunning [*astucia santa*].[45]

Similarly, Mariano Lebrón Saviñón, a professor of medicine at the University of Santo Domingo, in his essay "La locura de Alonso Quijano el Bueno"

43. *A mi señor Don Quijote* (Mexico: [n.p.], 1966), 68. On the knight's bearing on Fabela's thought, see David Vela, "El Quijote y Fabela," *Homenaje a Isidro Fabela* [no ed. named], 2 vols. (Ciudad Universitaria: Universidad Nacional Autónoma de México, 1959), 2:713–17.
44. *Anales Cervantinos* 4 (1954):77–100; see 77.
45. *Los mitos del Quijote* (Madrid: Aguilar, 1953), 107.

(1960, The madness of Alonso Quixano the Good), diagnoses the knight as a paranoic who,

> like Christ on the mountain, had the power of persuasion, and by that means came to take over his only apostle: Sancho. He departed by himself on his adventures, and after them attracted not only the squire, but all characters from their normal lives: priest, barber, students, inn-keepers, duke and duchess. But none won salvation through faith as Sancho did.[46]

These works by Rodríguez, Fabela, Fernández Suárez, Maldonado de Guevara, and Lebrón Saviñón have four things in common: all are by Hispanic authors (albeit not all from Spain); all were written during the first decade and a half after the war; all contain passages that contribute to the religious trend in *Quixote* criticism; and all show the influence of Unamuno. However, the perpetuation of the religious trend during that decade and a half was not confined to Hispanic authors. The trend also flourished in three studies by authors writing in German, each of whom likens Don Quixote to Christ: Michael Brink's *Don Quichotte: Bild und Wirklichkeit* (1946, Don Quixote: image and reality);[47] Paul Wildi's *Das christliche Zeugnis Don Quijotes* (1953, The Christian testimony of Don Quixote);[48] and Walter Nigg's chapter on the *Quixote* in his *Der christliche Narr* (1956, The Christian fool).

Nigg, a Swiss Protestant theologian whose interpretation crystallizes the religious readings by Brink and Wildi, considers Cervantes and his knight as exemplary "Christian fools" on a par with Symeon of Ydessa, Jacopone da Todi, Erasmus, Philipp Neri, Heinrich Pestalozzi, and Dostoevsky's Prince Myshkin. He regards the *Quixote* as "a disguised portrait of the soul of the author" (*ein nuanciertes Seelengemälde des Autors*) expressing "the inner

---

46. "La locura de Alonso Quijano el Bueno," *Anales de la Universidad Autónoma de Santo Domingo* 23, nos. 87–88 (1958):309–29; 25, nos. 89–92 (1959):93–116; 26, nos. 93–96 (1960):23–31; here 30.

47. *Don Quichotte: Bild und Wirklichkeit* (2d ed., Heidelberg: Schneider, 1946), 86: "[I]n Don Quichotte ein Anbild des Menschensohnes selbst vor uns steht und . . . der Christ ihm auf dem gleichen Wege nachfolgt. Als ich den Krieg kommen sah, der das Ende des Abendlandes bedeuten kann, sah ich Don Quichotte über die Felder des Grauens wandern, aufrecht und mit einem überirdisch leuchtenden Antlitz."

48. *Das christliche Zeugnis Don Quijotes* (Buenos Aires: Deutschweitzerische Evangelisch-reformierte Kirche, 1953); see esp. chap. 10 ("Christus im Don Quijote"), 89–95.

imitation of Christ in Don Quixote" (*Der christliche Narr,* 235). Much like Kierkegaard in his journals, Nigg sees the *Quixote* as "a fool's novel [*Narren-roman*], which proclaims with eloquent language that even in the beginning of modern times, the true Christian [*der echte Christ*] can still go through the world only as the pure fool [*als der reine Tor*]" (236)—a phrase with a Parzivalian ring. Cervantes was himself "an altruistic man, a true Christian" (274), and the knight he created is "a brother of the great mystics" (249), a "man sent from Heaven" (250), and "a man with a new Christian soul" (272). Pursuing his "chiliastic goal" of restoring the Golden Age, which is for him "a religious category" (253), the knight is accompanied by the dual forces of "eternal fate": the condition of "being weighed down by the earth" (*Erden-schwere*), embodied by Sancho, and "ethereal essence" (*ätherisches Wesen*), represented by Dulcinea (247), who is for Don Quixote what Beatrice was for Dante. The knight's story turns out to be a "Christian Passion in modern garb" (259), in which the episode of the knight's entrapment in the cage becomes "a Passion-scene" (260), and his renunciation of chivalry books in the end is his "final self-crucifixion" (261). In sum, "The marked Christianity in the life of Don Quixote is a modified imitation of Christ [*modifizierte Nachfolge Christi*]" (274). Had St. Teresa read the *Quixote,* she would have called the knight her "brother" (282).

Nigg's reading falls in line with what he calls "the religious track of Don Quixote interpretation" (*Die religiöse Fährte der Don-Quijote-Deutung*) (266), which for him includes Dostoevsky, Unamuno, Brink, and Wildi. But Nigg departs from Unamuno's mystical reading in the equal emphasis that he places on Don Quixote's humorous and serious aspects. In Nigg's opinion, Unamuno exaggerates the serious aspects and ignores the humorous, thereby eliminating the very quality that makes the knight a "holy fool" (*heilige Narr*) (266). An heir of Kierkegaard, for whom humor constitutes the boundary between the ethical and the religious stages of existence, Nigg ranks Cervantes "among the greatest humorists of Christianity," and finds the *Quixote* to contain a "Christian" or "religious humor," through which the reader "overcomes false seriousness, that affliction which does not even know the true seriousness of eternity" (268). At the same time, acknowledging that "on Dostoevsky, Don Quixote had no longer a humorous effect, but indeed, a frightening [*erschreckend*] one" (268), Nigg finds the book's humor to be counterbalanced by another aspect:

Over Cervantes's work is spread a Christian melancholy [*christiche Wehmut*] which is certainly unmistakable if one reads carefully. Whoever does not begin to shed tears from reading of Don Quixote, and indeed, tears of the heart and not of the eyes, has completely missed the meaning of the work. There is so inexpressibly much sadness contained in the book, that one can hardly comprehend it at once, because the poet conceals it behind a smiling countenance. Don Quixote is melancholy; one is almost tempted to speak of Christian pessimism [*christlichen Pessimismus*]. (269)

As it combines "Christian humor" and "Christian sadness," so the *Quixote* also "embraces in their polarity both the comic and the tragic" (270).[49]

The question of the knight's relation to the comic and the tragic is also addressed, albeit from a different angle, by the first and most important English-speaking contributor to the religious trend after the war, W. H. Auden, in his essays "The Ironic Hero: Some Reflections on Don Quixote" (1949), and "Balaam and the Ass: The Master-Servant Relationship in Literature" (1954). No less so than Unamuno's interpretation, Auden's shows the direct influence of Kierkegaard, whose thought and works he knew well and wrote upon elsewhere,[50] though the Dane goes unmentioned in these two essays.

After the manner of *Fear and Trembling,* which sets Abraham apart from the tragic hero as a knight of faith, Auden characterizes Abraham as a Christian saint and distinguishes him from three types of conventional hero: epic, tragic, and comic. In doing so, he draws on four crucial strands of Kierkegaard's theological thought. First, there is the distinction between two of Kierkegaard's three stages of existence, the aesthetic and the religious, which Auden employs to interpret the *Sitz im Leben* and transformation of the gentleman whom we meet in Cervantes's opening chapter—a gentleman who "is (a) poor, (b) not a knight, (c) fifty, (d) has nothing to do except hunt and read romances. . . . His situation, in fact, is aesthetically uninteresting except in one thing: his passion is great enough to make him sell land to buy books.

49. Wildi, *Das christliche Zeugnis,* 31, likewise remarks on "die Mischung von Ernst und Humor im Don Quijote."

50. That Auden associated Kierkegaard with Don Quixote is evidenced by the title of his review-essay of volume 1 of the Hongs' translation of Kierkegaard's *Journals and Papers,* "A Knight of Doleful Countenance," *New Yorker,* 25 May 1968.

This makes him aesthetically comic. Religiously he is tragic; for he is a hearer, not a doer of the word." However, "suddenly he goes mad, i.e., he sets out to become what he admires. Aesthetically this looks like pride; in fact, religiously, it is a conversion, an act of faith, a taking up of his cross."[51]

The second Kierkegaardian strand in Auden's interpretation is the antithesis of faith and despair, which is invoked to explain how Don Quixote can persist in his illusion despite his constant misfortunes. On the one hand, "People are tempted to lose faith (a) when it fails to bring worldly success, (b) when the evidence of their senses and feelings seem against it." On the other hand, "Don Quixote (a) is constantly defeated yet persists, (b) between his fits of madness sees that the windmills are not giants but windmills, etc., yet, instead of despairing, says, 'Those cursed magicians delude me' " (91).

Third, in distinguishing Don Quixote from epic heroes, Auden adopts the concept of the knight of faith from *Fear and Trembling:* Don Quixote "uses the language of the epic hero, but reveals himself to us as the Knight of Faith, whose kingdom is not of this world" (93).

Finally, the concept of irony, so pervasive in Kierkegaard's thought, furnishes Auden with his titular notion of "the ironic hero." Through this phrase, Auden means to allude to two things: his assumption that the Christian saint, with whom he equates Don Quixote, "is ironically related to suffering" (89); and the "ironic vision," which transforms the saint into "a Don Quixote" (94).

Despite Kierkegaard's impact on Auden's overall approach to the *Quixote,* Auden's reaction to the ending of the novel is the very opposite of Kierkegaard's. Whereas Kierkegaard, as noted earlier, objects to Don Quixote's repossession of sanity and suggests that the knight's adventures should continue endlessly, Auden contends: "However many further adventures one may care to invent for Don Quixote—and, as in all cases of a true myth, they are potentially infinite—the conclusion can only be the one which Cervantes gives, namely, that he recovers his senses and dies" (93).

In "Balaam and the Ass," Auden surveys the master-servant relationship in literature and ranks the "harmonious" and "dialectical" relationship of Don Quixote and Sancho above the unharmonious one of Shakespeare's Prospero and Caliban, and the undialectical one of Tamino and Papageno in Mozart's *The Magic Flute,* as "the greatest of spirit-nature pairs and the most orthodox." For Auden, "both they and their relationship are comic; Don Quixote is

51. "The Ironic Hero: Some Reflections on Don Quixote," *Horizon* 20 (1949): 86–94; here 89.

comically mad, Sancho Panza is comically sane, and each finds the other a lovable figure of fun, an endless source of diversion." Consistent with Kierkegaard, and anticipating Nigg, Auden links the *Quixote's* comic dimension to what he regards as its essentially Christian nature: "The man who takes seriously the command of Christ to take up his cross and follow Him must, if he is serious, see himself as a comic figure, for he is not the Christ, only an ordinary man, yet he believes that the command, 'Be ye perfect,' is seriously addressed to himself."[52] Like Kierkegaard, for whom the discrepancy between Don Quixote and his world epitomizes comic contradiction, Auden claims:

> If someone, for instance, were to let his hair and beard grow till he looked like some popular pious picture of Christ, put on a white linen robe and ride to town on a donkey, we should know at once that he was either a madman or a fake. At first sight Don Quixote's madness seems to be of this kind. He believes that the world of the Romances is the real world and that, to be a knight-errant, all he has to do is imitate the Romances exactly. (262)

Auden's comparison of Don Quixote to someone whom we would recognize on the street as a "mad" would-be Christ, or "fake" Christ, should be distinguished from the analogies that Kierkegaard said would exist between Don Quixote and Christ if the latter were to appear in the modern secular world. The contradiction inherent in Auden's fake Christ is that the fake is trying to be someone he is not, whereas the contradiction in Kierkegaard's true Christ in the modern world is that he would be historically and existentially out of place. Auden admits that the comparison of Don Quixote and the fake Christ is not wholly accurate as it does not take into account Don Quixote's self-conception. Rather than to view the knight's insanity as symptomatic of a fake, Auden construes it as "holy madness," reasoning that "amour-propre has nothing to do with his delusions" (262).[53] Juxtaposed with Don Quixote the "holy" madman is Sancho the "holy" realist, and it is only their companionship that makes the knight's madness "Christian":

---

52. "Balaam and the Ass: The Master-Servant Relationship in Literature," *Thought* 29 (1954): 237–70; here 261.

53. This last point is disputable. One could attribute self-love to Don Quixote on the basis of his repeated boasts of strength and courage, and his apparent notion that his chastity is constantly threatened by admiring ladies. Some critics have even construed him as a megalomaniac.

Don Quixote's lack of illusions about his own powers is a sign that his madness is not worldly but holy, a forsaking of the world to follow, but without Sancho Panza it would not be Christian. For his madness to be Christian, he must have a neighbor, someone other than himself about whom he has no delusions but loves as himself. (264)

After Auden, symptoms and elements of the religious trend appear in some works on the *Quixote* written by other authors in English during the period from the 1950s through the 1970s. For example, Vladimir Nabokov, lecturing at Harvard in the spring of 1952, expressed a disdain of the *Quixote* as a work of art, but appreciated "the pathetic, poignant, divine element which radiates from Don Quixote" (*Lectures,* 42). And Robert M. Adams, whose essay "Two Lines from Cervantes" (1958) examines the influence of the *Quixote* on Flaubert and Stendhal, agrees with Nigg's view of Don Quixote as a holy fool. As Nigg ponders the "rationally unexplainable paradox" of the knight's being "foolish and exemplary at the same time" (*töricht und vorbildlich zugleich*) (*Der christliche Narr,* 240), so Adams perceives in him "the paradox of the Divine Simpleton, who, because he knows nothing of the world's complexities, is all the more fitted to bring Christ's simplicity to the absurd, the hopeless test of action and practice" (*Strains of Discord,* 78–79).

The examination of Don Quixote as a holy fool is taken up again by the Swiss Catholic theologian Hans Urs von Balthasar as part of his "Ästhetik der Transzendentalen Vernunft" (Aesthetic of transcendental judgment) in the third and last tome (1965) of his monumental opus on theological aesthetics, *Herrlichkeit* (1961–), known in English as *The Glory of the Lord: A Theological Aesthetics* (1982–). Von Balthasar's chapter on "Narrentum und Herrlichkeit" (Foolishness and God's Glory) places Cervantes in the company of Symeon, Andreas, Jacopone da Todi, François Villon, Johannes von Tepl, Wolfram, Erasmus, Grimmelshausen, Dostoevsky, and Rouault — four of whom were discussed by Nigg, on whose work von Balthasar draws considerably. The latter's analysis of the *Quixote* is significant not so much for its approaching the knight as a Christ-like holy fool (that approach is not new), as for its assimilating the discussion of the knight into the vast enterprise of a systematic, Roman Catholic exploration of theological-philosophical aesthetics:

[Don Quixote's] madness is the closing of the abyss [*Kluft*] between the "ideal" of God's salvation in Christ and the "reality" of the earthly,

allegedly world-transforming achievement of Christ; the abyss, which
Don Quixote, in his "naive" faith and in his well-meaning action, sees
bridged, gapes open, ridiculously evident for everyone, precisely in the
face of his destiny and his lack of success. Don Quixote thus becomes
the true patron saint (*Schutzpatron*) of Catholic action; even more,
he is one of those Catholic theologians neglected because of his
dogmatism, which can be construed as Catholic only with and through
humor.[54]

Though von Balthasar's discussion of Cervantes has been generally neglected
by *Quixote* critics, he was by no means the last author to view the Manchegan
knight in a religious light, or specifically as a holy fool associated with religious
paradox. An accordant interpretation crops up in Serrano-Plaja's *"Magic"*
Realism in Cervantes (Spanish, 1967; English trans., 1970), which attempts
to examine the *Quixote* "through" (*desde*) *Tom Sawyer* and *The Idiot.*
Serrano-Plaja compares Don Quixote and Myshkin as exemplars of the sort of
childlike innocence espoused by Christ, and, in reference to "that most bitter of
endings of the First Part" of the *Quixote,* he denies that "there is any doubt
about Cervantes' intention of alluding, in some way, to the Passion of Our
Lord: such is the sarcasm and contempt with which he makes Don Quixote
enter his village" (*"Magic" Realism,* 129). Even closer to the views of Nigg
and von Balthasar is the one expressed by Frederick R. Karl in his study
(1974) of the eighteenth-century English novel as an "adversarial" genre that
grew out of the *Quixote;* Karl characterizes the knight as "one of [God's]
fools, a lunatic or madman with his own particular wisdom, and therefore a
danger to a normative society" (*Adversary Literature,* 61). For Karl, Don
Quixote's role in the lion adventure falls in a direct line of descent from
Christ and the Christian martyrs (see 63–64). Taking the deification a step
further, William Byron in his biography (1978) of Cervantes asserts that the
Quixote is held together by the knight's refusal "to face what Cervantes saw as
the basic contradiction of human effort: man may not be God. To presume to
try is madness. Yet he is impelled to usurp God's function by the God within

54. *Herrlichkeit: Eine theologische Ästhetik* (Einsiedeln: Johannes, 1961–), vol. 3, pt. 1: *Im
Raum der Metaphysik* (1965), pt. 2 ("Auswirkungen"), division B ("Ästhetik der Transzendentalen
Vernunft"), chap. 3 ("Narrentum und Herrlichkeit"), section e ("Die Lächerlichkeit und die
Gnade. *Cervantes*"), 517–28. The translation of this portion will be included in the fifth volume
of the projected seven-volume edition of *The Glory of the Lord: A Theological Aesthetics* (San
Francisco, Calif.: Ignatius, 1982–), 7 vols., which is not yet complete.

him" (*Cervantes,* 425). If Don Quixote cannot be God, he and Sancho nevertheless are linked in a way that is analogous to the Christ-Peter relationship, and "come to form a single whole in our minds, as the human and divine identities coincide in the figure of Christ" (428).

In addition to the strictly critical works from the post-World War II period that discuss Don Quixote and Sancho in religious terms, there are religiously suggestive fictional transformations of that pair: for example, the spiritually expectant but ultimately despairing tramps, Vladimir and Estragon, in Samuel Beckett's drama *En Attendant Godot* (premiere 1953); the figure of St. Francis, who combines fanaticism and gentleness, and Brother Leo, who is practical and dull-witted, in Kazantzakis's novel *Saint Francis* (Greek, 1956; English trans., 1962); and the idealistic radio and television editor, Anton Schmitz, and his practical-minded friend, Peter Scheel, who are depicted at one point as Christ and Peter, and at another as Don Quixote and Sancho, in Paul Schallück's novel *Don Quichotte in Köln* (1967, Don Quixote in Cologne).[55]

The most obvious exegetical contribution to the religious trend in *Quixote* criticism from the past decade is Rielo's *Teoría del Quijote.* Anticipated by Pierre Groult's essay "Don Quijote místico" (1954),[56] not to mention Unamuno, Rielo examines the text's affinities with the Spanish mystical tradition, and the "equations" of Don Quixote = Christ, and Dulcinea = Mary. An awareness of what Rielo calls the knight's "christification" (*cristificación,* in *Teoría,* 135) also informs Robertson Davies's entry, "The Novel as Secular Literature," in Eliade's *The Encyclopedia of Religion* (1987), which says of Don Quixote: "We love him, because his folly is Christlike, his victory is not of this world" (8:575–80; here 576). This most recent critical inscription of the religious trend would apply just as well to the knight's latest religious transformation in fiction, a case where sanctification becomes ordination: *Monsignor Quixote.*

55. See Frederick A. Busi, " 'Waiting for Godot': A Modern 'Don Quixote'?" *Hispania* 57 (1974):876–85; Jo Anne Englebert, "A Sancho for Saint Francis," *Hispania* 46 (1963):287–89; Alan Frank Keele, *Paul Schallück and the Post-War German Don Quixote: A Case-History Prolegomenon to the Literature of the Federal Republic* (Bern: Herbert Lang, 1976).

56. In *Estudios dedicados a Menéndez Pidal* (Madrid: CSIC, Patronato M. Menéndez y Pelayo, 1954), 231–51.

6

Don Quixote's Religious Transformation in Monsignor Quixote

The momentous religious implications of *Monsignor Quixote* do not arise wholly from its relation to the *Quixote*. Its double theme, the comedy of the true Christian in an unchristian world, and the conflict of faith and doubt, crystallizes the sanctifying tendencies in *Quixote* criticism which find their origins in Kierkegaard and Dostoevsky, and reflects the impact of Unamuno's interpretation on Greene. However, this is not to deny that another priest comparable to the knight appears in an earlier novel of Greene's, one he wrote long before he was impressed by Unamuno: the whiskey priest in *The Power and the Glory* (1940) is, as Theodore Ziolkowski puts it, obsessed by the "quixotic ambition of being the sole representative of the Church in an otherwise godless state (*Fictional Transfigurations,* 286). Nor is it to be denied that the central theological concern that *Monsignor Quixote* shares with Unamuno (the concern with faith, doubt, and their interrelationship) was not new to Greene when he came under Unamuno's sway in the early 1960s. In his autobiography (1980), Greene recalls having begun his struggle with these problems more than a decade earlier.[1]

According to Greene, it was *after* he wrote *A Burnt-Out Case* (1960) that he first read *The Tragic Sense,* where he found "the same distrust of theology" he had already portrayed in two of his characters, the titular protagonist of "A Visit of Morin" (1957) and Querry, the hero of *A Burnt-Out Case.* He had read Unamuno's *The Life of Don Quixote and Sancho* thirty years before "with no particular interest—it left no memories. But perhaps the book which I so quickly forgot had continued to work its way through the cellars of the unconscious," with the result that "I found myself, in 'A Visit to Morin' and *A Burnt-Out Case,* in that tragicomic region of La Mancha where I expect to stay" (231). Greene's vision of Don Quixote's world as a "tragicomic region" was undoubtedly encouraged by the closing chapter of *The Tragic Sense,* "Don Quixote in the Contemporary European Tragicomedy," which discusses the knight's plight as a "comic" and "irrational tragedy."

The thematic bearing of Unamuno, Kierkegaard, and Dostoevsky on *Monsignor Quixote* cannot be overemphasized. On one level, the comedy of the true Christian in an unchristian world, a Kierkegaardian theme analogous to that of "The Grand Inquisitor," evolves through Father Quixote's increasing identification with his "ancestor" as his thoughts, beliefs, and actions bring him into constant conflict with the political and ecclesiastical establishment. On another level, the dialogue between the priest and his Sancho-like companion, the mayor, over faith and doubt, belief and uncertainty, gradually elicits the Unamunian paradox that doubt is essential to faith.

The following analysis is divided into three sections focused on (1) *Monsignor Quixote*'s correspondence to the *Quixote,* especially in its presentation of the quixotic priest and the sanchopanzaesque mayor; (2) the thematic continuity of Greene's novel with Kierkegaard's concept of the true Christian, and with Karamazov's portrayal of Christ in "The Grand Inquisitor"; and (3) Unamuno's influence on the novel's theme of faith and doubt.

---

1. *Ways of Escape* (1980; New York: Washington Square, 1982), 226–27.

Analysis of the Text

At the opening of *Monsignor Quixote,* which like the *Quixote* has two parts, we learn of the peculiar problem presented by Father Quixote, the parish priest of El Toboso: he believes himself to be a descendant of Don Quixote, and drives a dilapidated Fiat that he calls Rocinante to commemorate his ancestor's horse. This issue is raised by Father Quixote's local bishop, whose moral condemnation of the *Quixote* corresponds to the disparaging views expressed by some of the characters in that novel toward chivalry books:

> "How can he be descended from a fictional character?" he had demanded in a private conversation which had been promptly reported to Father Quixote.
>
> The man to whom the bishop had spoken asked with surprise, "A *fictional* character?"
>
> "A character in a novel by an overrated writer called Cervantes—a novel moreover with many disgusting passages which in the days of the Generalissimo would not even have passed the censor."[2]

Greene's plot is set in motion by a genial Italian ecclesiastic whose Mercedes happens to break down in front of Father Quixote's house, and whom the latter kindly invites in for dinner. Unlike Father Quixote's bishop, who admitted he "never got beyond the first chapter" of the *Quixote* (170), this bishop of Motopo evidently knows well and admires the novel. When Father Quixote goes outside to fix the bishop's car and then returns, he finds his guest leafing through "a copy of Cervantes' work which Father Quixote had bought when he was a boy, and he was smiling over a page as Father Quixote's own bishop would certainly not have done" (24). Touched by the priest's charitableness, the bishop on departing exhorts him to emulate his ancestor in service of the church:

> "We are here to bring sinners to repentance and there are more sinners among the bourgeois than among peasants. I would like you to go forth like your ancestor Don Quixote on the high roads of the world...."

2. *Monsignor Quixote* (New York: Simon and Schuster, 1982), 16. All quotations are from this edition.

"He was a madman, monsignor."

"So many said of Saint Ignatius. . . . "

"He was a fiction, my bishop says, in the mind of a writer. . . . "

"Perhaps we are all fictions, father, in the mind of God."

"Do you want me to tilt at windmills?"

"It was only by tilting at windmills that Don Quixote found the truth on his deathbed," and the bishop . . . intoned in Gregorian accents, " 'There are no birds this year in last year's nests.' " (25-26)

This exchange contains the first signs of Unamuno's influence, with the bishop serving as a mouthpiece for the philosopher's views. The bishop's comparison of Don Quixote to Ignatius falls in line with parallels drawn between them in Unamuno's commentary, and his suggestion that humans are "fictions" in God's mind plays on Unamuno's notion that all existence is a dream dreamed by God (see *Life of Don Quixote,* 2:74; *Our Lord Don Quixote,* 319-20)—a notion derived from Calderón de la Barca's philosophical drama *La vida es sueño* (1635). By the same token the bishop's affirmation that the knight had to tilt at windmills to find the truth agrees with Unamuno's conviction that "Truth," as symbolized by Don Quixote, "is that which, after moving us to act in one way or another, makes the result conform to our intent."[3] Finally, in quoting Don Quixote's cryptic deathbed utterance about "no birds this year in last year's nests," the bishop invokes a line that Unamuno compares at length to certain passages from the Calderón play, Pedro de Ribadeneira's life of Ignatius (Latin, 1572; Castilian, 1583), and St. Teresa of Jesus (*Life of Don Quixote,* 2:74; *Our Lord Don Quixote,* 314-16).

The import of that quotation is not implied until many weeks after the bishop's visit. Informed that he has been promoted by the Vatican to the rank of monsignor upon the bishop's recommendation, Father Quixote plans to travel with his friend the mayor to Madrid in order to purchase there the purple socks and bib that symbolize his new office. But he is uneasy about leaving El Toboso, and one night dreams that "he had been climbing a high tree and he had dislodged a nest, empty and dry and brittle, the relic of a year gone by" (37). The oneiric allusion to his ancestor's deathbed utterance portends that Father Quixote will precariously ("climbing a high tree") assume

3. *Life of Don Quixote,* 1:31; *Our Lord Don Quixote,* 129. Cf. 1:50, 154; 2:40-43, 221; 2:58, 257-58.

for himself ("dislodge") the legacy of his renowned ancestor ("the relic of a year gone by").

Correspondences between the priest and the hidalgo present themselves in the opening pages of their stories. Like that unmarried gentleman, Father Quixote lives alone with a housekeeper, Teresa, whose sassiness is reminiscent of some of Cervantes's peasant women. The priest's parlor, where he keeps "his missal, his breviary, the New Testament, a few tattered volumes of a theological kind, the relics of his studies, and some works by his favorite saints" (18), is a counterpart to his ancestor's reading room. And the disclosure that the priest has spent all his life in El Toboso, except during his studies for the priesthood, recalls the isolated, provincial life-style of the hidalgo before he went mad and took up chivalry.

Two developments allow for the priest's character to undergo a change that makes him become more and more like the *mad* Don Quixote after his transformation: the unexpected visit of the Italian bishop, and the priest's friendship with the communist ex-mayor of El Toboso, whom he calls Sancho. The bishop, in exhorting him to set forth into the world like his ancestor, and later recommending his promotion to monsignor, is the prime mover behind the priest's transformation. But the bishop never reappears after departing, and the mayor becomes the catalyst to Father Quixote's identification with his ancestor.

As it would make perfect sense for a Marxist to regard a representative of the Catholic church (or any other religious institution) as quixotic, so the communist mayor delights in linking Father Quixote to the famous knight. We are told that after the priest once inadvertently aided the escape of some of Franco's imprisoned enemies through an act of charity, the mayor "clapped him on the back and called him a worthy descendant of his great ancestor who had released the galley slaves" (28). The mayor now continues to draw such analogies; early on he likens Father Quixote's favorite religious reading material to the Don's anachronistic books, and the priest resists the comparison:

> "You know, father, you remind me of your ancestor. He believed in all those books of chivalry, quite out of date even in his day. . . . "
> "I've never read a book of chivalry in my life."
> "But you continue to read those old books of theology. They are

your books of chivalry. You believe in them just as much as he did in his books."

"But the voice of the Church doesn't date, Sancho."

"Oh yes, father, it does. Your second Vatican Council put even Saint John out of date." (34)

When the mayor observes that Father Quixote no longer quotes at the end of the mass the line from Saint John that he used to cite (" 'He was in the world and the world was made by Him and the world knew Him not' " [34]), the priest protests:

"I still say those words."

"But you don't say them aloud. Your bishop wouldn't allow it. You are like your ancestor who read his books of chivalry secretly so that only his niece and his doctor knew until—"

"What a lot of nonsense you talk, Sancho."

"—until he broke away on Rocinante to do his deeds of chivalry in a world that didn't believe in those old stories."

"Accompanied by an ignorant man called Sancho," Father Quixote replied with a touch of anger which he immediately regretted. (35)

That the mayor is the one to propose that they take a trip together reverses the roles of their Cervantine counterparts. Don Quixote lured Sancho along on his journeys by promising him the governorship of an island. In contrast, Father Quixote is reluctant to go on a trip. Concerned about their ideological differences, he asks the mayor:

"You still believe in our travels? I doubt very much whether we are the right companions, you and I. A big gulf separates us, Sancho."

"A big gulf separated your ancestor from the one you call mine, father, and yet...." (36)

It becomes apparent that the mayor has catalyzed in Father Quixote a sense of spiritual kinship with his ancestor. Despite his earlier resistance to the mayor's analogy between the books that he and Don Quixote read, Father Quixote uses that same analogy in conversing with Father Herrera, the cocky young priest dispatched by the local bishop to look after El Toboso in Father Quixote's absence. Herrera, who recently received his doctorate in moral theology from the University of Salamanca, is Greene's replica of Cervantes's bachelor Sansón Carrasco, a divinity graduate of that same institution. As they discuss moral theology, the younger priest notices a copy of Heribert Jone's *Moral Theology* on his host's shelf and indicates his approval of that stodgy German theologian by asserting that a priest's "instinct" in parish work "must have a sound basis." Father Quixote replies:

> "Yes. But like my ancestor, perhaps I put my trust most in old books written before Jone was born."
> "But your ancestor's books were only ones of chivalry, surely?"
> "Well, perhaps mine—in their way—are chivalry too. Saint John of the Cross, Saint Teresa, Saint Francis de Sales. And the Gospels, father. 'Let us go up to Jerusalem and die with Him.' Don Quixote could not have put it better than Saint Thomas." (39–40)

Father Quixote's appeal to this analogy betrays his sense of spiritual kinship to his ancestor. Both Don Quixote, as imitator of Amadís, and Father Quixote, as follower of Christ ("Let us . . . die with Him"), lead lives that seem contradictory, comical, or even "mad" in their own ages. Thus the priest is known to celebrate the early-morning Mass "in an empty church" (19).

Father Quixote's feeling of affinity with his ancestor betrays itself again on the day of their departure. To his declaration that he "can't afford to waste money on purple socks" at Madrid, the mayor responds with another analogy:

> "Your ancestor had a proper respect for the uniform of a knight errant, even though he had to put up with a barber's basin for a helmet. You are a monsignor errant and you must wear purple socks."
> "They say my ancestor was mad. They will say the same of me. I will be brought back in disgrace. Indeed I must be a little mad, for I am mocked with the title of monsignor and I am leaving El Toboso in charge of that young priest." (41)

Father Quixote's sense that his monsignorial title is a mockery accounts for why he has already asked Herrera not to call him by it (see 39). Like his ancestor, who sometimes questioned his own worthiness as a knight, Father Quixote will say: "I think—perhaps—I am unworthy to be a priest" (50), and "I am unworthy to be called your monsignor" (61).

As soon as the two protagonists are on the road, more correspondences emerge between them and their Cervantine prototypes. Sancho Panza's gluttony is recalled in the mayor's complaints: "I am hungry and thirsty," and "If only we could find an inn" (44). Later, he draws another analogy between Father Quixote and Don Quixote by invoking Marx's idea of religion as the people's opiate: "Ah, you indulge too much, father, in a dangerous drug—as dangerous as the old Don's books of chivalry" (48).

While representing a *conjunctio oppositorum,* Father Quixote's relationship with the mayor does not simply polarize Catholicism and communism, thesis and antithesis. As the aim of dialectics is synthesis, so a mutual and conciliatory understanding is the end toward which the dialogues between these two protagonists continually press. The priest dreams "of how their journey would go on and on—the dream of a deepening friendship and a profounder understanding, a reconciliation of their disparate faiths" (61). Their conversations evoke affinities between the original ideals of Catholicism and communism, ideals often obscured by the distorted and inimically opposed forms which they have taken in human history. In a way comparable to the so-called quixotization of the squire and sanchification of the knight, Father Quixote and the mayor lead each other to a conciliatory understanding of each other's faith.

This movement toward conciliation first becomes apparent while they are eating lunch beside a crumbling wall on which is painted a red hammer and sickle. When the priest laments, "I would have preferred a cross," the mayor reminds him that *both* symbols are "protests against injustice" (45). And when the priest counters with the claim that "One created tyranny, the other charity" (45), the mayor retorts that, for communism's Stalin, there has been Catholicism's Torquemada. Father Quixote later points out that Marx was not so hostile to religion as the mayor seems to think he was. When the mayor attacks Father Quixote's belief in God by invoking Marx's claim that "religion is the opium of the people," the priest contends: "But you take it out of context. . . . Just as our heretics have twisted the words of Our Lord" (48). He urges the mayor to recall Marx's defense of English monastic orders in *Das Kapital:* "Opium then was not an evil drug—laudanum was a tranquilizer, nothing worse. . . . Religion is the Valium of the poor—that was all he meant" (48). Shortly thereafter each of the two characters explains a particular tenet of his own theological or philosophical doctrine in a way that his companion can easily comprehend: Father Quixote explicates the Holy Trinity by using three wine bottles for illustration, while the mayor illustrates the concept of class struggle and the oppressiveness of bourgeois materialism by retelling the tale of the Prodigal Son in Marxist-Leninist terms.

The priest's quixotism comes to the fore upon their arrival at Madrid. While his communist companion (ironically) wishes to stay at the glittering Palace Hotel, the priest refuses, protesting that "I wouldn't feel comfortable here" (60). When they end up taking a room in a dingy old hostelry in a poorer section of the city, the priest's insistence on staying among the destitute smacks not only of Jesus, but also of Don Quixote, who stays at low-class inns that his insanity leads him to mistake for castles. This is even suggested by the mayor once they are alone in their gloomy room with no hot water. Fearing that they will have their throats cut in such a place, he tells the priest: "You are mad" (60). Later the mayor wakes Father Quixote from a brief siesta by announcing, "I am Sancho," and explains: "You have become a knight. We must find your sword, your spurs, your helmet—even if it is only a barber's basin" (61, 62). His facetious allusion is to the monsignorial socks and bib they must purchase for Father Quixote. Later, when their hostess at the hostelry demands that they record their intended destination on a piece of paper, the mayor tells the priest to write "Barcelona"—significantly, the farthest point from La Mancha reached by Don Quixote and Sancho.

From Madrid, the two companions head not toward Barcelona, but instead, at the mayor's urging, to the Valley of the Fallen, situated on the way westward toward Salamanca. While this itinerary differs markedly from Don Quixote's, their travel talk calls the *Quixote* constantly to mind. The mayor tells a tale about a rich man who arranges to take regular advantage of a loophole in Jone's *Moral Theology* that makes *coitus interruptus* permissible upon the intervention of a third party. The tale's content, to be sure, has nothing to do with the *Quixote;* the mayor wants to mock the book by Jone that Father Quixote has brought along. But formally, the tale serves as a hilarious analogue to the interpolated stories in the *Quixote*'s first part. And when, in reaction to the tale's irreverence, Father Quixote accuses the mayor of mocking him, the mayor compares him to the knight:

> "Remember what the canon said to your noble ancestor. 'Nor is it reasonable for a man like yourself, possessed of understanding, your

reputation and your talents, to accept all the extravagant absurdities in these ridiculous books of chivalry as really true.' "

The Mayor stopped speaking and glanced sideways at Father Quixote. He said, "Your face has certainly something in common with that of your ancestor. If I am Sancho you are surely the Monsignor of the Sorrowful Countenance." (76–77)

Another analogy suggested by the mayor soon follows, this one linking the priest with his ancestor's irrationalism:

> "Would you want to live in a wholly rational world?" Father Quixote asked. "What a dull world that would be."
> "There speaks your ancestor." (78)

That the two companions' friendship has begun to transcend their ideological differences becomes clear as they are eating another of their eucharistic lunches with wine beside the road. The mayor tries on Father Quixote's clerical collar, joking: "If I remember right, Sancho became governor of an island, and so with your help I will become a governor of souls" (82). A moment later he adds:

> "How odd, father, without your collar I would never take you for a priest and certainly not for a monsignor."
> "When his housekeeper took away his spear and stripped Don Quixote of his armor you would never have taken him for a knight errant. Only for a crazy old man. Give me back my collar, Sancho." (83)

Father Quixote and the mayor are interrupted and interrogated by two officers of the Guardia Civil who have been trailing them. In their comical stupidity, these officers, and others who appear later, resemble the unintelligent officers of the Holy Brotherhood who pursue the knight and squire in the *Quixote*. When the officers finally depart the mayor casts the incident in a Cervantine light by describing the Guardia as "windmills" that they have "conquered," since "The Guardia revolve with every wind" (91).

Through the mayor's analogies Father Quixote has been forced to imagine himself in the light of his ancestor's mad persona: he has his own books of chivalry (theology books); his own knightly accouterments (clerical socks and bib); his own Dulcinea (St. Teresa); and had his own adventure with "windmills" (the Guardia), which was, as its counterpart was for the knight, his first adventure with a squire (the mayor). The mayor continues fostering the priest's sense of spiritual kinship to Don Quixote during their brief stop in Arévalo. Noticing some torn circus posters that picture a huge wrestler named "El Tigre," the mayor assures the priest:

> "We shall have our adventures on the road, father, much as your ancestor did. We have already battled with windmills and we have only missed by a week or two an adventure with the Tiger. He would probably have proved as tame when challenged as your ancestor found the lion."
>
> "But I am not Don Quixote, Sancho. I would be afraid to challenge a man of such a size."
>
> "You underrate yourself, father. Your faith is your spear. If the Tiger had dared to say something derogatory of your beloved Dulcinea. . . . "
> (96)

The mayor's last line will prove prophetic when Father Quixote later tries to block a church procession that blasphemes the image of the Holy Virgin.

Unamuno and his relation to Don Quixote are discussed when the two companions cross the river Tormes into Salamanca, where the philosopher taught as a university professor. The mayor, we learn, studied there as a youth because his parents wanted him to be a priest. Their visit to the university's campus and the square outside the house where Unamuno died occasions his revelation that he studied for two years with the philosopher. Gazing at the imposing statue of Unamuno in the square, the mayor remarks to Father Quixote: "You know how he loved your ancestor and studied his life" (98).

In the remaining episodes of part 1, Father Quixote's naïveté and the contradiction between his sacred profession and his profane circumstances reveal themselves in ways that link him to his ancestor. The first episode resembles the scene in the *Quixote* (1:2) where the knight arrives at an inn, mistakes it for a castle, and addresses two prostitutes as damsels. Father Quixote and the mayor lodge at a Salamanca brothel, which the priest finds "quiet and friendly" and mistakes for a "hotel" with a "truly welcoming" *patrona,* a "large staff of charming young women," and "real family atmosphere" (101). When, in his room, he marvels over the provision of "a foot-bath" (102), and mistakes one of the mayor's prophylactics for a balloon and playfully blows it up, we are again reminded of Don Quixote's tendency to misperceive reality.

The next day, the two companions pay tribute to Cervantes—as they already paid tribute to Unamuno—by traveling to Valladolid to visit the house where Cervantes completed the *Quixote.* Afterwards, Father Quixote suggests that the documented arrest of Cervantes on his false implication in a murder might have influenced his writing of the book. When he speculates that Cervantes's experience of imprisonment may account for the scene where Sancho Panza as governor lets a suspected criminal go free rather than imprisoning him, the mayor cynically observes that the contemporary Civil Guard lacks such leniency. Following this exchange, the priest, who knows that Don Quixote and his squire shared a great sympathy for criminals and prisoners, implies that the mayor's "prophet," Marx, had something in common with Don Quixote:

> "You know, I think my ancestor would have got on well with Marx. Poor Marx—he had his books of chivalry too that belonged to the past."
> "Marx was looking to the future."
> "Yes, but he was mourning all the time for the past—the past of his imagination." (108)

To illustrate his point, the priest quotes two passages from *The Communist Manifesto* regarding the spiritual vacuity of the modern bourgeoisie, and a strikingly similar remark from Don Quixote's speech to the goatherds about the degeneracy of the present Age of Iron (see Cohen translation, 108-9).

There ensue two episodes that place Father Quixote in profane circumstances that comically contradict the sacredness of his profession and make him seem particularly quixotic. First, he hears a stranger's confession in the men's room of a bar, with a toilet stall serving as the confessional. Second, he finds himself with the mayor in a theater watching a soft-core pornographic film, having been attracted by its innocent-sounding title, "A Maiden's Wish." Here again he betrays traits inherited from his ancestor: inexperience in the world ("I have never been to a cinema before" [121], he tells the mayor), and sexual innocence ("What a lot of exercise they were all taking" [122], he remarks of the copulating couples on the screen). We are reminded of Don Quixote's platonic nature as a lover when the priest confides that he has "never been troubled with sexual desires" (124).

It seems that the mayor now feels as deeply akin to Sancho Panza as the priest feels to Don Quixote. The protagonists stop in a field beside a river on their way to León because of the mayor's claim of having "great thirst," which proves to be "only a subterfuge to break the silence of Father Quixote which was getting badly on his nerves" (126). Like Sancho Panza, who rebels against the extended silences that his melancholy master tries to force him to maintain, the mayor grows impatient at the sight of "Father Quixote staring gloomily" (126) and chides him for it. The mayor then alludes to the original Sancho as his "ancestor" for the first time, and characterizes the contrast between his own Marxist materialism and the priest's lofty spirituality by describing Sancho and Leon Trotsky as analogues in opposition to Don Quixote (see 126–27). The mayor's identification with Sancho here is especially appropriate, given what happens next. Father Quixote informs him that he has hidden in the trunk of his car a wounded man who has been accused by the Guardia of robbery and murder and is fleeing arrest. The mayor's consternation at this matches that which Sancho expressed after his master liberated the galley slaves; like the squire, who worried that the guards whom Don Quixote chased away would report the incident to the Holy Brotherhood, who would pursue the culprits, the mayor warns the priest about the penalty of imprisonment "for hiding a fugitive from justice," and asks: "Whatever induced you . . . ?" (129). Invoking the knight's words, Father Quixote defends his deed by urging the mayor to recall

> " . . . what my ancestor told the galley-slaves before he released them, 'There is a God in heaven, who does not neglect to punish the wicked nor to reward the good, and it is not right that honorable men should be executioners of others.' That's good Christian doctrine." (130)

The conclusion of the episode is patterned after that of the galley-slave adventure. Before freeing the prisoners, Don Quixote listened to several of them give their own humorously modified accounts of their crimes. Likewise, the fugitive tells the priest and the mayor that the Guardia trumped up the charges against him. And just as the freed galley slaves stoned their liberator and his squire, robbed them and then fled, so the fugitive whom Father Quixote has concealed pulls a gun and robs him of his shoes.[4] He then forces the priest and the mayor to drive him to León, where he exits from the car and flees after threatening to kill them. "At least he didn't assault me," remarks Father Quixote afterwards, "like the galley-slaves assaulted my forebear" (133).

Two more developments in part 1 are directly analogous to the denouement of the *Quixote's* first part. As Don Quixote was pursued by the Holy Brotherhood for freeing the galley slaves, so Father Quixote is hunted by the Guardia, who suspect him (hilariously) of involvement with Basque separatists. And, as the priest and the barber enacted a plan to retrieve the knight from his mad adventures, so Father Quixote's bishop and Father Herrera, deeming the priest "mad" and worthy to "be shut in a madhouse to save the honor of the Church" (136), devise a strategy to bring him home.

When Father Quixote hears this news from his housekeeper over the phone and relates it to the mayor, the latter comes up with another analogy: "Well there's no harm in that. They thought your ancestor was mad too. Perhaps Father Herrera will behave like the canon and start burning your books" (137). The next time the mayor draws such an analogy, Father Quixote loses his temper. This occurs when the two stop to drink some wine on their way from León to Osera, where they hope to take refuge in a monastery. When the mayor jovially suggests that Father Quixote is a more suitable travel companion than Don Quixote must have been, as the priest, unlike the knight, enjoys wine, the priest snaps:

> "Why are you always saddling me with my ancestor?"
> "I was only comparing—"
> "You talk about him at every opportunity, you pretend that my

4. The parallel is unmistakable: just as we are told that the galley slaves "stripped him [Don Quixote] of a jacket . . . , and would have taken off his stockings too if his leg armour had not prevented them" (Miguel de Cervantes Saavedra, *Don Quixote,* trans. J. M. Cohen [Middlesex: Penguin, 1950; repr. 1978], 1:22, 180), so the fugitive in *Monsignor Quixote* tells the priest after taking the latter's shoes: "I'd take your pants too if they would only fit" (131). All quotations of the *Quixote* in Part III of this book are from this edition of Cohen's translation, which Greene acknowledges in the front of his novel. The colon separates the part and chapter numbers, which are followed by the page.

saints' books are like his books of chivalry, you compare our little adventures with his. Those Guardia were Guardia, not windmills. I am Father Quixote, and not Don Quixote. I tell you, I exist. . . . I go my way—my way—not his. I have free will. I am not tethered to an ancestor who has been dead these four hundred years." (141)

When the mayor tries to apologize, the priest complains: "Oh, I know what you think. You think my God is an illusion like the windmills. But He exists, I tell you. I don't just believe in Him. I touch Him" (141).

There are several ironies about Father Quixote's drunken outburst. Despite his claim, "I exist," his existence is no less fictional from the reader's vantage than is Don Quixote's. Despite his claim to a "free will" that distinguishes him from his ancestor ("I go my way—my way—not his"), the priest's character, journey, and adventures have been shown by the mayor's analogies to conform with the *Quixote*. And despite the priest's insistence that God "exists" because "I touch Him" (which paraphrases a claim made by an actual acquaintance of Greene's[5]), God seems as illusory as Don Quixote's fantasies to the mayor, who slyly asks: "Is he soft or hard?" (142).

Father Quixote's outburst betrays his awareness of the transformation he has undergone through his experiences with the mayor. After they reconcile themselves, the priest acknowledges the mayor's effect upon him: "You worry me, Sancho. Four days of your company worry me." Recalling some of their more humorous experiences together, he reflects: "El Toboso seems a hundred years away. I don't feel myself at all, Sancho. There's a giddiness" (142). When the mayor assures him that intoxication is not the sinful vice that Jone defines it as, the drunken priest utters: "You are my moral theologian, Sancho" (144).

Though the shift from part 1 to part 2 in *Monsignor Quixote* encompasses only a single night and morning, as opposed to the period of at least a month that passes between the *Quixote's* two parts, there are rough correspondences between these two transitions. At the opening of Greene's second part, the priest wakes up in bed at home in El Toboso, finding himself in the presence of his housekeeper and his kindly physician, Dr. Galván. He learns that the doctor

5. Greene has spoken of "a friend of mine, a Spanish priest with whom I go traveling every year," who, when asked to describe his own "absolute faith," replied—as quoted by Greene—"I do not believe in God, I touch Him" (Marie-Françoise Allain, "The Uneasy Catholicism of Graham Greene," *New York Times Book Review*, 3 April 1983, 1).

and Father Herrera, acting on a plan masterminded by his bishop, tracked him down on the previous night, injected him with a tranquilizer in his sleep, abducted him without waking the mayor, and brought him home—a stunt that recalls the forced retrieval of Don Quixote to his village by the priest and the barber at the end of Cervantes's first part. Father Quixote himself is aware that his predicament matches that of the knight:

> "My ancestor . . . was at least spared the bishop when the priest brought him home. And I prefer Dr. Galván to that stupid barber who told my ancestor all those tales about madmen. How could such stories of madmen have cured him if he had been really mad, which I don't for a moment believe. Oh well, . . . I don't think they will try to burn my books." (159)

In reversing the opinion he expressed earlier to the bishop of Motopo, the priest's denial that Don Quixote was "really" mad reveals that his journey with the mayor has nurtured in him a new sympathy toward his ancestor.

A clear sign of Father Quixote's changed character is his defiance toward his bishop when the latter accuses him of having jeopardized the church's dignity through unpriestly conduct during his journey. Father Quixote refutes the charge, and when the bishop insinuates that the mayor "led" him to think in "dangerous" ways, he retorts: "It wasn't that he *led* me, Excellency. He gave me the opportunity" (167). The bishop departs in a fury after announcing his refusal to "listen to the ravings of a sick mind" (168), that is, like Don Quixote's. The mayor promptly shows up in the priest's car—as Sancho Panza showed up at the house of his "recovering" master (*Quixote,* 2:2)—and together they flee from El Toboso, much as Don Quixote and Sancho fled into the Sierra Morena after the adventure of the galley slaves in order to escape the Holy Brotherhood. Alluding to Father Quixote's "grave crime" of hiding the fugitive from the Guardia, the mayor reminds him, "You've freed a galley-slave," and insists: "We have to get into the mountains" (178).

When the two protagonists stop to eat beside the road in the mountains, their conversation reveals that each of them now believes more in a particular ideal (Catholicism or communism) than in that ideal's historical agency (Rome or the party).

"It seems to me," he told the Mayor, "that you have more belief in Communism than in the Party."

"And I was just going to say almost the same, father, that you seem to have more belief in Catholicism than in Rome."

"Belief? Oh, belief. Perhaps you are right, Sancho. But perhaps it's not belief that really matters."

"What do you mean, father? I thought . . . "

"Did the Don really believe in Amadis of Gaul, Roland and all his heroes—or was it only that he believed in the virtues they stood for?" (179)

The priest's speculation about his ancestor helps explain why he no longer deems his ancestor mad: he now identifies not with the sane Alonso Quixano who "died in bed," but with the "mad" Don Quixote who "would have lived longer if he had stayed on the road" (184).

The chapter entitled "How Monsignor Quixote Had His Last Adventure Among the Mexicans" draws on two episodes from the *Quixote:* the visit to the house of the gentleman in green, and the adventure of the penitential procession. It is here that the knight's religious transformation culminates.

Upon entering Galicia, Father Quixote and the mayor go in search of good wine and find themselves in front of the secluded ramshackle home of a vineyard-owner whose name, Señor Diego, connects him to Don Diego de Miranda, the gentleman in green who entertained Don Quixote and Sancho at his house (*Quixote,* 2:18). Like Don Diego, Señor Diego lives in the country, and is even associated with the same pastoral color: his vineyard's "southern slopes were green with vines" (187). The man whom the priest and the mayor meet in front of a ramshackle house turns out to be a gerontic, world-weary version of the middle-aged gentleman in green: "An old man with great dignity," bearing "the sad and weary face of a man who has seen too much life for far too long" (190). No less hospitable than Don Diego, the melancholy old man immediately has his grandson serve them food and wine. Any reader familiar with the *Quixote* is bound to feel a strange sense of literary déjà vu when the old man requests his guests' names:

"I am very happy," Señor Diego said, "to welcome under this fig tree Monsignor . . . Monsignor . . . "

"Quixote," the Mayor said.

"Quixote? Not surely—"

"An unworthy descendant," Father Quixote interrupted him.

"And your friend?"

"As for myself," the Mayor said, "I cannot claim to be a true descendant of Sancho Panza . . . —but I can assure you that Monsignor Quixote and I have had some curious adventures. Even if they are not worthy to be compared . . . " (192)

As their feasting and conversing continue, another correspondence emerges. Matching Don Diego's expressed regret over his son's aspiration to be a poet, Señor Diego tearfully confides how sorry he is that his grandson became a priest. Nonetheless, like Don Diego, Señor Diego is an extremely reverential man. He and Father Quixote drink a toast "to the Holy Father and his Intentions," which leads to a dispute between Señor Diego and the mayor over the latter's refusal to join in:

"Surely even a Communist can toast the Holy Father's intentions?"

"Would you have toasted Stalin's intentions?" the Mayor demanded. "One can't know a man's intentions. . . . Do you think that the monsignor's ancestor really represented the chivalry of Spain? Oh, it may have been his intention, but we all make cruel parodies of what we intend." (194)

The mayor's outburst complements the one Father Quixote had near the end of part 1. As Father Quixote's outburst signified a crucial point in his spiritual transformation, which had been catalyzed by the mayor, so the priest now senses in the mayor's voice "a note of sadness and regret" that betrays "a form of despair, of surrender, or even perhaps of change. He thought for the first time: Where will this voyage of ours finally end?" (194).

This question anticipates the climax of the journey. After the mayor's outburst Señor Diego has his grandson inform his guests of a corrupt church celebration held in a nearby village, whose greedy priests "prey" on the superstitious poor and rich alike by auctioning the image of the Virgin Mary to the highest bidders, who in winning the right to carry her in the procession "believe they can buy their way into Heaven" (194-95). This information spurs

Father Quixote on to his final adventure. He bids adieu to Señor Diego, who, true to the generosity of his Cervantine namesake, sends them off with two cases of wine. Father Quixote drives with the mayor to the village to see for himself the blasphemous celebration. Upon their arrival he dons his clerical bib and collar, indicating his readiness to assume his ancestor's role: "We are going into battle, Sancho. I need my armor. Even if it is as absurd as Mambrino's helmet" (196).

The ensuing incident is modeled after the adventure with the penitents in the *Quixote* (1:52). As Don Quixote, against Sancho's objections, disrupted the procession of penitents whose image of the Virgin he mistook for an abducted lady, so Father Quixote, despite the mayor's protestations,[6] tries to block the church procession whose participants have blasphemed Mary's image by covering it with paper money. In the ruckus that follows, the priest announces himself as Monsignor Quixote of El Toboso, paraphrasing his ancestor's full title, Don Quixote of La Mancha, and just as Don Quixote was knocked unconscious by a head-blow dealt with a stick by one of the bearers of the Virgin's image, so Father Quixote's head is bloodied by a censer swung by one of the priests leading the procession.

Greene's final chapter is set at the Trappist monastery of Osera, where two new characters are introduced: Father Leopoldo, a Spanish monk who wants "to question everything, in the manner of Descartes, searching for an absolute truth" (205), and Professor Pilbeam, an American Hispanist from the University of Notre Dame, "perhaps the greatest living authority on the life and works of Ignatius Loyola" (205), who is doing research at the monastery's library. In the monastery's church this unlikely pair engages in a conversation that establishes the relevance of Ignatius, the exemplar of unquestioning religious faith, and Descartes, the spokesman for philosophical doubt, to the *Quixote*. When Pilbeam suggests that Ignatius was "a good soldier" who found "useful ways of suffering" (206), the monk contradicts him, citing Unamuno's comparison of the Spanish saint to Don Quixote:

6. This analogy between the mayor and Sancho Panza is made explicit as Father Quixote begins to approach the procession:

> "The Mayor . . . said, 'Come away, Father.'
> " 'No, Sancho.'
> " 'Don't do anything foolish.'
> " 'Oh, you are talking like that other Sancho, and I say to you as my ancestor said when he saw the giants and you said they were windmills—"If you are afraid go away and say our prayers." ' " (*Monsignor Quixote*, 198)

"I am not sure that Saint Ignatius was all that concerned with what was useful. A soldier can be very romantic. . . . All Spaniards are romantic, so that sometimes we take windmills for giants."

"Windmills?"

"You know that one of our great modern philosophers compared Saint Ignatius to Don Quixote. They had a lot in common."

"I haven't read Cervantes since I was a boy. Too fanciful for my taste. I haven't much time for fiction. Facts are what I like. . . . "

"Fact and fiction—they are not always easy to distinguish. As you are a Catholic . . . " (206–7)

Having broached the Cervantine theme of "fact and fiction," Leopoldo promptly links it to the question of faith. When the professor asks him what brought him to the monastery, he replies:

"I suppose Descartes brought me to the point where he brought himself—to faith. Fact or fiction—in the end you can't distinguish between them—you just have to choose."

"But to become a Trappist?"

"I think, you know, professor, that when one has to jump, it's so much safer to jump into deep water." (207)

Leopoldo, who has "taken a greater leap than Descartes" (205) by becoming a monk, and Pilbeam, who "decided long ago that [he] was not a jumper" (207), are promptly confronted by an incident to which they react in accordance with their different inclinations toward faith and doubt. Interrupted by the sound of an explosion and crash, they go out to find a small car smashed against the wall of the church, and a man with a bloody head who is yelling angrily at two armed officers of the Guardia while trying to free an unconscious priest from the driver's seat. When one of the officers announces that the two men are being arrested for causing a riot and stealing, Father Leopoldo protests:

"Nonsense. The man in the car is a monsignor. . . . What's your friend's name?" he asked the stranger.

"Monsignor Quixote."

"Quixote! Impossible," Professor Pilbeam said.
"Monsignor Quixote of El Toboso. A descendant of the great Don Quixote himself."
"Don Quixote had no descendants. How could he? He's a fictional character."
"Fact and fiction again, professor. So difficult to distinguish," Father Leopoldo said. (209)

What happens next strangely inverts the pattern of the *Quixote*'s final scene. Whereas Don Quixote regains his sanity and becomes Alonso Quixano, Father Quixote lapses into delusion in a bed at the monastery and assumes a role analogous to that of the mad knight. After sleeping deeply under a doctor's sedative, the priest awakes momentarily in the presence of the monk, the professor, and the mayor, thinking that he is at home in El Toboso. Addressing the monk, whom he mistakes for Doctor Galván, he expresses his fear that Father Herrera might be burning his books. When he again awakes he mutters a cryptic monologue mixing references to some of his theology books, remonstrations aimed at his bishop, and an allusion to the *Quixote:* "Mambrino's helmet. Give it me" (213). Moments later the delusive priest wanders to the church, where he goes to the altar and—just as Don Quixote often spoke in the elevated, outdated dialect of his chivalry books—begins to recite a peculiarly abridged form of the old Latin Mass, which was abrogated by the Second Vatican Council. Accordingly, the curiosity expressed by many of the *Quixote*'s "sane" characters about the madman's state of mind, is matched by the inquisitive utterances of the monk and the professor: "Dreaming or delirium?" (213), "Sleep? Delirium? Madness?" (216).

The scene culminates when Father Quixote gives the Catholic Communion to the Marxist mayor with a nonexistent Host, addressing him as *Compañero* (the codeword of the Communist Party), while the mayor kneels and accepts the invisible Host on his tongue. This bizarre sacramental act, a symbolic bonding of the two protagonists' selves, is somewhat analogous to the knight's sanchification and the squire's quixotization in the *Quixote.* But while "Don Quixote's end came, after he had received all the sacraments" (Cohen trans., 2:74, 938), Father Quixote dies immediately after he *gives* the communional sacrament, leaving the mayor to wonder why "love, the love which he had begun to feel for Father Quixote, seemed now to live and grow in spite of the final separation and the final silence" (221).

Father Quixote, Kierkegaard's Christian, and Karamozov's Christ

Monsignor Quixote expresses a profound insight into the quixotism of true Christianity in the modern world, and thus accords with Kierkegaard's conception of the knight of faith, and Karamazov's portrayal of Christ in "The Grand Inquisitor": as Christ finds himself condemned in sixteenth-century Catholic Seville, so the true Christian, as Kierkegaard observed, would seem comically out of place in modern Christendom. For Dostoevsky (explicitly in his letter to Sofia, implicitly in his creation of Myshkin) and Kierkegaard (explicitly in his journals, implicitly in his conception of the knight of faith), Christ and the true Christian find an analogue in Don Quixote, who embodies a comical anachronism.

Father Quixote becomes commensurable with Karamazov's Christ and Kierkegaard's knight of faith upon the disclosure that his bishop once called him "a fool—a term which Christ had deprecated" (28), for inadvertently helping some incarcerated enemies of Franco to escape. Rebuked by such a high church official, Father Quixote resembles Karamazov's Christ, whom the Inquisitor condemns for having liberated mankind. In calling Father Quixote "a fool," the bishop is like the Inquisitor, who denigrates Christ's work as "madness." At the same time, the mayor praised Father Quixote for assisting the prisoners, calling him "a worthy descendant of his great ancestor who had released the galley slaves" (28). In that adventure the knight acts in what Kierkegaard would describe as a religious (as opposed to ethical) manner. Viewed as a knight of faith, Don Quixote engages in a teleological suspension of the ethical of the sort that Kierkegaard attributes to religious existence. In freeing the prisoners, he ignores the king's law of ethics, according to which criminals are to be punished by the government, and appeals instead to divine law, which holds that the wicked are punishable by God alone. As Unamuno points out, the sort of "abstract justice" represented by the guards is "based on cold theological arguments," and is therefore "repugnant to quixotic Christianity" (*Life of Don Quixote*, 1:22; *Our Lord Don Quixote*, 103–4).

The priest again associates himself with the galley-slave adventure when he helps the fugitive to avoid arrest by the Guardia. Father Quixote's action brings him and the mayor into conflict with the Guardia in the way that Don Quixote's action brought him and his squire into conflict with the Holy Brotherhood. While neither action can be properly called ethical, both are truly Christian. In justifying his action to the mayor, Father Quixote cites as "good Christian doctrine" his ancestor's statement to the galley slaves about "God in heaven, who does not neglect to punish the wicked nor to reward the good," and about the wrongfulness of men who become "executioners of others" (130).

Father Quixote's inclination toward the religious mode is also suggested by his special fondness for the books of Saints Teresa, John of the Cross, and Francis de Sales. Christian mysticism, especially the sort exemplified by these saints, places an emphasis on love and is not laden by moral or ethical dogma. This is precisely why Father Quixote is attracted to them. He at one point recalls what he used to do whenever he tired of teaching doctrinal concepts which he did not understand: "I went home and read my saints. They wrote of love. I could understand that. The other things didn't seem important" (142). The mystic's experience of rapture, ecstasy, and union with God would be inconceivable without divine love, but has little to do with the concept of God's justice, a chief category for any moralist or ethicist. Father Quixote betrays an aversion to Father Herrera's emphasis on the justice of God, reminding him that "another sound base is God's love" (40). Elsewhere Father Quixote alludes to God as "a loving parent" (68), and comes close to questioning the existence of Hell: "I believe [in Hell] from obedience, but not with the heart" (68). He concurs with another character's speculation that because "millions" die each moment, God must lack "the time to bother or to condemn" (157).

Father Quixote's preference for God's love over God's justice accords with Unamuno's repeated equations of God with love,[7] and underscores his own distaste for sterile moralism. To Father Herrera he admits his own weakness in moral theology: "Ah, I always found that a very difficult subject. I very nearly failed to pass" (39). He later makes the same admission to the mayor and the bishop (see 81, 167), and we learn that Augustine's *City of God* is one of his favorite "old books" because its author "was a sinner and a saint, . . . not a

7. See *Tragic Sense,* esp. chap. 8 ("From God to God"), 172–203.

moral theologian" (91). In contrast to Herrera, who, like Judge William of Kierkegaard's *Either/Or,* seems set in the ethical stage of existence, Father Quixote tends toward the religious, which transcends the moral and ethical and brings him to a closer, more personal relationship with God—hence his remark: "I touch Him."

In fact, there are compelling parallels between Father Quixote and the Christ of the Gospels. These begin to show themselves when he insists on staying overnight at a low-class hostelry in one of Madrid's poorer quarters rather than in the luxurious Palace Hotel favored by the mayor. That Father Quixote views the poor as his flock, as did Jesus, is clear when he reminds the mayor that the poor not only fall under the purview of Marxists, but "are my people too" (61). In Valladolid Father Quixote correlates himself with Christ when he thinks aloud upon realizing the true function of the place in which the mayor has them spending the night: "A monsignor in a brothel. Well, why not? Christ mixed with publicans and sinners" (104). This correlation anticipates the dream the mayor has on the night of the priest's abduction:

> He was searching for Father Quixote, who was lost. The Mayor . . . was worried because the mountainous path Father Quixote had taken was very rough for a man barefooted. Indeed, he came here and there on traces of blood. . . . Suddenly he emerged onto a great marble paving and there in front was the church of El Toboso from which strange sounds were coming. He went into the church, . . . and perched up on top of the altar like a sacred image was Father Quixote, and the congregation laughed and Father Quixote wept. (144)

Specific images from this dream—"the mountainous path," "a man barefooted," "traces of blood"—suggest Jesus' climbing of Calvary, and the comparison of Father Quixote to the "sacred image" and the laughter of the "congregation" place him in the role of the crucified and mocked Christ. When the mayor has this dream, he and Father Quixote have been on the road for four days, a number that suggests Christ's resurrection on the fourth day after his crucifixion. And just as Mary and the disciples did not know Jesus' whereabouts when they found his tomb empty, so the mayor, unaware of Father Quixote's abduction, is mystified the next morning when he discovers that the priest is gone.

Father Quixote soon finds himself in a situation that recalls Christ's predicament in "The Grand Inquisitor." Consistent with the tale's message that the true Christian is liable to seem mad and subversive to most people, especially to the high officials of the Catholic church, the theme of Greene's novel culminates in Father Quixote's encounter with his censorious bishop. A modern Inquisitor, the bishop reproves the errant priest for everything he did on his journey. The priest, in disputing the bishop's charge that he has been corrupted by the mayor, broaches the question of "freedom," and tries to articulate how he has benefited from the mayor's company:

> " . . . but on this holiday I have felt a freedom. . . . "
> "A very dangerous freedom it seems to have been."
> "But He gave it to us, didn't He—freedom? That was why they crucified Him."
> "Freedom," the bishop said. It was almost like an explosion. "Freedom to break the law? You, a monsignor? Freedom to go to pornographic films? Help murderers?" (167–68)

This passage repeats the pattern of Karamazov's tale, albeit in an altered way. Like the Inquisitor, who condemns Christ for *giving* freedom to mankind, the bishop reprimands Father Quixote for *accepting* that freedom. In calling that freedom "dangerous," the bishop accords with the Inquisitor, who, aligned with Satan, deems the Church's aim to be the enslavement of mankind.

Karamazov's tale is also pertinent to the Unamunian theme of faith and doubt in Greene's novel. The Inquisitor's argument that Christ, by miraculously descending from the cross, would have robbed mankind of the freedom inherent in faith, is borne out by Father Quixote's agony after his dream that Christ was rescued from the cross by a legion of angels. This dream, as we will see, leads the priest to his Unamunian conclusion that uncertainty and doubt are essential to faith.

Faith and Doubt: The Influence of Unamuno

Unamuno's influence on *Monsignor Quixote* is most obvious in its treatment of the theme of faith and doubt, belief and uncertainty. Greene once wrote that his aim in *A Burnt-Out Case* was "to give expression to various states or moods of belief and unbelief," so that one character (Father Thomas) represents "an unsettled form of belief," and another (Querry), "an unsettled form of disbelief" (*Ways of Escape,* 228). Likewise the twin protagonists of *Monsignor Quixote* represent specific modes of faith and doubt, finding their prototypes in Unamuno's interpretation of Don Quixote and Sancho Panza in *The Tragic Sense:* "Our Lord Don Quixote is the prototype of the vitalist whose faith is founded on uncertainty, and Sancho is the prototype of the rationalist who doubts his own reason" (133). This formula, which sums up Unamuno's *The Life of Don Quixote and Sancho* and illuminates the characterization of Greene's protagonists, must be understood in the context of Unamuno's voluntarist notion that "faith is in essence no more than a matter of will, not one of reason, just as to believe is to want to believe, and that to believe in God is to wish, above all and before all, that there may be a God" (*Tragic Sense,* 127).

In *Monsignor Quixote* the Unamunian paradox that faith thrives on uncertainty is introduced through the bishop of Motopo's attempt to explain to Father Quixote the reason we can never know why God created mosquitoes and fleas: "These are great mysteries. . . . Where would our faith be if there were no mysteries?" (23). That Father Quixote "believes" in Unamuno's voluntarist sense of that word (i.e., to believe is to *want* to believe) is apparent in his first conversation with the mayor, who charges:

> "All the same, you do believe in all that nonsense. God, the Trinity, the Immaculate Conception. . . . "
> "I *want* to believe. And I want others to believe." (32)

The priest's faith, like Don Quixote's, is clearly—in Unamuno's terms—"founded on uncertainty." As the mayor observes: "Belief dies away like desire for a woman. I doubt if you are an exception to the general rule" (33).

Consistent with Unamuno's view of Don Quixote, Father Quixote is led by his companion's constant queries to betray the uncertainty underlying his own faith. The mayor's suspicion that Father Quixote's faith is dying away is substantiated by the priest's failure to affirm the invulnerability of his faith. As they are driving to Madrid, the priest admits:

"We have just left La Mancha and nothing seems safe any more."

"Not even your faith?"

It was a question which Father Quixote did not bother to answer.
(43)

While Father Quixote struggles with his faith, the mayor is outspoken about his own disbelief in God. As attested by his willingness to "understand" but not "believe" (51) in the Holy Trinity, the mayor's rationalism accords with Unamuno's view of Sancho Panza as the "rationalist who doubts his own reason." That the mayor secretly doubts his reason, just as Father Quixote feels uncertain about his own faith, was suggested when they both admitted their vulnerability to "despair." Having answered affirmatively when the mayor questioned whether he hoped that the Catholic religion would ever "lead men to a happy future," the priest returned the question:

"Do you hope that Communism—I mean the real Communism your prophet Marx spoke about—will ever arrive, even in Russia?"

"Yes, father. I hope, I do hope. But it's true . . . I do sometimes despair."

"Oh, despair I understand. I know despair too, Sancho. Not final despair, of course."

"Mine isn't final either, father. Or I wouldn't be sitting here on the ground beside you."

"Where would you be?"

"I would be buried in unconsecrated ground. Like other suicides."

"Let us drink to hope then," Father Quixote said and raised his glass. They drank. (46)

This discussion revolves around Unamuno's basic notions of despair, suicide, and hope. As they were for Kierkegaard, despair and hope are crucial categories for Unamuno;[8] in his view, suicide results from the despairing victim's failure to find "motives and incentives for life and action" (142). However, seeing Don Quixote as a symbol of despair and hope, Unamuno holds that "it is despair and despair alone which engenders heroic hope, absurd hope, mad

8. See *Tragic Sense,* chap. 6 ("In the Depths of the Abyss"), 118–45; chap. 9 ("Faith, Hope, and Charity"), 204–35.

hope" (352). Despite the marked despair in Greene's priest and mayor,[9] their denials that theirs is a "final despair" suggests that they have found "motives and incentives for life and action." Father Quixote comes to realize that "sharing a sense of doubt can bring men together perhaps even more than sharing a faith" (55). It dawns on him that doubt is essential to faith. After he dreams of Christ being rescued from the cross by a legion of angels, he realizes that such an event, in proving beyond doubt that Christ was the Son of God, would have precluded the need for faith:

> It was only a dream, . . . but nonetheless Father Quixote had felt on waking the chill of despair felt by a man who realizes suddenly that he has taken up a profession which is of use to no one, who must continue to live in a kind of Saharan desert without doubt or faith, where everyone is certain that the same belief is true. He had found himself whispering, "God save me from such a belief." (70)

The idea that uncertainty is essential to faith preoccupies Father Quixote for the rest of the novel, and exposes the verso of the problem of faith that Holbein's picture of the dead Christ elicited for Myshkin and Ippolit: for Father Quixote, the thought of there being "no ambiguity" about Christ's divinity causes a "chill of despair," whereas for Myshkin and Ippolit, the grimly *un*ambiguous image of Christ's mortality destroyed the possibility for faith. In their next discussion of faith and doubt, after arguing that the mayor's faith in the future would be impossible for his great-great-grandson if communism were to arrive in the world by the latter's age (as "The future would be there before his eyes"), Father Quixote asks rhetorically: "Can a man live without faith?" (73). Although the mayor dodges this question, the expected negative answer finds support in Unamuno's claim that "Faith makes us live by showing us that life, though dependent on reason, has its wellspring and source of power outside itself, in something supernatural and miraculous" (*Tragic Sense,* 210).

Father Quixote applies his idea of the impossibility of faith without doubt to

9. Before Father Quixote's encounter with his bishop we are told: "He felt as though he had been touched by the wing-tip of the worst sin of all, despair" (*Monsignor Quixote,* 160). After the mayor's outburst at Señor Diego, in which Father Quixote senses "regret," we are told that the latter "had been accustomed to aggression from the Mayor . . . , but regret was surely a form of despair" (194).

the mayor's faith in Marxism by intimating that if all uncertainty about the theories of Marx and Lenin were ever eradicated, their writings would lose the value they hold for their believers:

"We can't always believe. Just having faith. Like you have, Sancho. Oh, Sancho, it's an awful thing not to have doubts. Suppose all Marx wrote was *proved* to be absolute truth, and Lenin's works too."
"I'd be glad, of course."
"I wonder." (73–74)

Unamuno's influence is again discernible when the priest defends his faith in the "fact" of Christ's resurrection in spite of its seeming absurdity:

"Whatever absurdities you can dig out of my books, I still have faith. . . . "
"In what?"
"In a historic fact. That Christ died on the Cross and rose again."
"The greatest absurdity of all."
"It's an absurd world or we wouldn't be here together." (77)

This affirmation of faith in the face of its absurdity falls in line with that tradition of Christian thinkers from Tertullian, through Kierkegaard, to Unamuno, who state their belief in Christ's resurrection precisely because that belief is absurd (see *Tragic Sense,* 82. Cf. 104, 116).

Despite his mockery of the priest's beliefs, the mayor admits that he himself "shared" such "superstitions" as a theology student at the University of Salamanca: "Is that why I seek your company now—to find my youth again, that youth when I half believed in your religion and everything was so complicated and contradictory—and interesting?" (81). The mayor recalls that he "still had a half belief" when he studied with Unamuno, a "professor with a half belief" (98), who "kept me in the Church for several years with that half belief of his which for a while I could share" (99). Father Quixote responds that the mayor's "complete belief" in Marx, for which the priest envies him, enables the mayor not to have to think for himself:

"There's only one thing you will ever lack—the dignity of despair," Father Quixote spoke with an unaccustomed anger—or was it, he wondered, envy?

"Have I complete belief?" Sancho asked. "Sometimes I wonder. The ghost of my professor haunts me. I dream I am sitting in his lecture room and he is reading to us from one of his own books. I hear him saying, 'There is a muffled voice, a voice of uncertainty which whispers in the ears of the believer. Who knows? Without this uncertainty how could we live?' "

"He wrote that?"

"Yes." (99)

Father Quixote clearly recognizes the affinity between the quandary to which he himself was led by his dream of Christ's rescue from the Cross ("Can a man live without faith?"), and the Unamunian problem that haunts the mayor ("Without this uncertainty how could we live?").

As Father Quixote's envy for the mayor stemmed from his having mistaken the mayor's uncertainty for utter belief, so the mayor now admits that he has envied the priest for the same unfounded reason. After telling him "You drew me to you because I thought you were the opposite of myself," the mayor confesses that he grew "tired" of himself and of all his Party comrades:

"We quoted Marx and Lenin to one another like passwords . . . , and we never spoke of the doubts which came to us on sleepless nights. I was drawn to you because I thought you were a man without doubts. I was drawn to you, I suppose, in a way by envy."

"How wrong you were, Sancho. I am riddled by doubts. I am sure of nothing, not even of the existence of God, but doubt is not treachery as you Communists seem to think. Doubt is human. Oh, I want to believe that it is all true—and that want is the only certain thing I feel. (180)

Not unlike the disbelieving Querry in *A Burnt-Out Case,* Father Quixote admits to always sensing "the shadow of disbelief haunting my belief" (173). But since his doubt does not negate his expressed will to believe, he exemplifies Unamuno's voluntarist form of belief. For Unamuno, nothing is worse than to believe with certainty. Accordingly, when the mayor tells Father Quixote that certainty "was the belief I thought you had" (180), the priest replies: "Oh no, Sancho, then perhaps I could have burnt my books and lived really alone, knowing that all was true. 'Knowing'? How terrible that might have been" (180-81).

In keeping with Unamuno's characterization of the knight and squire, Father Quixote's "faith" is revealed to be "founded on uncertainty," and the mayor proves to be a "rationalist who doubts his own reason." The dialogue between Father Leopoldo and Professor Pilbeam sets this theme against its sixteenth- and seventeenth-century background: Ignatius, in whom Pilbeam claims expertise, and Descartes, to whose thought Leopoldo devotes himself, are cited often by Unamuno as classic exemplars of faith and doubt. The dialogue also links this theme to the problem of fact and fiction. As Leopoldo points out to the professor, who refuses to believe that Father Quixote can be descended from a fictional figure, fact and fiction cannot be distinguished "with any certainty" (218). Implied is that one can be no more certain in differentiating fact and fiction than in opting for God or reason. When Pilbeam objects to Leopoldo's suggestion that the mayor could have received Communion from Father Quixote without the presence of actual bread or wine, the monk recasts the question of faith and doubt in the same way as did the bishop of Motopo. The latter asked, "Where would our faith be if there were no mysteries?"; the monk now wonders: "Do you think it's more difficult to turn empty air into wine than wine into blood? Can our limited senses decide a thing like that? We are faced by an infinite mystery" (220). The mayor, still struggling to retain his faith in Marxist rationalism, resists the monk's argument.

> The Mayor said, "I prefer to think there was no Host."
> "Why?"
> "Because once when I was young I partly believed in a God, and a little of that superstition still remains. I'm rather afraid of mystery, and I am too old to change my spots. I prefer Marx to mystery, father." (220)

Despite this claim, the mayor has changed, because the doubt instilled in him by the priest has cost him the illusion of "freedom" that Marxism once provided: "He wanted to feel free, but he had the sense that somewhere on the road from El Toboso he had lost his freedom. It's only human to doubt, Father Quixote had told him, but to doubt, he thought, is to lose the freedom of action" (220). Father Quixote's effect on the mayor adds a twist to the analogy between the priest and Karamazov's Christ as liberators; the priest has inverted the role of liberator insofar as he inadvertently caused the mayor to lose his freedom by teaching him that it is "human to doubt." Despite his association with Unamuno's image of Don Quixote, Father Quixote seems more a knight of doubt than a knight of faith. In the end, the twist given to Unamuno's view could not be more ironic: the mayor, instilled with doubt by Father Quixote, is left "fighting for a certainty" (221) after the priest's death, whereas Don Quixote's squire was—to repeat Unamuno's words—"left to replace" his deceased master, whose faith had been "stored up in Sancho."

Conclusion

The Quixotism
of
Religious Existence

It is frequently said that if Christ were to come again now he would once more be slain. This is perfectly true; but qualified more precisely, it would have to be added that he would be sentenced to death and slain because what he proclaimed was not Christianity *but a lunatic, wicked, blasphemous, misanthropic exaggeration and caricature of that gentle doctrine, Christianity, the true Christianity, which is found in Christendom and whose founder was Jesus Christ.*

—*Søren Kierkegaard*[1]

Most important is the unexamined assumption in most Western societies that there must be a "rational motive" for every human action—and that "God told him to do it" is not rational. When "it" refers to killing people, we all quickly agree. But that still leaves the question, Is Mother Teresa mentally ill?

—*Don Wycliff*[2]

Scholars and critics often call attention to the secularizing tendency of modern literature, and, within that literature, they note the numerous fictional transfigurations of Jesus on the one hand, and the innumerable literary descendants and clones of Don Quixote on the other. However, my study is the first to examine a lineage of characters in whom the images of the alleged savior and the mad knight are combined. While, as Kierkegaard never tired of stressing, contemporaneity with Christ was of no advantage to the first-century disciples, since faith is always a gift from beyond any earthly situation, the mixing of his image with Don Quixote's implies that Christ would find himself even more

1. Entry of 1850, *Journals*, 1:147–48.
2. "When Reason Blocks Out the Divine," *New York Times,* 21 July 1986, 16.

out of place and misunderstood if he were to appear in the modern world—a place where true adherence to his message can seem quixotic.

The question posed in our introduction was How and why did Don Quixote come to be seen by Fielding, Dostoevsky, and Greene as an appropriate model for depicting their religious paragons in *Joseph Andrews, The Idiot,* and *Monsignor Quixote?* It should now be clear that Don Quixote's sacred aura stems largely from the image of Christ latent in his character—an image that was not apparent to Cervantes's contemporaries, but revealed itself through an interpretive trend traceable from the sympathetic view of the knight in the eighteenth century, through the Romantic approach in the nineteenth century, to the religious interpretation in our own century. More specifically, the knight's adaptability as a vehicle for religious expression in these novels can be explained by Fielding's discernment of the knight's primitive Christian qualities (faith, innocence, charity, compassion, benevolence, good works); by Dostoevsky's appreciation of those same qualities in the knight, together with the latter's kenotic suffering, his tendency toward humiliation, and hence his comparability with Christ's "beauty"; and by Greene's recognition of the knight's bearing on the problem of faith and doubt, belief and uncertainty.

Certain interpretive tendencies were essential for conditioning these particular views. Had Fielding gone the same direction as Graves and other eighteenth-century opponents of religious fanaticism who passed Don Quixote off as an "enthusiast," rather than following the new trend of sympathetic readings of the *Quixote,* he would never have become aware of the knight's pertinence to his own latitudinarian ethic and notion of good nature. Had the exaltation and idealization of Don Quixote in the nineteenth century not coincided with the humanization and naturalization of Christ's image, Dostoevsky's comparison of the two figures would have been inconceivable. Had Greene not read Unamuno, whose writings on Don Quixote furnish the nexus between Kierkegaard and the religious trend in twentieth-century *Quixote* criticism, he might never have perceived the knight's bearing on the problem of faith and doubt.

It was Kierkegaard who first suggested that Christ, the apostles, and the earnest ascetic, were they to enter modern Christendom, would appear as "counterparts" to Don Quixote. This notion bears out our general supposition that the sanctification of Don Quixote in *Joseph Andrews, The Idiot,* and *Monsignor Quixote* reflects the struggle of religious faith and ideals in the modern world. Effected by the relentless encroachment of secularity and skepticism, the general decline of Western religious faith since the Renaissance is presaged in the *Quixote* by the diminishment of the knight's faith in his illusions under the constant challenges of reality and reason, and reduplicated through his sanctification in Adams, Myshkin, and Father Quixote.

Along with a descending line that might be drawn to follow the progressive questioning of God's existence since the eighteenth century, we could draw a line tracing a decline of faith exemplified by those three characters. Chronologically, our line would begin with Abraham Adams, who, like the patriarch from whom his given name is taken, sustains an unshakable faith in providence. At a height equal to that of Adams's faith, our line might also pass through Goldsmith's Dr. Primrose (in *The Vicar of Wakefield*), another quixotic clergyman whose faith proves equally unshakable. From Primrose, the line would descend to Myshkin, who, while resembling Christ, fails to give a direct answer when asked whether he believes in God, and who later admits that he sometimes loses his faith. Then, falling through Unamuno's representation of the knight as a man of faith struggling with doubt, the line would find its terminus in Father Quixote, who, while also approximating the image of Christ, is plagued by doubt, and resolves that uncertainty is essential to belief.

This does not imply that the sequence of Don Quixote's religious transformations ends in atheism; even Father Quixote asserts that he can "touch" God. (Strictly speaking, quixotism and atheism would be incompatible in the world today, because atheism conforms to the secular tone of modernity, while quixotism by definition must stand at odds with whatever tone characterizes the contemporary world.) Nor do the differing kinds or degrees of faith displayed by the characters suggest that one of them is any more or any less Christian than the others. Despite their differing affiliations as Anglican parson, lay adherent to Russian Orthodoxy, and Roman Catholic priest, all three prove to be exemplary Christians in ways that link them to both Christ and Don Quixote. It is of course highly paradoxical that the bookish hidalgo whose lapse from sanity led him to act upon "the strangest notion that ever a madman hit upon," would some day seem comparable to the alleged "Son of God." Yet, as we have seen, that comparison has been drawn repeatedly, beginning with Kierkegaard, Turgenev, and Dostoevsky, and the images of both figures emerge to varying degrees of explicitness, like pentimenti, in Adams, the good man and perfect clergyman; Myshkin, the positively beautiful man; and Father Quixote, the Unamunian knight of doubt.

Don Quixote and his religious transformations all share an abundance of Jesus' virtues, including chastity, idealism, compassion, charitableness, innocence, simplicity, concern for the victims of injustice, and a disregard for the claims of money, property, and worldly law, when such law would override some "higher" law. In addition, the knight and the parson inherit the sterner side of the savior's personality, while the prince and the priest take after his gentler side. The sort of sternness that Jesus was capable of displaying (e.g., toward the Pharisees and scribes) is manifest in Don Quixote, as when he rebukes the ecclesiastic at the duke's dinner table, and in Adams, as when he chastizes the "roasting" squire and his cronies, but totally absent from Myshkin and Father Quixote. At the same time, the prince's *smirenie* or nonresistance to evil, and Father Quixote's absorption in the Spanish saints and mystics, bespeak a Christ-like humility, gentleness, and submissiveness that are missing in Don Quixote and Adams, both of whom exhibit vainglory—the one in his knighthood, the other in his sermons and worth as a pedagogue—and are ever ready for a fight. (This is not to deny the capacity of Myshkin and Father Quixote to intervene against evil: as Christ overturned the tables of the money-changers and drove the merchants from the temple, so the prince steps in to prevent Ganya from striking Varya, and to block the officer from striking Nastasya, while the priest intervenes to halt a blasphemous church procession. Yet neither Myshkin nor Father Quixote display the pugnaciousness of Don Quixote or Adams.)

As if to make explicit their connection with Christ, Don Quixote and his religious transformations all, at one point or another, paraphrase some key statement from the Gospels. Echoing what Jesus said to the doubting Peter (Matt. 14:31), Don Quixote exclaims to the carter who wants to flee before the knight does battle with a lion: "O man of little faith" (Ormsby trans., 2:17, 513). Adams, sermonizing to Joseph against "the indulgence of carnal appetites," is quick to cite Christ as his authority: "The text will be, child, Matthew the 5th, and part of the 28th verse: 'Whosoever looketh on a woman so as to lust after her' " (4:8, 264). In telling the jealous Aglaya not to "cast a stone" at Nastasya, Myshkin borrows the phrase that Christ uttered to dissuade the scribes and Pharisees from punishing the adulterous woman. And Father Quixote appeals to the Gospels (Matt. 9:10; Luke 7:34; 15:1) when he justifies his presence in a brothel by recalling that "Christ mixed with publicans and sinners."

Despite these connections, however, there is one trait shared by Don Quixote and his religious transformations that distinguishes them most essentially from Christ, and through which they will be seen to find their greatest theological import. The trait I have in mind is not, as one might guess, Don Quixote's madness, which has its modified counterparts in Adams's absentmindedness and eccentricity; in Myshkin's epilepsy and "idiocy"; in Father Quixote's expressed fear that he himself "must be a little mad" like his ancestor, and later, in the priest's delirium before dying. Jesus was surely sane, but he was viewed as mad by some of the people of his day, as attested by Mark 3:21, and in this respect he was no different from the Hebrew prophets or Muhammad; the latter, in one of his Meccan revelations, must go so far as to defend his own sanity.[3] Besides, the distinction between "sane" and "insane" becomes blurred by the end of the *Quixote,* whose narrator is even willing to suggest that those who play jokes on the knight and squire are "as crazy as the victims" (2:70, 810).

The most essential difference between Christ and Don Quixote is that the latter, insofar as his chivalric career becomes his raison d'être, finds himself temporally misplaced, as the former did not. Viewed as savior (*soter*), Christ embodies the problematic notion of the eternal stepping into the temporal; however, this problem can be resolved by the concept of his "fulfillment of time," or *kairos,* as explicated by theologians like Tillich.[4] While it may seem logically inevitable that a God-Man should find himself out of place and literally out of time within any earthly, human situation, regardless of the particular point in history at which he enters that situation, the Gospels present Christ as having fit perfectly into the historical moment of his era insofar as that *kairos* proved utterly ripe for his mission by providing him the appropriate conditions in which to fulfill the prophecies of the Hebrew scriptures. Even the most obsessive doubting Thomas or confirmed atheist would have to accept the centurion's remark, "Truly this was the Son of God!" as a plausible deduction *within* the context of the biblical accounts, if not necessarily as a valid assessment of the historical Jesus *outside* that context. In contrast, the "softest" reader of the *Quixote,* despite all the sympathy he or she might muster for the hero, could remain faithful to the narrative only by acknowledging with its narrator and its characters: "Truly this man is mad, not a knight!"

Here we arrive at our culminating question, How is Don Quixote to be understood theologically?

3. *Al-Qur'an: A Contemporary Translation,* trans. Ahmed Ali (1984; rev. ed. Princeton: Princeton University Press, 1988), sûrah 81, lines 22-25. On the alleged "madness" of the Hebrew prophets, see Max Weber's section, "Psychological Peculiarities of the Prophets," in his *Ancient Judaism,* trans. and ed. Hans H. Gerth and Don Martindale (New York: Free Press, 1967), 286-96. For a different view see Abraham J. Heschel, *The Prophets* (New York: Harper & Row, 1962), chap. 23 ("Prophecy and Psychosis"), 390-409, esp. 403-5.

4. Paul Tillich, *Systematic Theology,* 3 vols. (Chicago: University of Chicago Press, 1951-63), 3:369-72.

Theological Significance

Don Quixote's highest theological significance emerges not in Cervantes's text, but in the myth that evolved out of several centuries of readings of that novel, and most exemplarily in the adaptations of that myth in *Joseph Andrews, The Idiot,* and *Monsignor Quixote.* Each of these novels contains a hero who, as a true Christian, appears quixotically out of place in the world he inhabits. While Adams, Myshkin, and Father Quixote embody respectively an ideal parson, a saintly fool, and an uncorrupted priest, their quixotism reflects the alleged anachronicity and tenuousness of religious faith and ideals in the modern world. This point deserves elaboration.

It is generally accepted, as we remarked in the introduction, that from Cervantes's time on, the authority of religion and religious faith steadily diminished under the social, institutional, and ultimately psychological impact of such often-discussed processes as disenchantment, demythologization, secularization, and rationalization. Directly or indirectly, these developments also discouraged and finally destroyed the Western inclination to accept as guidelines for salvation any of those examples of past virtue, happiness, or perfection that Huizinga terms "historical ideals of life"; that is, "any concept of excellence man projects into the past."[5] From classical antiquity to the end of the eighteenth century, five main ideals of this kind gained ascendancy in gradual succession: the Golden Age; the lives of Christ and the apostles, and evangelical poverty; pastoral life; chivalry; classicism. But since the time of the French Revolution,

> historical cultural ideals of a general human purport have apparently passed out of the picture. Even romanticism was never completely serious in its imitation of the Middle Ages. . . . The plain reality of history—and the unquenchability of the desire—became too clearly conscious for modern humanity to continue to seek its salvation in the imitation of an imagined past. (91)

While the pertinence of Huizinga's remarks to the doom of the chivalric ideal is borne out by the *Quixote,* which he describes as "merely the last,

5. "Historical Ideals of Life," in *Men and Ideas: History, the Middle Ages, the Renaissance,* trans. James S. Holmes and Hans van Marle (1959; Princeton: Princeton University Press, 1984), 77–96; here 80.

supreme expression of that irony" that "[t]hose who upheld the chivalric ideal were aware of its falsity" (89), the relevance of his thesis to the apparent obsoleteness of the ideal of *imitatio Christi* and evangelical poverty in the modern world may be illumined by Weber's assertion in 1915 that "in the midst of a culture that is rationally organized for a vocational workaday life, there is hardly any room for the cultivation of acosmic brotherliness." He goes on: "Under the technical and social conditions of rational culture, an imitation of the life of Buddha, Jesus, or Francis seems condemned to failure for purely external reasons."[6] Thirteen years earlier, William James had made a comparable observation in lecture 15 of *The Varieties of Religious Experience* (1902), "The Value of Saintliness":

> [W]e must not confound the essentials of saintliness, which are those general passions of which I have spoken [e.g., purity, charity, asceticism], with its accidents, which are the special determination of these passions at any historical moment. In these determinations the saints will usually be loyal to the temporary idols of their tribe. Taking refuge in monasteries was as much an idol of the tribe in the middle ages, as bearing a hand in the world's work is to-day. Saint Francis or Saint Bernard, were they living to-day, would undoubtedly be leading consecrated lives of some sort, but quite as undoubtedly they would not lead them in retirement. (*Varieties,* 286)

These observations are consistent with Huizinga's claim that the imitation of Christ and other historical life-ideals of Western culture have been abandoned in the modern age. Weber and James differ in their methodological viewpoints: James as psychologist is no less interested in the internal, psychological "essentials of saintliness" than in its sociohistorical "accidents," whereas Weber as sociologist is more exclusively concerned with "purely external" factors. Nevertheless, the two scholars arrive at provocatively similar conclusions: the one, that the classic religious founders and saints could not be successfully *imitated* in a "rational culture"; the other, that such lives could not be *repeated* unaltered in such a culture by the individuals who originally lived them.

Given the seeming obsolescence of the imitation of Christ in modernity, we

6. "Religious Rejections of the World and Their Directions," *From Max Weber: Essays in Sociology,* trans. and ed. H. H. Gerth and C. Wright Mills (New York: Oxford University Press, 1946; repr. 1978), 323–59; here 357.

may assume that were any of the great Christian saints living today, or were someone today to pursue their ideal with the fervor of a Francis or Bernard, that imitator would appear as a "Quixote" in the sense (defined in our introduction) of "a person who is idealistic beyond practicality, or inspired by ideals that are lofty, Romantic, and chivalrous, but also false, unrealizable, and rash." Indeed, religious ideals, faith, and religion itself might seem "quixotic" insofar as they appear "false, unrealizable, and rash" in the modern secular view, which is often associated with that triumvirate of what Ricoeur has labeled the "hermeneutic of suspicion": Marx, Nietzsche, Freud.

Marx's well-known assessment of religion revolves around his notion that life determines consciousness. Because he considered all ideas as reflections of socioeconomic circumstances in the "real" world, he, like Ludwig Feuerbach before him, viewed religion as an ideology abstracted from reality: "*Man makes religion,* religion does not make man."[7] From this viewpoint the concept of God represents the divine qualities that man has "alienated" from himself. Marx observes in his early treatise *On the Jewish Question* (1843): "Religion is simply the recognition of man in a roundabout fashion; that is, through an intermediary. . . . Christ is the intermediary to whom man attributes his own divinity and all his religious *bonds.* "[8]

Though Marx's interest in religion diminished as he grew older and his main concerns shifted from philosophy and theology to economics and politics, it seems appropriate that his death (1883) came just one year after the publication of Nietzsche's *The Gay Science* (1882), whose aphorism no. 125 contains the famous pronouncement, "God is dead." Several years later, in *Beyond Good and Evil* (1886) and *Toward a Genealogy of Morals* (1887), Nietzsche elaborated his well-known critique of religion, which Ricoeur sees as "a good introduction to the hermeneutics of Freud": "The murder of the moral God is what Nietzsche described as a cultural process, the process of nihilism, and what Freud described in more psychological terms as the work of mourning applied to the father image."[9]

Freud's first essay on religion, "Obsessive Actions and Religious Practices" ("Zwangshandlungen und Religionsübungen," 1907), focuses on the ties between

7. "Toward the Critique of Hegel's Philosophy of Law. Introduction" (1844), in *Karl Marx on Religion,* ed. Saul K. Padover (New York: McGraw, 1974), 35.

8. *The Marx-Engels Reader,* ed. Robert C. Tucker (1972, 2d ed., New York: Norton, 1978), 26–52; here 32. Cf. Marx, *Capital,* vol. 1, *Reader,* 294–442; see 326.

9. "Religion, Atheism, and Faith," in Paul Ricoeur and Alistair MacIntyre, *The Religious Significance of Atheism* (New York: Columbia University Press, 1969), 63, 67.

its titular subjects: "In view of these similarities and analogies one might venture to regard obsessional neurosis as a pathological counterpart of the formation of a religion, and to describe that neurosis as an individual religiosity and religion as a universal obsessional neurosis."[10] This formula—which Ricoeur sums up as meaning that "man is neurotic insofar as he is *homo religiosus* and religious insofar as he is neurotic"[11]—plants the seed for Freud's whole critique in his later tetralogy on religion: *Totem and Taboo* (1913), *The Future of an Illusion* (1927), *Civilization and Its Discontents* (1930), and *Moses and Monotheism* (1939).

Two of Freud's propositions pose threats to any theology. The first, submitted in *Totem and Taboo* and *Moses and Monotheism,* is that "God" signifies nothing other than an exalted father, and that the "religious" phase in the phylogeny of mankind's view of the universe (following the "animistic" and preceding the "scientific" stage) corresponds to the "neurotic" or "object-choice" phase in the ontogeny of the human individual (after the "narcissistic" and before the "mature" stage). Even more intimidating is the proposition that religion is nothing other than an "illusion" (*Illusion*), as *The Future of an Illusion* construes it, or a "mass-delusion" (*Massenwahn*), as *Civilization and Its Discontents* argues.

At this point, we should recall the analogies drawn in our introduction between Don Quixote in his relation to reality, and religious faith in its relation to the modern secular world: namely, that each is governed by a particular representation of the world; each seeks to act in accordance with that representation; and each must confront forces that deny or undermine the legitimacy of that representation. With these analogies in mind, we cannot but be struck by the fact that Freud, one of our century's foremost antagonists of religion, defines religion in terms that aptly sum up Don Quixote's vision of the world: illusion and delusion. Freud theorizes that the "most fundamental purpose" behind any neurosis is the person's desire "to take flight from an unsatisfying reality into a more pleasurable world of phantasy."[12] Regardless of whether Don Quixote is diagnosed as neurotic, these same terms could describe his condition after he lapses from sanity and seeks to transform his

10. "Obsessive Actions and Religious Practices," *The Standard Edition of the Complete Psychological Works of Sigmund Freud,* trans. under the general editorship of James Strachey, in collaboration with Anna Freud, 24 vols. (London: Hogarth, 1953–74), 9:117–27; here 126–27.

11. *Freud and Philosophy: An Essay on Interpretation,* trans. Denis Savage (New Haven: Yale University Press, 1970), 232.

12. *Totem and Taboo,* trans. James Strachey (New York: Norton, 1950), 74.

bleak surroundings ("an unsatisfying reality") into a chivalric realm ("a more pleasurable world of phantasy"). This affinity between Don Quixote and Freud's theory of neurosis, together with Freud's neurosis-religion analogy, supports a correlation between Don Quixote and the psychoanalyst's theory of religion. The knight's stated conviction that "[c]hivalry is a religion" (2:8, 467) seems to furnish a case in point of Freud's notion that "an obsessional neurosis presents a travesty, half comic and half tragic, of *a private religion*" ("Obsessive Actions," 9:119, emphasis mine). An analogy emerges between the way Sancho Panza's constant questioning and skepticism threaten to subvert his master's illusions, and the way the realistic worldview of science, according to Freud, follows and replaces the illusory Weltanschauung of religion. The knight's sanchification, which guides him from illusion to reality, could correlate with that aspect of science Freud cherishes most: its function as a means for an "education to reality."[13]

Our purpose is not to psychoanalyze Don Quixote, as some doctors and critics have done.[14] Nor is it to intimate that such an approach to the knight would be any more or any less valid than others. Rather, our interest in the psychoanalytic analogy between religion and neurosis, as well as in the correspondences between neurosis and Don Quixote and between Don Quixote and religion, lies in their demonstration that religion appears quixotic when viewed from Freud's quintessentially modern atheistic perspective. Like Don Quixote, religion is identified with illusion and delusion. As Don Quixote is led by his obsessive fantasies into continual conflicts with reality, so religion, conceived as an illusion (or "the universal obsessional neurosis of humanity" [Freud, *Future,* 43]), seems utterly maladapted to the actual world. And just as the mad knight would seem a bizarre remnant from the past in seventeenth-century Spain, so religion, conceived by Freud as the second of mankind's three phylogenic phases, appears obsolete in the context of the third, "scientific" phase.

It is to the illusory, anachronistic, i.e., quixotic status of religion in the modern secular world that the sanctification of Don Quixote testifies, and it is in bearing such witness that his religious transformations find their greatest

13. *The Future of an Illusion,* trans. James Strachey (New York: Norton, 1961), 49.

14. E.g., José Goyanes [M.D.], *La tipología de el Quijote: Ensayo sobre la estuctura psicosomática de los personajes de la novela* (Madrid: Aguirre, 1932); Helene Deutsch [M.D.], "Don Quijote und Donquijotismo," *Almanach der Psychoanalysis* 10 (1935):151–60; Carroll B. Johnson, *Madness and Lust: A Psychoanalytical Approach to Don Quixote* (Berkeley: University of California Press, 1983).

theological significance. To be sure, the first of these transformations, Adams, was created well over a century before Freud was born, and the second, Myshkin, appears in a book that was written while the founder-to-be of psychoanalysis was still a child. But the hermeneutic of suspicion that underlies the Freudian theory finds earlier exemplars in Marx and Nietzsche, and has roots in European philosophy that extend back to Descartes (Ricoeur, *Freud and Philosophy,* 33), who is identified with Cervantes as a cofounder of the modern Age of Doubt. If, as Américo Castro suggested, once an art form is launched by genius, as the genre of the novel was launched by Cervantes, "the atmosphere becomes impregnated with its properties," then it must also be true that when a revolutionary scientific insight or philosophical problem is enunciated by genius, like Copernicus's hypothesis of a heliocentric universe or Descartes's method of doubt, it can condition a civilization's thinking for centuries to come. Though it was not until the discovery of the unconscious and the founding of psychoanalysis in our own century that religion could be diagnosed as "neurotic," it need come as no surprise that in the increasingly skeptical, agnostic post-Galilean and -Cartesian world the insane knight of La Mancha could already have appeared to Fielding and Dostoevsky as a suitable model for the two exemplary Christian figures of Adams and Myshkin. Let us conclude by considering the special sort of suffering which Don Quixote bequeathed to them.

Homo Religiosus *and Quixotic Suffering*

In the chapter of Joseph Campbell's *Creative Mythology* entitled "The Death of 'God,'" the section on Don Quixote opens by citing Henry Adams's reference to the year 1600—the year Giordano Bruno was burned—as marking the climax of the transition from the religious to the "Mechanical Phase" of mankind's history.[15] Adams observes that the prime movers of this transition, including Gutenberg, Columbus, Luther, Calvin, Bruno, Galileo, Kepler, Spinoza, Descartes, Leibnitz, and Newton, were unaware that in their search for truth, they were contributing to the destruction of the very "Unity" upon which their

15. Henry Adams, *The Degradation of the Democratic Dogma,* ed. Brooks Adams (New York: Macmillan, 1919; rpt. Peter Smith, 1949), 293; cited incorrectly by Joseph Campbell, *The Masks of God,* 4 vols. (New York: Viking Press, 1960–68), vol. 4: *Creative Mythology,* 600–601.

religious faith was based. What replaced that unity? According to Adams, "This persistence of thought-inertia is the leading idea of modern history. Except as reflected in himself, man has no reason for assuming unity in the universe, or an ultimate substance, or a prime-motor."[16] Elaborating on Adams's thesis, Campbell states:

> Essentially what has happened is that in the physical field—the field of matter understood as distinct from spirit—an order of law has been recognized that is apparently not the same as that of the human will and imagination. As in the Freudian view of the forces operative in the structuring of the psyche the *wish* of the growing child is countered by the *prohibition* of the parent, and as in Adler's view the child's *wish* is frustrated by his own *impotence* to achieve, so here the symbols of the soul's dynamic structure, projected upon the universe, are met and broken by an irrefragable order in diametric opposition. Whereas in the soul, or heart, there is the sense of freedom—freedom of choice and to will—out there, in the field of its action, a mechanical determinism prevails. Whereas here there would seem to be intelligence and intention, there there is only blind, irresponsible, unknowing, unfeeling momentum. (602)

It is by the force of precisely such "momentum" that Don Quixote is knocked from his horse in his encounter with a mill whose wind-blown sail, in hitting him, functions as a "prohibition" to his "wish" that it be a giant. As a vivid symbol of the transition from the religious to the "Mechanical Phase" (Adams), or from the "religious" to the "scientific" view of the universe (Freud), this scene involves a clash not only between knight and windmill, lance and sail, but also between the two ages and worldviews reflected in the dialogue of the knight and squire. On the one hand, Sancho's contention that the "giants" are windmills could be exchanged for Lord Bacon's argument that thought must be evolved from the universe rather than the universe from thought. On the other hand, Don Quixote's insistence, based on the authority of chivalry books, that the windmills are giants—or, as he revises his argument after the incident, that they are giants whom a sorcerer has transformed into

16. *The Education of Henry Adams* (New York: Random House, 1931), 484; quoted by Campbell, *Creative Mythology*, 601-2.

mills—could be exchanged for Ignatius's injunction for the Catholic adherent to believe that white is black, and black white, if ordered to do so by the Church. The contradiction between Don Quixote's chivalric "wish" and the anti-chivalric "prohibition," which he meets in the form of brute reality, beatings, stonings, mockery, and the rational argumentation of other characters, causes him great suffering. Nonetheless, he repeatedly maintains that as a knight he expects to suffer, accepts his suffering, and, during his penance in the Sierra Morena, *wants* to suffer. One is tempted to compare him with Christ as sufferer, as we did in discussing the *Quixote*'s bearing on Dostoevsky's religious thought. After all, Don Quixote's repossession of sanity and reconciliation with the Church in the end imply that his suffering had for him the same kind of redemptive worth that is attributed to Christ's suffering. The two men's sufferings are reflected similarly in their moods. As John Chrysostom taught that Christ never laughed,[17] so Cervantes's narrator presents his *Schmerzens Mann* as having laughed only rarely. Don Quixote's otherwise constant "melancholy" (*melancolía*) makes apt the title conferred on him by Sancho: Knight of the Sad Countenance. Usually he can be imagined to appear as he does when Roque Guinart beholds on him "the saddest and most melancholy face that sadness itself could produce" (2:60, 758). In this respect he again seems like an anachronism left over from the late Middle Ages when, as Huizinga observes, "a sombre melancholy weigh[ed] on people's souls," a depression manifest in the physiognomies depicted in "the portraits of the time, which for the most part strike us by their sad expression."[18]

As similar as the sufferings of Christ and Don Quixote may seem, their causes are different: whereas Christ's agony at Gethsemane and his pain throughout the Passion stem ultimately from his earthly predicament as Word become flesh, the eternal within the temporal, the absolute amidst the conditional, Don Quixote's sufferings all result, directly or indirectly, from the conflict of his illusions with reality. And whereas Christ's sufferings are ultimately resolvable (in the Gospel context) by virtue of his being the "Son of God," Don Quixote's sufferings are resolvable only by his ceasing to conceive of himself as a knight. The human agony expressed in Christ's prayer in the garden, "O my Father, if it be possible, let this cup pass from me," finds its divine resolution in

---

17. *Patrologiae cursus completus, Series graeca,* 162 vols. (1857–66), ed. J.-P. Migne, 57:69; cited by Ernst Robert Curtius, *European Literature and the Latin Middle Ages,* trans. Willard R. Trask (New York: Pantheon Books, 1953), 420.

18. *The Waning of the Middle Ages* (1949; Garden City, N.Y.: Doubleday, 1954), 31, 34.

the next clause: "nevertheless not as I will, but as thou wilt" (Matt. 26:39). Accordingly, Christ's cry of mortal despair on the cross, recorded in Matthew 27:46, is counterbalanced by his expression of immortal resignation in Luke 23:46. But no such compensation is possible for Don Quixote; as long as he remains a knight his suffering must stay unresolved because the chivalric life and adventures he seeks are unreal and unattainable. In him we find—as Ortega puts it—"a strange dual nature, whose two elements belong to opposite worlds: the will is real but what is willed is not real" (*Meditations,* 148). This tension makes Don Quixote heroic in Ortega's sense of the term:

> Perhaps it is not possible, but it is a fact that there are men who decide not to be satisfied with reality. Such men aim at altering the course of things; they refuse to repeat the gestures that custom, tradition, or biological instincts force them to make. These men we call heroes, because to be a hero means to be one out of many, to be oneself. . . . The hero's will is not of his ancestors nor of his society, but his own. This will to be oneself is heroism. (149)

In embodying such individualistic "heroism"—epitomized in his indignant assertion to the neighbor who tried to convince him that he was not a knight: "I know who I am" (*Quixote,* 1:5, 46)—Don Quixote indeed becomes "one out of many." He is, the narrator reminds us, "the first in our age and in these evil days to devote himself to the labor and exercise of the arms of knight-errantry" (1:9, 66). Of course the narrator is speaking facetiously here; Don Quixote is not just the "first" knight of his age, but the only one. As such, he must endure a unique sort of mental pain: the suffering of a temporally misplaced person. Such suffering stems from his yearning for chivalry and the Golden Age of yore, a feeling that seems almost a parody of the "Nostalgia for Paradise in the Primitive Traditions" discussed in one place by Eliade,[19] though the knight experiences nothing like the "Normality of Suffering" that Eliade elsewhere attributes to the archaic man who succeeds in "annulling time" through periodic ceremonies revealing *illud tempus.*[20] A spiritualized form of such nostalgia is expressed by Kierkegaard when he laments: "O, they were better, much better times when men let Christianity be what it is" (entry

19. *Myths, Dreams, and Mysteries: The Encounter between Contemporary Faiths and Archaic Realities,* trans. Philip Mairet (New York: Harper & Bros., 1960), chap. 3, 59–72.

20. *Myth of the Eternal Return,* chap. 3 ("Misfortune and History"), sec. 1, 95–102.

of 1854, *Journals,* 2:226). Anticipating Kierkegaard, who attacked contemporary "Christendom," and complained of the "leveling" of individuality and the lack of religious passion in his day,[21] Don Quixote feels a distinct discomfort from existing in his own unchivalric age, the Age of Iron. In this connection, it is instructive to recall the Greek etymology of "nostalgia": *nostos* (a return home or homeward), and *algos* (pain, grief, distress).

Don Quixote's suffering of nostalgia, or return-pain, is distinct from the redemptive suffering of Christ and the Christian ascetics, saints, and martyrs. *Quixotic suffering,* if we may coin the term, can have redemptive effects (as the *Quixote*'s ending suggests), but it is something sui generis, definable as *the pain of a temporally misplaced person who has found the reality of his will to be at odds with the unreality of that which he wills, and who yearns to return to, or to restore, some paradisiacal past age when, in his view, his will and that which he wills would have been real and in accord.* As a painful longing for return, quixotic suffering is analogous to the nostalgia felt by the archaic person or *homo religiosus* who longs for the eternal return; and yet, quixotic suffering is a definitively modern phenomenon insofar as it could only be experienced in an age when such a yearning might seem illusory or delusive, and hence ridiculous.

It follows that Adams, Myshkin, and Father Quixote, as embodiments of the knight's sanctification, should experience the same quixotic suffering that would be felt by any *homo religiosus* or primitive Christian if such a person were to find herself or himself misplaced in the modern secular world. The mental and spiritual suffering of the quixotic hero is not nearly so explicit in the comical context of *Joseph Andrews* as it is in *The Idiot,* which has been viewed as a Christian tragedy,[22] or in the seriocomic atmosphere of *Monsignor Quixote;* Adams experiences nothing that resembles the kenotic suffering of Myshkin, or Father Quixote's *Angst*-ridden conflict with faith and doubt. Yet Fielding was no less concerned with the vulnerability of good nature to the guiles of the wicked, the contempt for religion and the clergy, and the corruption of clergymen, than was Dostoevsky with the spiritual vacuity of the

---

21. See Kierkegaard's *Attack Upon "Christendom" 1854–1855,* trans. Walter Lowrie (Princeton: Princeton University Press, 1944); and his *Two Ages: The Age of Revolution and the Present Age: A Literary Review,* trans. Howard V. Hong and Edna H. Hong (Princeton: Princeton University Press, 1978), esp. pt. 3, sec. 3: "The Present Age," 68–112.

22. Nathan A. Scott, Jr., "The Tragic Vision and the Christian Faith," *The Broken Center: Studies in the Theological Horizon of Modern Literature* (New Haven: Yale University Press, 1966), 119–44; see 144.

Russian aristocracy and the threat posed to religious faith by nihilism and atheism, or than is Greene with the tension of faith and rationalism, and what he portrays as the excessive moral harshness of the Catholic hierarchy. Hence the spectacle of the good Parson Adams suffering ill-treatment at the hands of fellow "Christians," being "roasted" by the "parson-hunting" squire, and suspecting that he is "sojourning in a country inhabited only by Jews and Turks,"[23] finds counterparts in *The Idiot* and *Monsignor Quixote.* On the one hand it corresponds to the spectacle of the positively beautiful man, Myshkin, being ridiculed and abused by his fellow Russians, desiring uncontrollably "to leave everything here and go away at once," and relapsing finally into idiocy. On the other hand it is analogous to the image of Father Quixote as the humble, innocent priest being called "fool" by his local bishop, pursued by the Guardia Civil, tormented by doubts about his own faith, and lapsing into delirium before his death.

These spectacles all reflect the paradigmatic image of Don Quixote's suffering. The misfortunes of Adams, Myshkin, and Father Quixote are understandable as part of the fate they must endure as religious paragons, or seeming denizens of the heavenly *civitas dei,* misplaced and highly vulnerable in the earthly world of modern human corruption manifest in Hanoverian England, czarist Russia, and post-Franco Spain. Their depictions would seem true to life to William James, the pragmatic psychologist, who warns that there is "no absoluteness in the excellence of sainthood," and that "as far as this world goes, any one who makes an out-and-out saint of himself does so at his peril. If he is not a large enough man, he may appear more insignificant and contemptible, for all his saintship, than if he had remained a worldling" (*Varieties,* 289).

The worst "peril" confronting the saint or *homo religiosus* today must surely be the suspicion that his or her leap of faith might be nothing more than a leap into illusion—that in pursuing, like the Abraham of *Fear and Trembling,* a religious existence, he or she might, like Kafka's "unsummoned" Abraham/ Quixote, be seeking something unreal. This peril inevitably bears with it a corollary analogous to the conviction of Kierkegaard's Climacus that "wherever there is contradiction, the comical is present" (*Postscript,* 459). For wherever the real aspiration to a religious existence is threatened by the possible unreality of that existence, the quixotic asserts itself.

---

23. It should go without saying that I emphatically disapprove of the pejorative implication that this phrase is meant to hold in the context of Fielding's novel.

Index